Affects in 21st-Century British Theatre

Mireia Aragay
Cristina Delgado-García • Martin Middeke
Editors

Affects in 21st-Century British Theatre

Exploring Feeling on Page and Stage

palgrave
macmillan

Editors
Mireia Aragay
University of Barcelona
Barcelona, Catalonia

Cristina Delgado-García
University of Glasgow
Glasgow, UK

Martin Middeke
University of Augsburg
Augsburg, Germany

University of Johannesburg
Johannesburg, South Africa

ISBN 978-3-030-58485-6 ISBN 978-3-030-58486-3 (eBook)
https://doi.org/10.1007/978-3-030-58486-3

Cover illustration: Getty Images: MATJAZ SLANIC

This Palgrave Macmillan imprint is published by the registered company Springer Nature Switzerland AG.
The registered company address is: Gewerbestrasse 11, 6330 Cham, Switzerland

Acknowledgements

The research underpinning the chapters by Mireia Aragay, Cristina Delgado-García, Clara Escoda, Martin Middeke and Clare Wallace was conducted within the framework of the research project "British Theatre in the Twenty-First Century: Crisis, Affect, Community" (FFI2016-75443). We are thankful to Spain's Ministry of Economy and Competitiveness (MINECO) and the European Regional Development Fund (ERDF), which funded the project between 2017 and 2021. This is the fifth research project undertaken by the Contemporary British Theatre Barcelona research group, recognised by the Catalan Research Agency AGAUR (2017 SGR 40), based at the University of Barcelona and led by Mireia Aragay. For more information on the group, please see www.ub.edu/cbtbarcelona/.

We also wish to thank América Martínez Gómez and, especially, Albert Méndez Panadés for supporting the project as copyediting assistants. América and Albert are PhD candidates at the University of Barcelona, and Albert is coinvestigator on the Contemporary British Theatre Barcelona research group.

Martin Middeke would like to express his gratitude to all participants in the stimulating, thought-provoking discussions in research seminars, master-classes and workshops at the universities of Augsburg, Johannesburg and Austin, TX, especially Bridget Grogan, David Kornhaber and Laura Cull.

Barcelona
Glasgow
Augsburg and Johannesburg
March 2021

Mireia Aragay
Cristina Delgado-García
Martin Middeke

Contents

Notes on Contributors

Mireia Aragay is Professor of English Literature, Drama and Theatre at the University of Barcelona. She is Principal Investigator of the Contemporary British Theatre Barcelona research group (www.ub.edu/cbtbarcelona/) and has published widely in the field, including the coedited volumes *British Theatre of the 1990s: Interviews with Directors, Playwrights, Critics and Academics* (2007), *Ethical Speculations in Contemporary British Theatre* (2014) and *Of Precariousness: Vulnerabilities, Responsibilities, Communities in 21st-century British Drama and Theatre* (2017), as well as the special issue "Theatre and Spectatorship" (*Journal of Contemporary Drama in English*, 2016).

Julia Boll is currently Associate Professor for British Studies at the University of Hamburg. Before, she held a research position at Konstanz University, where she investigated the diachronic representation of bare life on stage. She has spoken and written on the representation of war, violence, grief and pornography; ethics in literature on science; neoliberalism in European playwriting; theatre and utopia; the relationship between Early English culture and nostalgic nationalism; and figurations of bare life. Her monograph *The New War Plays* was published in 2013.

Cristina Delgado-García is Lecturer in Theatre and Performance at the University of Glasgow. Her research focuses on twenty-first-century playwriting, dramaturgy and ideology. She is the author of *Rethinking Character in Contemporary British Theatre: Aesthetics, Politics, Subjectivity* (2015) and is working on a monograph on theatre-maker Tim Crouch. Cristina has been coinvestigator on three research projects undertaken by the Contemporary British Theatre Barcelona research group (www.ub.edu/cbtbarcelona/). She coconvenes the Political Performances Working Group at the International Federation for Theatre Research (IFTR).

Clara Escoda is Lecturer in English Literature and Drama at the University of Barcelona. She is author of *Martin Crimp's Theatre: Collapse as Resistance to Late Capitalist Society* (2013), and her articles on Alice Birch and Crimp have appeared in journals such as *Contemporary Theatre Review*, *New Theatre Quarterly* and *Performing Ethos*. Her current research focuses on the intersections between feminism, neoliberalism and aesthetics in plays by emergent female writers. She is coinvestigator on the research group Contemporary British Theatre Barcelona (www.ub.edu/cbtbarcelona/).

Marissia Fragkou is Senior Lecturer in Performing Arts at Canterbury Christ Church University. Her research explores the politics of gender and precarity in contemporary theatre. Her essays have appeared in *Contemporary Theatre Review*, *Performing Ethos*, *Modern Drama* and volumes on British and European theatre and performance. She is the author of *Ecologies of Precarity in Twenty-First Century: Politics, Affect, Responsibility* (2019) and coeditor of the special issue "Dramaturgies of Change Greek Theatre Now" (*Journal of Greek Media and Culture*, 2017).

Lynette Goddard is Professor of Black Theatre and Performance at Royal Holloway, University of London. Their research focuses upon contemporary Black British playwriting with a focus on the politics of race, gender, sexuality and social issues. Their book publications include *Staging Black Feminisms: Identity, Politics, Performance* (2007), *Contemporary Black British Playwrights: Margins to Mainstream* (2015) and *Errol John's Moon on a Rainbow Shawl* (2017). They are researching Black British Theatre directors and how race is portrayed in contemporary plays.

Martin Middeke is Professor and Chair of English Literature at the University of Augsburg and Visiting Professor of English at the University of Johannesburg. His coedited volumes include the Methuen Drama Guides to *Contemporary Irish, British, American*, and *South African Playwrights* (2011–2015), *Of Precariousness: Vulnerabilities, Responsibilities, Communities in 21st-Century British Drama and Theatre* (2017) and *Drama, Theatre and Philosophy* (2018). His current projects include a *Handbook of Theatre Philosophy* and a website on theatre philosophy located at the Harry Ransom Center, University of Texas at Austin. He is coinvestigator on the research group Contemporary British Theatre Barcelona (www.ub.edu/cbtbarcelona/).

Mark Robson is Chair of English and Theatre Studies and Director of the Centre for Critical and Creative Cultures at the University of Dundee, Scotland. He has published widely on theatre, literature, philosophy and visual culture. His most recent publications include *Theatre & Death* (2019), *Shakespeare, Jonson, and the Claims of the Performative* (with James Loxley, 2013) and essays in journals such as *Contemporary Theatre Review*, *Studies in Theatre and Performance* and *Anglia*.

Korbinian Stöckl is Lecturer in English Literature at the University of Augsburg. He studied English, History and Social Sciences and was awarded a doctorate in English literature in 2019 for his thesis "Concepts of Love in Contemporary British Drama," which investigates historical continuities and contemporary peculiarities in treatments of love in British drama since the mid-1990s.

Liz Tomlin is Professor of Theatre and Performance at the University of Glasgow, where she specialises in British and European contemporary theatre. Her works include *Acts and Apparitions: Discourses on the Real in Performance Practice and Theory 1990–2010* (2013), *Political Dramaturgies and Theatre Spectatorship: Provocations for Change* (2019) and the edited volume *British Theatre Companies 1995–2014* (2015). She was previously a playwright and director with Point Blank Theatre and has published that body of work in *Point Blank* (2007).

Clare Wallace is Associate Professor at the Department of Anglophone Literatures and Cultures, Charles University. She is author of *The Theatre of David Greig* (2013) and *Suspect Cultures: Narrative, Identity and Citation in 1990s New Drama* (2006). She is coinvestigator on the research group Contemporary British Theatre Barcelona (www.ub.edu/cbtbarcelona/) and Key Researcher on the European Regional Development Fund project "Creativity and Adaptability as Conditions of the Success of Europe in an Interrelated World" (No. CZ.02.1.01/0.0/0.0/16_019/0000734).

Philip Watkinson is an independent scholar whose research examines contemporary performance and the politics of abstraction in neoliberal capitalism. He holds a PhD in Drama from Queen Mary University of London, and his work has been published in *Theatre Journal*, *Performance Research* and *Theatre Research International*.

CHAPTER 1

Introduction: Thinking-Feeling Our Way

Mireia Aragay, Cristina Delgado-García and Martin Middeke

From Aristotle and Bharata Muni through Antonin Artaud, Bertolt Brecht and Augusto Boal, to a range of twenty-first-century scholars, there seems to be a widespread agreement that feeling is an essential part of what matters in the theatre. The cultural significance of theatre, Erin Hurley contends, lies in the fact that it performs both "feeling labour"—since it makes, manages and moves feelings—and "feeling work"—since it intervenes in how a society understands its values and, ultimately, itself (2010, 9–10). In this respect, Hurley argues elsewhere, theatre might be seen as a "Public Feeling

M. Aragay (✉)
University of Barcelona, Barcelona, Catalonia
e-mail: aragay@ub.edu

C. Delgado-García (✉)
University of Glasgow, Glasgow, UK
e-mail: Cristina.DelgadoGarcia@glasgow.ac.uk

M. Middeke (✉)
University of Augsburg, Augsburg, Germany

University of Johannesburg, Johannesburg, South Africa
e-mail: martin.middeke@uni-a.de

M. Aragay et al. (eds.), *Affects in 21st-Century British Theatre*,
https://doi.org/10.1007/978-3-030-58486-3_1

Project" (2014a, 3).[1] In his introduction to *The Palgrave Handbook to Affect Studies and Textual Criticism*, Donald R. Wehrs provides a detailed, highly informative genealogy—or, rather, genealogies, in the plural—of the study of the interface between feeling and textual dynamics from "pre-Axial" through "Axial" worldviews to twenty-first-century "post-Axial" perspectives (2017, 1–93).[2] Rather than attempt a similar feat for the study of the relations between feeling and theatre, the aim of this introduction is far more modest. First, a brief overview of how twenty-first-century theatre scholarship has engaged with feelings enables us to delimit and justify this volume's specific contribution to the field, namely, its focus on playwright's theatre in the new millennium. This is followed by a succinct critical presentation of what seem to us to be, from the point of view of theatre studies, two particularly relevant strands within the early twenty-first-century "explosion of interest in how texts represent, reflect on, enact, and elicit affect, and in how affect/text dynamics bear on emotions, cognition, aesthetics, and culture's relation to ethics and politics" (Wehrs 2017, 1). The twelve chapters in this collection position themselves in relation to both the tensions and the resonances between these two strands. Finally, a brief conclusion draws their various explorations of feeling in/and theatre together around the notion of disturbance as an organising principle.

Theatre Scholarship and Affects: Recent Interventions

Surprisingly given the above-mentioned consensus on the centrality of affects, emotions and sensations to theatre, a sustained scholarly interest in examining the interface between theatre and feeling cannot really be said to have come into its own until the 2010s.[3] As regards contemporary theatre in particular, publications such as Nicholas Ridout's *Stage Fright, Animals and Other Theatrical Problems*—which defines theatre as "an apparatus for the production of affect" (2006, 168)—James Thompson's *Performance Affects: Applied Theatre and the End of Effect* (2009), Nicola Shaughnessy's *Applying Performance: Live Art, Socially Engaged Theatre and Affective Practice* (2012) and her edited collection *Affective Performance and Cognitive Science: Body, Brain and Being* (2013), Martin Welton's *Feeling Theatre* (2012), Adam Alston's *Beyond Immersive Theatre* (2016), Joanne 'Bob' Whalley and Lee Miller's *Between Us: Audiences, Affect and the In-Between* (2016), Elin Diamond, Denise Varney and Candice Amich's edited volume *Performance, Feminism and Affect in Neoliberal Times* (2017) or Bryan Reynolds's *Intermedial Theater:*

Performance Philosophy, Transversal Poetics, and the Future of Affect (2017), among others, demonstrate the growing interest in exploring the relationship between theatre and feeling. At the same time, they testify to a broad tendency to focus on a diverse body of performance-making strategies—including applied, socially-engaged and activist theatre, immersive theatre and intermedial theatre—production practices—from the visual and aural "feeling-technologies" of theatre (Hurley 2010, 28) to rehearsal, acting and embodiment—and, importantly, the affective dimensions of spectatorial engagement and reception. Invaluable as this kind of scholarship is, it is also indicative of a propensity to disregard playwright's work when it comes to the study of the operations of affects in theatre. In this respect, this collection is an invitation to reroute the current critical and theoretical interest in the feeling/theatre interface to address British playwright's theatre in the twenty-first century, by examining how affects are inscribed in the poetics of playtexts as well as in their iterations on stage in our historical conjuncture.

The Many Affective Turns in the Humanities

The so-called "turn to affect" in the humanities and social sciences, often viewed as a response to perceived omissions in poststructuralist thought with regards to embodiment, materiality and (ethical) responsibility (see, for example, Wehrs 2017, 34–35), is in fact "a set of many turnings that are problematically lumped together in a false unity that imagines that one single intellectual arc could describe them all" (Brinkema 2014, xii). In the present context, two salient threads within the twenty-first-century scholarly "turns to affect" seem to us to be particularly relevant and are discussed in this section.[4]

Affects as Autonomous Intensities

Described by Ruth Leys as "one of the most influential theorists in the humanities and social sciences today" (2011, 435), Brian Massumi's work on affect, stretching back to the publication of "The Autonomy of Affect" in *Cultural Critique* in 1995, has evolved and mutated in ways that we can only begin to sketch out here. The most "tenacious," yet arguably "increasingly incomplete" (Stanley 2017, 108), legacy of Massumi's contribution to affect theory is his positioning of the notion of affect in explicit contrast to that of emotion in his influential *Parables for the*

Virtual: Movement, Affect, Sensation (2002), which reprints "The Autonomy of Affect" as its first chapter. Via Gilles Deleuze and Felix Guattari's reading of Baruch Spinoza's *Ethics* ([1677] 2001), Massumi opens *Parables for the Virtual* by defining "affect" as "a body's *capacity* to enter into relations of movement and rest"—Spinoza's *affectus*; Deleuze and Guattari's *affect*—and as a bodily "intensity"—Spinoza's *affectio*; Deleuze and Guattari's *affection* (Massumi 2002, 15–16; italics in the original). Subsequently, in the first chapter, he states that "intensity will be equated with affect" (2002, 27), in other words, that his focus will be on *affectio*/affection. On this basis, in *Parables for the Virtual* Massumi goes on to define affect as a physiological, prelinguistic experience, an "unformed or unstructured" (2002, 260) "intensity" that is disconnected from "meaningful sequencing, from narration" and is embodied in "purely autonomic reactions most directly embodied in the skin" (2002, 25). Affect is celebrated by Massumi as a "threshold of potential" (2015a, 3), both prepersonal and asocial (2002, 30). He carefully distinguishes affect from emotion: "Emotion is qualified intensity, the conventional, consensual point of insertion of intensity into semantically and semiotically formed progressions, into narrativizable action-reaction circuits, into function and meaning. It is intensity owned and recognized," whereas affect is "irreducibly bodily and autonomic" (2002, 28). Emotions, that is, are discursive/social/cultural constructs that are organised cognitively, epistemologically, linguistically and narratively, while affect lies outside culture, epistemology, cognition or intentionality; it is part of a different order of experience—"it is not ownable or recognizable and is thus resistant to critique" (2002, 28). For the Massumi of *Parables of the Virtual*, in sum, it is crucial to set affect and emotion apart from each other so that "psychological categories" will not obscure the former concept, thus "undoing the considerable deconstructive work that has been carried out by poststructuralism" (2002, 27).

From this perspective, affect's autonomy or radical difference from social/epistemological/cognitive structures underpins its capacity to productively transform those structures. In other words, as an ontological, embodied, material order of experience that is uncontaminated by any cognitive, cultural, learned phenomena, it provides the individual body with an unpredictable "capacity to interrupt social logic" (Hemmings 2005, 552). "Affect" is here often used in the singular, thus framing it as a universal condition—it is "the capacity for movement or disturbance in general" (Brinkema 2014, xiii), found "in those intensities that pass body to body (human, nonhuman, part-body, and otherwise), in those resonances that circulate about, between, and sometimes stick to bodies and worlds, *and* in the very passages or variations between these intensities and resonances themselves" (Seigworth and Gregg 2010, 1; italics in the original). Affect is "[c]ast forward by its open-ended in between-ness" and is "integral to a body's perpetual *becoming* [...] otherwise" (Seigworth and Gregg 2010, 3; italics in the original), thus destabilising the notion of a coherent, intentional subjectivity. In terms of aesthetic analysis, viewing affect as "autonomous to the degree to which it escapes confinement in the particular body whose vitality, or potential for interaction, it is" (Massumi 2002, 35) opens up the possibility of exploring its manifestations through an aesthetics of the sublime: the affective event cannot be grasped by consciousness (thought) and is instead "deposed" in the sublime (Lyotard 1991, 90; see also Baraniecka 2013, 67).

In later work, Massumi has modulated his position in ways that are worth noting. "If I am guilty of romanticizing anything," he states in *Semblance and Event: Activist Philosophy and the Occurrent Arts*, "it would be *intensity*" (2011, 84; italics in the original). Overall, Kate Stanley detects in *Semblance and Event* an increased emphasis on affect as *affectus*, that is, on Spinoza's "embodied, relational, action-oriented definition of affect" and, hence, "on the embodied political activation" enabled by affect (Stanley 2017, 102). This was subsequently confirmed in both the collection of interviews *Politics of Affect* (2015a) and in Massumi's study of the affective dimensions of the post-9/11 politics of "preemption," *Ontopower: War, Powers, and the State of Perception* (2015b). From a conceptual point of view, this "turn" in Massumi's work is inseparable from a rethinking of the key, and highly vexed, question of temporality in relation to the pair (of terms) *affect* and *emotion*, as well as of the equally controversial issue of the link between affect (*affectio*/affection) and (political) action. While in *Parables for the Virtual* Massumi viewed affect (*affectio*/affection), via his Deleuzian reading of Spinoza, as "a suspension of action-reaction circuits and linear temporality" (2002, 28), in later work he acknowledges the "embeddedness of affect in a larger field of life" (2015a, 6) through a turn towards Spinoza's "fundamental understanding of an integrative mind-body loop" (Stanley 2017, 106). This move, Stanley contends, is inspired by William James's seminal, Spinoza-inspired work in the fields of psychology and philosophy. In sum, Massumi's recent writings take on James's important emphasis on the "conflicted temporal circuitry" (Stanley 2017, 107) of affect, self-reflection, emotion, cognition and action in ways that deserve continued exploration.

The Cultural Circulation of Affects

A different affective turn may be traced in the work of theorists such as Sara Ahmed, Lauren Berlant, Rustom Bharucha, Teresa Brennan, Ann Cvetkovich, Eva Illouz, Clare Hemmings, Sianne Ngai or Carolyn Pedwell. These scholars take as a starting point the claim that, paradoxically given its Spinozan point of departure, a sharp distinction between affect and emotion runs the risk of reinscribing the Cartesian dualism between body/materiality/ontology and mind/cognition/epistemology, as affect is often connected to the former while emotion is frequently associated to the latter (see Leys 2011, 468; La Caze and Lloyd 2011, 6).[5] As Bruce McConachie points out in *theatre & mind*, contrary to the binary vision of a disembodied mind (*cogito*) and a body/material world that constitute the thing thought about (*res cogitans*), most contemporary cognitive scientists and philosophers see cognition as a thoroughly embodied process: "[o]ur minds," McConachie succinctly states, "do not float above the messiness of material reality" (2013, 2).[6] Michael Hardt suggests that "affects refer equally to the body and the mind" (2007, ix). In a similar vein, affect theorists working in the fields of gender and/or race and transnational studies are generally wary of the binary body/materiality/ontology vs. mind/cognition/epistemology, and their respective correlations with affect and emotion. For Ahmed, famously, the distinction between affect and emotion "can only be analytic," as if "bodily sensation, emotion and thought [...] could be 'experienced' as distinct realms of human 'experience'" (2004a, 6). Ngai, for her part, sees "the difference between affect and emotion [...] as a modal difference of intensity or degree, rather than a formal difference of quality or kind. [...] [A]ffects are less formed and structured than emotions, but not lacking form and structure altogether; less 'sociolinguistically fixed', but by no means code-free or meaningless" (2005, 27). In Pedwell's words, "the relation between emotion and affect in sensorial practice remains one of contingency, blurring and imprecision" (2014, 20); affects/emotions are relational practices that imbricate "'the discursive' and 'the material', 'the cultural' and 'the biological', 'the personal' and 'the impersonal'" (2014, 21). Cvetkovich employs the term *feeling* "in part because it is intentionally imprecise, retaining the ambiguity [and continuity] between [...] embodied sensations and [...] psychic or cognitive experiences" (2012, 4).[7]

These theorists see affects, in the plural, as operating within existing power structures and social narratives, within culture and across differently situated bodies. They insist that affects do not work equally among, or attach equally to, all subjects. They pay close attention, for instance, to the heteronormative regulation of affect (Hemmings 2005, 560), to processes of affective racialisation (Ahmed 2006) or to the functioning and faultlines of the neoliberal affective regime (Ngai 2005). Using the term *feeling*, Ngai notes:

> [M]ost critics today accept that far from being merely private or idiosyncratic phenomena, or reflecting a "romantically raw domain of primitive experiential richness" that materialist analysis will be unable to grasp (Massumi, *Parables of the Virtual*, 29), feelings are as fundamentally "social" as the institutions and collective practices that have been the more traditional objects of historicist criticism (as Raymond Williams was perhaps the first to argue, in his analyses of "structures of feeling"), and as "material" as the linguistic signs and significations that have been the more traditional objects of literary formalism [from semiotic analysis to poststructuralism]. (2005, xx)[8]

In terms of how this may translate into aesthetic analysis, film scholar Eugenie Brinkema adds that since life is always "enacted in the definite particular," "[t]here is no reason to assume that affects are identical aesthetically, politically, ethically, experientially and formally" (2014, xv). She argues that the only way of articulating such differences is by "reading specific affects as having and being bound up with specific forms"; in other words, through "close reading" (2014, xv). To treat affects in such a way, she adds, "deforms any coherence of 'affect' in the singular, general, universal and transforms it into something not given in advance, not apprehendable except through the thickets of formalist analysis" (2014, xv). This, she claims, returns us to "the spirit of Deleuze—the minor, inconsequential, secret, atomic" (2014, xv).

The strong correlation Massumi and related scholars establish between affect and "movement" or "becoming" underpins their focus on the radical, transformative potential of affect. However, it is not difficult to think of "affective responses that strengthen rather than challenge a dominant social order" (Hemmings 2005, 551), or that rather than lead to "processes of subject-constitution which [...] induce [...] *becoming*," bring about modes of being defined by "*becoming-stuck*" (Blackman 2008, 47; italics in the original). Being mindful also of Massumi's recent claim that the "affect modulation" of power has taken the place of "old style ideology" (2015a, 32) so that meaningful resistance "has to learn to [...] meet affective modulation with affective modulation" (2015a, 34), it would appear that the relationship between affect, power relations and injustice deserves further work. It is worth noting in this connection that the "mobile body" that can "do things" because it is characterised by ease of movement is a body that takes up a very particular orientation towards the world and others, one that is more often than not based on the normative embodiment of heterosexuality and whiteness (Ahmed 2004b, 2006).

A Capacious Understanding of Affects

This edited collection seeks to mobilise a malleable understanding of affect, concerning both physiological sensations and psychological states, that is, affects, emotions and feelings. We conceive affect as the capacity—of a human, non-human or inanimate body, of an incorporeal phenomenon—to disturb and be disturbed. Studying affects can, we feel, contribute to critically unpicking the various sensations, multiple intensities, diverse valences, (aesthetic) dissonances and interior processes that are at work in and that, at the same time, collide with pressures and energies of what Berlant calls the "affective *scenarios*" of twenty-first-century human life and culture (2011, 9; italics in the original). Avoiding theoretical prescriptivism on either side of Spinoza's legacy, we invited our contributors to be influenced by, and potentially contribute to, competing theorisations of affect as they think about and are moved by new writing for the theatre in twenty-first-century Britain.

According to Jo Labanyi, "[i]f structuralism made us think about 'what texts are' rather than 'what texts mean,' the affective turn can make us attentive to 'what texts do' and what texts do is communicate all manner of things. So affect takes us back to meaning, but to forms of meaning that are not restricted to the cognitive" (2010, 230). Each in its own way, the four chapters in Part I, titled "Affects and Cognition: Thought, Intention, Empathy," trouble cognition/feeling and mind/body dualisms that, as noted above, persist in the work of some affect theorists, but have been contested by scholars that work in the fields of gender, race and/or transnational studies. Mireia Aragay's opening essay examines the intricate workings of empathy in debbie tucker green's *hang* (2015) through a four-faced critical prism encompassing recent debates about affect/emotion, Ngai's exploration of "ugly feelings" (2005), Deleuze and Guattari's notion of lines of flight (see O'Sullivan [2005] 2010 and Parr [2005] 2010a) and Ahmed's reflections on the relationship between emotions and (in)justice (2004a, 191–203). Methodologically, Aragay takes on board Brinkema's defence of "the formal dimension of affect" (2014, xv) and close reading, which, even if "utterly unfashionable" (2014, xv), permits a way into the dense, plural, aesthetically inscribed specificities of affects. On this basis, Aragay suggests that *hang*, like the rest of tucker green's theatre, invites spectators to feel *and* think, think *and* feel in an open-ended process of mutual accretion between bodily/affective/emotional responses and cognitive/reflective judgements that has the potential to "press" on their bodies (Ahmed 2004a, 6) and maybe alter their position or orientation vis-à-vis existing affective and epistemological frames.

Starting from the claim that "it is no news that feelings and emotions matter to and are the matter of theatre," Clare Wallace's contribution is similarly underpinned by a view of affect/emotion and cognition as mutually implicated systems. Framing her analyses of Caryl Churchill's *Love and Information* (2012), Tim Crouch and Andy Smith's *what happens to the hope at the end of the evening* (2013), Lucy Kirkwood's *The Children* (2016) and James Fritz's *Parliament Square* (2017) within the "thinking-feeling" sensorium of neoliberalism, Wallace's essay also addresses the mutual entanglement of affect and aesthetic form—she claims, in this regard, that the formal diversity of the four plays she examines indicates that "the affective" has a potential to be "magnetised by various modes of representation." The chapter shows that Churchill's, Crouch and Smith's, Kirkwood's and Fritz's plays share a profound ambivalence about the future and about ideas of agency, intention and efficacy. This, Wallace argues, marks them as interventions "in the sensorium of a present in which disempowerment is strongly felt."

Korbinian Stöckl's examination of Lucy Prebble's *The Effect* (2012) and tucker green's *a profoundly affectionate, passionate devotion to someone (-noun)* (2017) takes on Leys's influential critique of the anti-intentionalist stance of "Deleuze-inspired affect theorists" (2011, 443). From a position that views affect and cognition as being "radically entwined" and theatre as involving "intentional mind/body interactivity," then, Stöckl proceeds to read the romance plot in Prebble's play as asking whether the experience of (falling in) love can be neatly divided into a purely bodily and a purely cognitive realm—in other words, as thematically addressing the question whether it makes sense to conceive of affects as strictly non-intentional, preconscious moments of potential. Conversely, Stöckl's analysis of tucker green's play in its Royal Court Jerwood Upstairs premiere incarnation focuses on how the play's aesthetics set out to elicit strong affective responses from spectators coalescing around the recognition of shared human vulnerability. Yet such responses, Stöckl argues, are still instances of mind/body interactivity in that they cannot be prised away from the cognitively grasped thematic content of the play.

In the chapter that closes Part I, Elizabeth Tomlin challenges Hans-Thies Lehmann's view that the political potential of the affect of shock operates most effectively "within dramaturgies that rupture the aesthetic boundaries of the theatre event (dramatic or postdramatic)" via the irruption of "real actuality" (Lehmann 2013, 99). In Anthony Neilson's *God in Ruins* (2007) and *The Wonderful World of Dissocia* (2004), Tomlin argues, the aesthetic representational framework remains ultimately intact beyond the rupture brought about by the (momentary and apparent) intervention of the real. And yet, such reinscription of the dramaturgical and theatrical frame is precisely what enables the spectator to cognitively process to political effect the visceral shock and intense sensory engagement evoked by Neilson's theatre of affect. Contrary to Lehmann, then—whose implicit understanding of (the politics of) affect resonates with the early Massumian, ontological view of affect as presocial, autonomous intensity—Tomlin claims that the political charge of the visceral affect of shock can only be realised through cognitive processing, and that this is precisely how Neilson's theatre operates.

Tomlin's chapter provides a suitable transition to Part II, "Affects and Politics: Identities, Institutions, Ideology." Lynette Goddard's chapter importantly vindicates the theoretical contributions to the study of affect that Black feminist scholars made in the 1980s and 1990s, whose work is "affective in nature *and* subject matter," and places them firmly alongside recent theorists such as Ahmed and Ngai. In so doing, the chapter not only highlights a theoretical genealogy but also a history of racialised distributions of rage, anger, grief, fear and emotional exhaustion that are attendant to experiences of racist violence and acts of resistance to it. Those are indeed the central affects in the London iteration of the international project *Black Lives, Black Words*, which Goddard's chapter examines across its three short seasons at the Bush Theatre between 2015 and

2017. The series, composed of rehearsed readings of short plays by Black authors in response to the #BlackLivesMatter movement, demonstrates that affect lies at the intersection between race relations, activism and politically inflected theatre.

Marissia Fragkou's chapter is similarly interested in legacies—those of feminism, postfeminism and neoliberal capitalism on contemporary women's theatre in Britain and the possibility of "feminist renewal." Such revitalisation, Frakgou argues, is only possible through a "disturbance to consensual forms of happiness" that work to occlude injustice: a determined disruption of the status quo that Ahmed's figures of the "feminist killjoy" (2017) and the "willful subject" (2014) embody well and that can be related to the "radical mischief" proposed by director Erica Whyman. Fragkou's two case studies, Alice Birch's *Revolt. She Said. Revolt Again.* (2014) and Sh!t Theatre's *Letters to Windsor House* (2016), illustrate such work.

Turning to political institutions and drawing from Chantal Mouffe's work on radical democracy (2000, 2013) and left-wing populism (2018), Cristina Delgado-García advocates for attention to the operations of feelings both in democracy and in theatre invested in democracy. To this aim, she offers a new set of questions to ask to a rich body of theatre works in the 2010s representing, responding to and seeking to supplement democratic politics: "What does liberal democracy feel like in the UK in the politically turbulent decade of the 2010s? For whom does it feel like this, and for whom may it feel otherwise? What models of democracy are presented in contemporary British theatre, and what are the affects that buttress them? How are those affects composed in the text and on the stage? And importantly, what is the function of such feelings in a historical conjuncture in which democracy is under stress?" Her reading of David Greig's version of Aeschylus's *The Suppliant Women* (2016; published in 2017) begins to address these questions.

Philip Watkinson's chapter closes Part II with a focus on abstraction as an operation of neoliberal capitalism that has material and affective consequences. Via Louis Althusser, Watkinson defines abstraction in this sense as the extrication of specific practices and relations from their context, a series of displacements that are "intimately bound to our affective capacities and well-being." Relatedly, Watkinson argues, the abstraction or indeterminacy characteristic of much twenty-first-century British new writing explores how the abstractions of neoliberal capitalism "unsettle the basis on which social and affective relations can be formed." This is the case of the two plays the chapter examines: tucker green's *a profoundly affectionate, passionate devotion to someone (-noun)* and Anders Lustgarten *The Sugar-Coated Bullets of the Bourgeoisie* (2016). For Watkinson, their formal abstraction is political insofar as it expresses the anxiety and fear generated by the abstractions of neoliberal capitalism.

The four essays in Part III, titled "Affects and Hope: From Crisis to Utopian Feelings," centre on manifestations of crisis and how the plays at issue open up avenues to utopian perspectives. These often appear through oscillations between stasis and development, affirmation and negation, pessimism and—the often last resort of—hope. Martin Middeke's affective reading of Penelope Skinner's *Eigengrau* (2010) and Mike Bartlett's *Game* (2015) focuses on the transpersonal dynamics of affect that both plays construct and that likewise appeal to their audiences and readers. Drawing mainly on the theoretical work of Massumi, Jane Bennett and Nigel Thrift, Middeke analyses the configuration of glamour in "affective arrangements" (Slaby et al. 2019) of theatrical, performative and textual space. He equates affect with intensity and vibrancy, detecting a physicality of structures and textures in both plays that turns the relation between affect, emotion and cognition into a likewise interrelated rather than mutually exclusive "intra-action" (Barad 2007). Configuring the process of affecting and being affected, the physical impact of textures on spectators and readers, he argues, reflects on and constitutes vibrant matter, that is, a dynamic intra-action between human and nonhuman actants. By accomplishing this, the plays generate vital hope as they become vibrant matter themselves.

Julia Boll's reading of Zinnie Harris's migration play *How to Hold Your Breath* (2015) also draws on Karen Barad's post-/transhumanist concept of intra-action in order to challenge the malformations of neoliberal structures in Western society. Boll identifies two structural narratives of affect that complement each other in Harris's play: while the first, individual-centred narrative sketches a way to adjust and achieve the flexibility or plasticity (Malabou 2008) necessary to follow one's own path in societal surroundings, the second narrative centres on the appeal to the spectator/reader to consider human and nonhuman beings and objects as intra-acting and, especially, mutually affecting each other. Boll argues that thinking about affective behaviour in intra-active terms transcends an understanding of affect as an "autonomous" process. From an ethical perspective, she suggests that the internalisation of intra-action can be a key to the utopia of human happiness.

Mark Robson's analysis of Stef Smith's *Swallow* (2015) and Kieran Hurley's *Heads Up* (2016) reflects on the ontological and epistemological difficulties and aporias involved in the construction of future and futurity. Robson interrogates the affective charge of ideas such as "the end of the world" and "catastrophe" which, from ancient aesthetic reflections on theatre—Plato, Aristotle, Horace—to more recent work—such as Antonin Artaud's *Theatre of Cruelty* (1993)—have been omnipresent and inseparable from affects that hover between reinforcing and resisting a pedagogical and political purpose. Both *Swallow* and *Heads Up* centre on the aporia of being affective and, at the same time, critical. Both plays pessimistically negate the present in that they engage with negative futures. Robson claims that this negation in the theatre, however, always contains the potentiality to transcend the negative image into a virtual and, after all, more hopeful future.

In fruitful dialogue with the symbolic hope emanating from the plays discussed in the three earlier essays in Part III, Clara Escoda closes the collection by bringing Berlant's understanding of the present as "mediated affect" (2011, 4) and Ahmed's concept of the "stickiness" of affects (2004a, 4) to bear on her reading of Kae Tempest's play *Wasted* (2011; published 2013), specifically regarding the protagonists' attempts to resist the neoliberal discourses of resilience and self-development. Rather than unambiguously presenting hopeful images of individual empowerment and agency, Escoda claims, the play traces the collision between "negative affects" (Ngai 2005, 3) and positive human "inclinations" (Cavarero 2011) in such a way that ultimately foregrounds the shared ontological condition of relationality and vulnerability at the—utopian—heart of human subjectivity. Like Robson, Escoda invokes Jean-Luc Nancy, specifically his reflections on "exposure" (2008), as essential for any hopeful (re)configuration of human subjectivity.

Although the chapters are organised around three clusters that focus, respectively, on the relation between affects and cognition, politics and hope, there are various kinds of resonances across the three sections. Among others, there is a shared concern with the legacies of feminism in Escoda and Fragkou, while Boll, Escoda, Robson and Wallace all take into consideration the future. Empathy features centrally or is identified as lacking in the chapters by Aragay, Middeke and Robson. Together, the chapters by Aragay, Stöckl and Watkinson make a significant contribution to the study of tucker green through the lens of affect. Finally, the notion of disturbance—in line with Brinkema's definition of affect (2014, xiii) discussed earlier—emerges as another common denominator across the twelve chapters in the collection. Indeed, each chapter records how the selected contemporary plays register and/or prompt affective irritations of hegemonic practices, discourses and states of feeling. Our contributors chart the disruption of normalised racism through manifestations of Black anger, grief and solidarity (Goddard); the interruption of female obedient compliance with patriarchal structures (Fragkou); the cracks in the fantasy of agency, control, self-enterprise and progress (Boll; Wallace; Watkinson); and the feelings that democracy stirs and the ones it suppresses (Delgado-García). Many question the very binary of thinking and feeling (Aragay; Delgado-García; Stöckl; Tomlin), while others highlight disturbances and disruptions as an aesthetic strategy to produce ethical appeals and effects (Middeke). In short, the volume sees affects as dynamic and disruptive, and capable of disturbing the very structures that they may have contributed to form and fossilise. The significance of such affective disturbances, even if small, cannot be disregarded. As Bennett puts it, "[t]here will be no greening of the economy, no redistribution of wealth, no enforcement or extension of rights without human dispositions, moods, and cultural ensembles hospitable to these effects" (2010, xiii).

Notes

1. As Sarah Crook explains, "[t]he Public Feelings project, which developed [in the US] in the early 2000s, sought to navigate and understand the emotional dynamics of contemporary life within the political and power structures from which they emerge" (2013). Cvetkovich's own *Depression: A Public Feeling* (2012) is an outcome of this project.
2. In pre-Axial ancient Greek or Sanskrit cultures, there is a strong correlation between the social/political and the moral/religious order; Axial civilisations, instead, including Christianity, "institutionally and discursively differentiate between mundane and transcendent spheres of being" (Wehrs 2017, 4). Both pre-Axial and Axial worldviews, however, place a "permeable" human self at their core, whereas post-Axial cultures substitute a "disengaged self" for whom the natural/material world "becomes raw material whose proper processing, Descartes claims, enables individuals to becomes the human world's masters and transformers" (Wehrs 2017, 16). Notwithstanding Wehrs's expansive historical and transcultural overview, *The Palgrave Handbook to Affect Studies and Textual* focuses almost exclusively on narrative fiction and poetry; of the thirty-one chapters the book

comprises, only Julia Reinhard Lupton's addresses theatre, with Shakespeare's *King Lear* as its main case study (Lupton 2017).

3. This belatedness might not be unrelated to the cultural preeminence of "[t]he arc of post-Axial reflection running from Descartes to Althusser [that] tends to obscure or ignore affect" (Wehrs 2017, 24), particularly damaging, perhaps, to an art form, theatre, that "traffics frequently and fundamentally in feeling in all its forms" (Hurley 2010, 4). Theatrical forms that most openly and actively mobilise feelings, such as nineteenth-century melodrama, Hurley contends, have traditionally been accorded a conspicuously low position in a cultural hierarchy of theatrical value, which "underscore[s] the dubiously regarded place of feeling and its undeniably somatic—or embodied—dimension in theatre practice and studies" (2010, 59).
4. For a more expansive taxonomy, see Seigworth and Gregg (2010, 6–9), who identify up to eight branches of contemporary theories on affect.
5. Wehrs pays scant attention to this strand: one paragraph (2017, 41) and one endnote (2017, 71).
6. Neuroscientist Antonio Damasio (2003, [1994] 2005) was a pioneer in this respect. As Wehrs notes, "Damasio suggested that cognition, emotion, reasoning, and evaluation are dialogically entwined through forms of mental processing carried on by both evolutionarily earlier and evolutionarily later anatomical-neurophysiological structures and systems" (2017, 36).
7. See also Rei Terada, who summarises a common understanding of the terms as follows: "by emotion we mean a psychological, at least minimally interpretive experience whose physiological aspect is affect. Feeling is a capacious term that denotes both physiological sensations (affects) and psychological states (emotions)" (2001, 4).
8. For Williams's concept of "structures of feeling," see his *Marxism and Literature* (1977, 128–35).

References

Ahmed, Sara. 2004a. *The Cultural Politics of Emotion*. London and New York: Routledge.

———. 2004b. "Affective Economies." *Social Text* 22 (2): 117–39.

———. 2006. *Queer Phenomenology: Orientations, Objects, Others*. Durham, NC and London: Duke UP.

———. 2014. *Willful Subjects*. Durham, NC and London: Duke UP.

———. 2017. *Living a Feminist Life*. Durham, NC and London: Duke UP.

Alston, Adam. 2016. *Beyond Immersive Theatre*. London: Palgrave Macmillan.

Artaud, Antonin. 1993. *The Theatre and Its Double*. Translated by Victor Corti. London: Calder.

Barad, Karen. 2007. *Meeting the Universe Halfway: Quantum Physics and the Entanglement of Matter and Meaning*. Durham, NC and London: Duke UP.

Baraniecka, Elżbieta. 2013. *Sublime Drama: British Theatre of the 1990s*. Berlin and Boston: De Gruyter.

Bennett, Jane. 2010. *Vibrant Matter: On the Political Ecology of Things*. Durham, NC and London: Duke UP.

Berlant, Lauren. 2011. *Cruel Optimism*. Durham, NC and London: Duke UP.

Blackman, Lisa. 2008. "Affect, Relationality and the 'Problem of Personality'." *Theory, Culture and Society* 25 (1): 27–51.

Brinkema, Eugenie. 2014. *The Forms of the Affects*. Durham, NC and London: Duke UP.

Cavarero, Adriana. 2011. "Inclining the Subject: Ethics, Alterity and Natality." In Elliot and Attridge 2011, 194–204.

Clough, Patricia T. with Jean Halley, eds. 2007. *The Affective Turn: Theorizing the Social*. Durham, NC and London: Duke UP.

Crook, Sarah. 2013. Review of *Depression: A Public Feeling, by* Ann Cvetkovich. *The History of Emotions Blog*, July 23. Accessed May 28, 2020.

Cvetkovich, Ann. 2012. *Depression: A Public Feeling*. Durham, NC and London: Duke UP.

Damasio, Antonio. 2003. *Looking for Spinoza: Joy, Sorrow, and the Feeling Brain*. New York: Harcourt Brace.

———. (1994) 2005. *Descartes' Error: Emotion, Reason and the Human Brain*. London: Penguin.

Diamond, Elin, Denise Varney, and Candice Amich, eds. 2017. *Performance, Feminism and Affect in Neoliberal Times*. London: Palgrave Macmillan.

Elliot, Jane and Derek Attridge, eds. 2011. *Theory After 'Theory'*. London and New York: Routledge.

Gregg, Melissa and Gregory J. Seigworth, eds. 2010. *The Affect Theory Reader*. Durham, NC and London: Duke UP.

Hardt, Michael. 2007. "What Affects Are Good For." In Clough with Halley 2007, ix–xii.

Hemmings, Clare. 2005. "Invoking Affect: Cultural Theory and the Ontological Turn." *Cultural Studies* 19 (5): 548–67.

Hurley, Erin. 2010. *theatre & feeling*. Basingstoke and New York: Palgrave Macmillan.

———. 2014a. "Introduction: Theatre Matters." In Hurley 2014b, 1–11.

———, ed. 2014b. *Theatres of Affect: New Essays on Canadian Theatre*. Toronto: Playwrights Canada.

Jürs-Munby, Karen, Jerome Carroll and Steve Giles, eds. 2013. *Postdramatic Theatre and the Political: International Perspectives on Contemporary Performance*. London: Bloomsbury.

La Caze, Marguerite and Henry Martyn Lloyd. 2011. "Philosophy and the 'Affective Turn.'" *Parrhesia* 13: 1–13.

Labanyi, Jo. 2010. "Doing Things: Emotion, Affect and Materiality." *Journal of Spanish Cultural Studies* 11 (3–4): 223–33.

Lehmann, Hans-Thies. 2013. "A Future for Tragedy? Remarks on the Political and the Postdramatic." In Jürs-Munby, Carroll and Giles 2013, 87–110.

Leys, Ruth. 2011. "The Turn to Affect: A Critique." *Critical Inquiry* 37 (3): 434–72.

Lupton, Julia Reinhard. 2017. "Trust in Theatre." In Wehrs and Blake 2017, 155–81.

Lyotard, Jean-François. 1991. *The Inhuman: Reflections on Time*. Translated by Geoffrey Bennington and Rachel Bowbly. Cambridge: Polity.

Malabou, Catherine. 2008. *What Should We Do with Our Brain?* Translated by Sebastian Rand. New York: Fordham UP.

Massumi, Brian. 1995. "The Autonomy of Affect." *Cultural Critique* 31 (Autumn): 83–109.

———. 2002. *Parables for the Virtual: Movement, Affect, Sensation*. Durham, NC and London: Duke UP.

———. 2011. *Semblance and Event: Activist Philosophy and the Occurrent Arts*. Cambridge, MA: MIT Press.

———. 2015a. *Politics of Affect*. Cambridge: Polity.

———. 2015b. *Ontopower: War, Powers, and the State of Perception*. Durham, NC and London: Duke UP.

McConachie, Bruce. 2013. *theatre & mind*. Basingstoke and London: Palgrave Macmillan.

Mouffe, Chantal. 2000. *The Democratic Paradox*. London: Verso.

———. 2013. *Agonistics: Thinking the World Politically*. London: Verso.

———. 2018. *For a Left Populism*. London: Verso.

Nancy, Jean-Luc. 2008. *Corpus*. Translated by Richard A. Rand. New York: Fordham UP.

Ngai, Sianne. 2005. *Ugly Feelings*. Cambridge, MA: Harvard UP.

O'Sullivan, Simon. (2005) 2010. "Subjectivity + Art." In Parr (2005) 2010b, 276–78.

Parr, Adrian. (2005) 2010a. "Lines of Flight + Art + Politics." In Parr (2005) 2010b, 149–51.

———, ed. (2005) 2010b. *The Deleuze Dictionary*. Edinburgh: Edinburgh UP.

Pedwell, Carolyn. 2014. *Affective Relations: The Transnational Politics of Empathy*. Basingstoke and New York: Palgrave Macmillan.

Reynolds, Bryan. 2017. *Intermedial Theater: Performance Philosophy, Transversal Poetics, and the Future of Affect*. London: Palgrave Macmillan.

Ridout, Nicholas. 2006. *Stage Fright, Animals and Other Theatrical Problems*. Cambridge: Cambridge UP.

Seigworth, Gregory J. and Melissa Gregg. 2010. "An Inventory of Shimmers." In Gregg and Seigworth 2010, 1–25.

Shaughnessy, Nicola. 2012. *Applying Performance: Live Art, Socially Engaged Theatre and Affective Practice*. Basingstoke and New York: Palgrave Macmillan.

———, ed. 2013. *Affective Performance and Cognitive Science: Body, Brain and Being*. London: Bloomsbury.

Slaby, Jan, Rainer Mühlhoff and Philipp Wüschner. 2019. "Affective Arrangements." *Emotion Review* 11 (1): 3–12.

Spinoza, Baruch. (1677) 2001. *The Ethics*. Trans. R. H. M. Elwes. *Full Text Archive: Free Classic E-Books*. Accessed February 12, 2020.

Stanley, Kate. 2017. "Affect and Emotion: James, Dewey, Tomkins, Damasio, Massumi, Spinoza." In Wehrs and Blake 2017, 97–112.

Terada, Rei 2001: *Feeling in Theory: Emotion after the 'Death of the Subject.'* Cambridge, MA: Harvard UP.

Thompson, James. 2009. *Performance Affects: Applied Theatre and the End of Effect*. Basingstoke and New York: Palgrave Macmillan.

Wehrs, Donald R. 2017. "Introduction: Affect and Texts: Contemporary Inquiry and Historical Context." In Wehrs and Blake 2017, 1–93.

Wehrs, Donald R. and Thomas Blake, eds. 2017. *The Palgrave Handbook of Affect Studies and Textual Criticism*. London: Palgrave Macmillan.

Welton, Martin. 2012. *Feeling Theatre*. Basingstoke and New York: Palgrave Macmillan.

Whalley, Joanne 'Bob' and Lee Miller. 2016. *Between Us: Audiences, Affect and the In-Between*. London: Palgrave Macmillan.

Williams, Raymond. 1977. *Marxism and Literature*. Oxford: Oxford UP.

PART I

Affects and Cognition: Thought, Intention, Empathy

CHAPTER 2

Feel and Think, Think and Feel: Complicating Empathy in debbie tucker green's *hang*

Mireia Aragay

Introduction: Framing the Argument

Judith Butler opens *Frames of War: When Is Life Grievable?* by drawing attention to the political import of epistemological framing: "the frames through which we apprehend or, indeed, fail to apprehend the lives of others as lost or injured (lose-able or injurable) are politically saturated" ([2009] 2010, 1). They are "operations of power" ([2009] 2010, 1), normative schemes that determine the limits of intelligibility and recognition ([2009] 2010, 5–12). In this chapter, I examine the workings of empathy in debbie tucker green's *hang* (2015) through the concept of *affective* frames, that is, in the light of the idea that framing is not just essential as regards the production and circulation of knowledge, but equally so when it comes to affects/emotions—which, in turn, also (re)produce frames of intelligibility and recognition. In fact, as will become

M. Aragay (✉)
University of Barcelona, Barcelona, Catalonia
e-mail: aragay@ub.edu

M. Aragay et al. (eds.), *Affects in 21st-Century British Theatre*,
https://doi.org/10.1007/978-3-030-58486-3_2

apparent, my argument questions any assumed opposition between knowledge/cognition and affects/emotions in favour of a model where feeling and thought feed back into one another in an ongoing, continuous process. This model is aligned with a strong tradition of feminist thought that, as Clara Fischer shows, has consistently sought to dismantle cognition/emotion and mind/body dualisms (2016, 812–15). I suggest it also resonates compellingly with tucker green's endlessly innovative dramaturgy, not least in terms of audience address and response.

Importantly in connection with the argument I propose in this chapter, the special issue of *Contemporary Theatre Review* on feminisms and performance—published, as its editors point out, in the context of "a significant resurgence and renewal of interest in feminism in Britain, the USA, and many other countries worldwide over the last five years" (Gorman et al. 2018, 278)—calls for an acknowledgement of "the power of affects" (Gorman et al. 2018, 282–83) to challenge the continuing ascendancy of neoliberal capitalism and white heteronormativity. Zooming in, Trish Reid's contribution to the same special issue, "'Killing Joy as a World Making Project': Anger in the Work of debbie tucker green" (2018), and her recent chapter "'What about the burn their bra bitches': debbie tucker green as the Willfully Emotional Subject" (2020) read tucker green's work as a dramaturgy of affect that rejects cause-and-effect realism in favour of foregrounding the intricate relationship between emotions and political power structures. In both instances, Reid brings tucker green's plays into conversation with cultural critic Sara Ahmed's work. Situated at the crossroads of feminist, queer and race studies, Ahmed's *oeuvre* is grounded in the claim that any binary distinction between affect and emotion "can only be analytic," as if "bodily sensation, emotion and thought [...] could be 'experienced' as distinct realms of human 'experience'" (2004, 6)—a view that is shared by other scholars that have "turned" to affect from feminist, queer and/or race-inflected perspectives (e.g., Ngai 2005, 27; Cvetkovich 2012, 4; Pedwell 2014, 21; Fischer 2016, 815). From this premise, in books such as *The Cultural Politics of Emotion* (2004), *The Promise of Happiness* (2010) and *Willful Subjects* (2014), among others, Ahmed's key contribution has been to examine the connections between affects/emotions, bodies, language and larger political configurations, and this, Reid perceptively notes, makes her work particularly resonant with tucker green's plays.

Specifically, Reid reads three frequently discussed aspects of tucker green's work—its formal adventurousness, its inventive, powerfully poetic use of language, and its focus on black women characters—through the lens of Ahmed's "feminist killjoy" (2010) and "willful subject" (2014) figures. She sees Dawta, the central black female character in *born bad* (2003), traumatised by her sexual abuse at the hands of her father, as a willful subject whose resistance manifests as "anger, defiance, irrationality, obstinacy and self-love" (2020, 48). In turn, she reads Three, the angry black woman at the centre of *hang*, as a black feminist killjoy that, like many other similar tucker green characters, "wilfully resist[s] the cultural imperative to follow gendered happiness scripts" (2018, 393). Above all, in dramaturgical terms, Reid views tucker green herself as a doubly willfull subject. Firstly, vis-à-vis black playwrights such as Bola Agbaje, Kwame Kwei-Armah or Roy Williams, whose work is also "consciously and purposefully racially inflected" (2018, 396) but who, as Elaine Aston also points out (2011, 197–98), do not share tucker green's thorough eschewal of social realism. Simultaneously, Reid argues, in relation to a mainstream, particularly English understanding of political theatre that deems rationality and its corollaries—"reasoned argument" in a social realist context—to be key to its value and effectiveness (2018, 397; 2020, 47–48).

This chapter contributes to the incipient conversation on the role of affects/emotions in tucker green's dramaturgy by focusing on the intricate workings of empathy in *hang*. The play is set in an unspecified time ("*Nearly now*"; tucker green 2015, 2) and place. A man, whom we never see but is probably white (we are told he has blue eyes), has violently assaulted a middle-aged woman and traumatised both her and her entire family. It gradually transpires that the woman—Three, described as being black and as having "*a slight, nervous tremble in her hand(s)*" (2)—has been summoned before two equally nameless officials, One and Two—"*any race*" and respectively "*female*" and "*male or female*" (2)—to decide how her aggressor will be executed. In a chilling satire of neoliberal consumer choice, Three is presented with a range of options, from "Passive Insertion," "Expiry by Inhalation," "Ballistic Expiry" or "Beheading" to the "Rope Option" she has settled on long before her interview with the two bureaucrats (51–59). In what follows, I approach the play through a four-faced critical prism, where the first face encompasses recent debates about the affect/emotion of empathy, the second embraces Sianne Ngai's exploration of "ugly feelings" (2005), the third comprises a series of concepts derived from Gilles Deleuze and Félix Guattari coalescing around the notion of "lines of flight," and the fourth and last is drawn from Ahmed's reflections on the relationship between emotions and (in)justice

(2004, 191–202). As I turn the prism, I position my reading of *hang* squarely within "the current debate on affect and emotion," where, in Fischer's words, "what is at stake [...] is the role cognition and representation are afforded therein" (2016, 815). I ultimately suggest that *hang* emerges as part of a body of work—tucker green's theatre as a whole—that "resists bifurcations of emotion/reason [...] that often continue in work by the new affect theorists" (Fischer 2016, 811).

Politicising Empathy

The workings of empathy in tucker green's work deserve further, more nuanced critical attention. So far, examples of "failures of empathy" within her plays have been pinpointed, either in general terms—for instance, "[tucker green] has been concerned to expose the failure in empathy that allows cruelty to persist and to give voice to the grief and anger that understandably proceed from such failure" (Reid 2018, 392)—or by specific reference to one of her plays—for example, "the body's failure to arouse empathy is particularly apparent in *dirty butterfly* where Jo's humanness is obliterated as Amelia refuses to hear Jo's story" (Fragkou 2012, 30). In my own work, *random*, one of her most frequently discussed plays, has been read as a call for empathy on the part of spectators (Aragay and Monforte 2013, 111). In what follows, instead, I proceed on the hypothesis that tucker green's work stages elaborate explorations of the complexity and ambivalence of empathy. In other words, her theatre may be viewed as engaging in what Ann Jurecic describes as "valuable work *with* empathy," thus intervening in "a continuing cultural conversation" about both its possibilities and its limits (2011, 18; italics in the original).

In *The Cultural Politics of Emotion*, Ahmed identifies the kernel of a contemporary affective frame according to which, based on a "Darwinian"—and, I would add, Cartesian—model, "emotions get narrated as a sign of 'our' prehistory, and as a sign of how the primitive persists in the present" (2004, 3). This *consensus* about emotions, in Jacques Rancière's sense of the term ([2010] 2015), sets the scene for two subsequent moves. In the first place, "[t]he hierarchy between emotion and thought/reason gets displaced [...] into a hierarchy between emotions: some emotions are 'elevated' as signs of cultivation, whilst others remain 'lower' as signs of weakness" (Ahmed 2004, 3). Secondly, and relatedly, "emotions may even be represented as good or better than thought, but only insofar as they are re-presented as a form of intelligence, as 'tools' that can be used by subjects in the project of life and career enhancement" (2004, 3). That is, only to the extent that they remain contained within a hierarchical affective frame of "emotional intelligence" wherein "good emotions" are to be "cultivated [...] worked on and towards," while "they remain defined against uncultivated or unruly emotions, which frustrate the formation of the competent self" (2004, 3). In sum, the normative frame privileges cognition/thought over affects/emotions, and occludes the "meaning" of "bad" affects/emotions—where they come from, which bodies they tend to "stick to" and why (Ahmed 2004).

In the wake of the discovery of the human mirror neuron system (MNS) in the 1990s, empathy—from Gr. *empatheia*; *en*-, "into," *pathos/-pathy*, "feeling, pity, passion"—has not only become "a hot-button topic" (Rifkin 2009, 14) in a range of fields, but has arguably taken pride of place within the hierarchical affective frame of "emotional intelligence." In *Affective Relations: The Transnational Politics of Empathy*, Carolyn Pedwell cogently argues that empathy has become "a Euro-American political obsession" (2014, ix) linked to the larger phenomenon of the "commodification of feelings" (2014, 32), which dictates that affects/emotions be "managed" in the interests of the global neoliberal workplace, marketplace and geopolitical order.[1] In the context of the dominant hierarchical affective frame, the existence of mirror neurons—"a type of brain cell that respond equally when we perform an action and when we witness someone else perform the same action" (Winerman 2005)—is interpreted as indicating that human beings are "hardwired" to "catch" others' emotions through embodied, unobtrusive imitation of their facial and vocal expressions, postures and overall behaviours. Allegedly, such mimicry is the bridge to empathy and altruism. This is the "empathy-altruism hypothesis" put forward by social psychologist C. Daniel Batson ([1991] 2014) and favoured by numerous neurologists, primatologists, social thinkers and developmental psychologists, including Frans de Waal (2009), Jeremy Rifkin (2009), and Paul Ehrlich and Robert Ornstein ([2010] 2012). To begin to complicate the picture, it is also espoused by thinkers who can hardly be described as champions of the global neoliberal order, either overtly or implicitly (Bauman [2000] 2012; Beck and Beck-Gernsheim 2001; Olson 2012; Clohesy 2014; Krznaric 2014; Standing [2011] 2014).

Within this framework, empathy is invoked either as essential "for affective dexterity and management in the capitalist marketplace" (Pedwell 2014, 40) or as "an affective bridge between social and cultural differences" (Pedwell 2014, 21) with a near magical capacity to bring about psychic healing, social justice and reconciliation and to foster global care and cooperation—or, indeed, as both. When viewed in this way, empathy can become "a kind of end-point" (Pedwell 2014, x): the linkage between empathy and altruism and the diagnosis of an "empathy deficit" are swiftly followed by a plea to cultivate it, while probing questions about its nature, limits and potential are sidestepped.[2]

Like theorists of affect and emotion who work in the fields of gender and/or race studies, such as Ahmed, Lauren Berlant, Rustom Bharucha, Ann Cvetkovich, Fischer, Ngai or Pedwell, among others, I am interested in what this narrative of empathy blocks from recognition or simply pushes outside the broader affective frame it forms part of. That is, I want to insert some measure of disturbance or dissensus into it, not in order to "dispense with empathy or dismiss its transformative potential" (Pedwell 2014, 42), but so as to explore and attempt to "explain the dynamics of its optimism and exclusions" (Berlant 2004a, 5). For Rancière, the political gesture of dissensus necessarily involves interrogating the dominant affective frame. As Steve Corcoran puts it, while "[t]he key operation of consensus for Rancière involves matching a *poiesis*, or way of doing, with an *aesthesis*, or horizon of affects/quality of speech" ([2010] 2015, 11), "[a]t the heart of dissensus [...] are processes of dis-identification, or of the undoing of [...] the various forms of privatization of speech and emotion" ([2010] 2015, 5). When the scholars mentioned at the start of this paragraph insist, as they do, on the relational character of affects/emotions—including empathy—they are engaged in precisely this kind of dissensual task. "[*D*]*is-sensus*," Corcoran adds, is "a process of re-ordering of the senses" leading to "the creation of a specific *sensorium* in which the rules that subordinate [...] bodies to places and corresponding horizons of affect, are reframed and suspended" ([2010] 2015, 4; italics in the original). When Ahmed foregrounds "unruly emotions" (2004, 3) or Ngai examines "ugly" or "dysphoric feelings" (2005, 1) such as anger, anxiety, disgust, envy, fear, hate, irritation, rage or shame, they are performing the equally dissensual operation of reframing an existing horizon of affect.

From a relational perspective that does not see affects/emotions as constitutive of the individual subject's interiority, but rather conceives them as cultural practices produced as "effects of circulation" (Ahmed 2004, 8) within specific geopolitical and social circumstances, affect theorists who conduct their work in the domains of feminist/queer and/or race studies delve into the tensions and ambivalences of empathy and their ethical and political implications. What does it mean, exactly, to "identify" with the Other? Does it involve a coercive, narcissistic appropriation of the Other by the (privileged) self in the context of current geopolitical and social divisions between (relative) safety and suffering? Led by questions such as these, their inquiry emphasises the complex imbrication of empathy in specific structures of power, currently still defined by neoliberal capitalism and white heteronormativity. "An unproblematized empathy," as theatre and performance scholar Bharucha points out, "can be unconsciously exclusionary" (2014, 64). On this basis, these critics proceed to "complicate empathy" in their analyses of cultural forms of representation.[3] That is, they jettison an approach that I would describe as "reading *for* empathy"—where empathy is not only assumed to be uncomplicatedly and universally positive and inseparable from altruism, but to always-already exist in the individual subject (reader, spectator), waiting to be tapped into—in favour of "reading empathy" as a complex, ambivalent, socially, culturally and politically mediated feeling.

Berlant's pioneering essay "Poor Eliza" (1998) is exemplary in this respect. Her sweeping historical excavation of the highly gender- and race-biased US discourse of "liberal sentiment" (1998, 636) leads her to the conclusion that "[b]ecause the ideology of true feeling cannot admit the nonuniversality of pain," the ethical and political "imperative toward social transformation is replaced by a civic-minded but passive ideal of empathy" (1998, 641). In the rest of this chapter, I take Berlant's statement as a starting point for a reading of the workings of empathy as it circulates—or, rather, is blocked from circulating—both within *hang* and, crucially, between the play and its spectators, in the process rubbing against "ugly" affects/emotions.

"You couldn't get anywhere near": Ugly Feelings and Trajectories of Repulsion

Marginalised or demonised within the dominant affective regime, ugly feelings ensue from situations of restricted or suspended agency (Ngai 2005, 2–3), the sort of subject positionality that is often occupied in neoliberal, white heteronormative societies by black women, doubly marginalised by sexism and racism. As Audre Lorde, one of the earlier-generation voices that has been revived by the recent renascence of feminism (Fischer 2016, 813 and 815; Gorman et al. 2018, 279), puts it, "[w]e operate in the teeth of a system for which racism and sexism are primary, established, and necessary props of profit" ([1984] 2007, 128). For Lorde, anger is the inevitable, indeed indispensable, ugly feeling in response to this ([1984] 2007, 124–33 and 145–75). tucker green's work, as Reid notes (2020, 49), is populated with angry black female characters, and *hang*'s Three is undoubtedly one of them. But before turning to the presence of ugly feelings in the play itself, I want to examine their circulation in terms of audience response.

To the extent that reviewers' reactions are helpful in gauging the wider affective/emotional impact of *hang*, it seems significant that a considerable number responded to the 2015 premiere production on the main stage at the Royal Court, directed by tucker green herself, with the ugly feelings of irritation and vexation. The play's opacity as regards character names, place, time period and the exact nature of the crime was described as frustrating (Hemming 2015; Maxwell 2015; Nathan 2015; Sierz 2015) or literally "irritating" (Letts 2015). Structurally, the play was perceived as "den[ying] us many of the traditional satisfactions of drama" (Billington 2015)—it was described as "repetitive" and "overextended" (Maxwell 2015), as feeling "longer" than its comparatively short running time of seventy minutes (Letts 2015) and as lacking "story," "conflict" and "drama" (Sierz 2015).[4] Overall, then, in affective/emotional terms, the play appears to have made its predominantly white, middle-class, male reviewers experience something akin to the ugly feelings (frustration, irritation) that tend to stick to less privileged bodies who routinely find themselves in positions of obstructed agency—they were unable to "master" the play in terms of their habitual epistemological frame.[5] In the next section I return to the structural objections mentioned by the reviewers. For now, of particular significance in the context of my argument is Aleks Sierz's pitting of thought and feeling against each other in his claim that "green doesn't want us to think; she just wants us to feel" (2015). That is, at least as far as *hang* is concerned, Sierz seems to concur with Reid's assessment of tucker green's dramaturgy as fundamentally affective. Yet contrary to Reid, in a Cartesian fashion that reinforces the hierarchical affective frame identified by Ahmed, he belittles the foregrounding of feeling to the detriment of thought as "a cop-out" (2015). At the same time, however, both Reid and Sierz keep affects/emotions and cognition/thought firmly separate on either side of a binary divide—a shared position I begin to unpick in the next paragraph.

In a line of reasoning that is partly inspired by Ngai's reading of Nella Larsen's 1928 novel *Quicksand*, a classic of the Harlem Renaissance, I see the reviewers' ugly feelings as indices of an "aesthetics of illegibility" (Ngai 2005, 175) that I suggest is at work in *hang* at both the textual and performative levels. In order to substantiate this proposition, I take on board Eugenie Brinkema's cogent defense of "the formal dimension of affect" (2014, xv). As noted in the introduction to this collection, an influential strand within the so-called turn to affect, often linked to Brian Massumi's early work (1995, 2002), views affect as entirely autonomous—a purely ontological, embodied, material order of experience uncontaminated by any cognitive, cultural, learned structures, which can, precisely by virtue of this, effectively resist and productively transform those structures. And yet, this complete reversal of the consensual affective frame that valorises thought/cognition over affect/emotion not only remains binary, but it "hold[s] on to the notion of a transcendental signified [...] that predates the linguistic turn" (Brinkema 2014, xiv). For Brinkema, the turn to affect "*does not obliterate the problem of form and representation*" (2014, xiv; italics in the original). On this basis, she makes an "utterly unfashionable" (2014, xv) call for close reading as the way into the dense, plural, formally inscribed specificities of affects. Conceptually, a methodological adherence to close reading chimes in with a nonbinary understanding of the relationship between affect/emotion and thought/cognition, according to which, as Clare Hemmings puts it in her critique of Massumi, bodily/affective/emotional response and reflective judgement form and "ongoing, incrementally altering chain," jointly "influencing the individual's capacity to act in the world" (2005, 564; also Fischer 2016, 819–21). In my view, this is an apt description of what tucker green's dramaturgy invites spectators to do—feel *and* think, think *and* feel, in an open-ended process of mutual accretion that has the potential to "press" on their bodies (Ahmed 2004, 6) and maybe alter their position vis-à-vis existing affective *and* epistemological (hence, political) frames.

Indeed, Ahmed's well-known argument that "emotions work to shape the 'surfaces' of individual and collective bodies" (2004, 1), leaving an "im*press*ion" on them (2004, 6; italics added), is perhaps particularly relevant to an art form, theatre, that depends on the physical presence of bodies on stage and in the auditorium. Like the rest of tucker green's work—not least *ear for eye* (2018), which opens with a scene where an African American son asks her mother's advice on how to hold his hands, only to be told that every conceivable possibility will be read by "them" as threatening, provocative, aggressive, insolent or defiant (tucker green 2018, 3–9)—both textually and performatively *hang* foregrounds "embodiedness." This, to cite Ahmed once more, has the potential to vividly allow spectators "to associate the experience of having an emotion with the very affect of one surface upon another" (2004, 6). Starting with the written text, Three's harrowing description of the consequences of the assault and subsequent bureaucratic "developments" on herself and her family is steeped in the vocabulary of affective/emotional embodiment: "We look at each other different. We talk to each other different. We move around each other carefully we're careful with each other, cautious with each other my son is scared of his shadow and my daughter pisses in her pants—how's that for a fuckin 'development'?" (tucker green 2015, 29–30). So is her excruciating account of how her children's bodies reacted to the attack and still bear its affective/emotional traces. Her seven-year-old daughter "couldn't stop shaking. For hours," while her nine-year-old son "was the one whose / scream only stopped when his voice ran out" (36). Now the boy "is / hollow. […] Like the rest of us" (37). Three's long speech ends with a question addressed to One and Two: "You tell me what do to then. / They are inconsolable. / When it is unexplainable. / When I am lost for words" (37). Admittedly, at first sight Three's description of herself as "lost for words" might appear to signal towards affect understood as prelinguistic, cognitively unassimilable experience. However, what seems fundamental in *hang*—and elsewhere in tucker green's work—is the deployment of a verbal and embodied grammar of ugly feelings that summons spectators to affectively perceive *and* cognitively process Three's predicament. This, to quote Fischer, "is not to deny that there are […] feelings that are not yet fully cognized," but to profess that "providing an ontology of affect, but not a social theory that might explicate […] how affects are culturally generated and transmitted, how they can be utilized for change […] deprives affects of political salience" (2016, 820).[6]

To begin to delineate the social and cultural generation and transmission of affects/emotions in *hang*, then, there seems little doubt that One and Two—Claire Rushbrook and Shane Zaza respectively in the premiere production—articulate the consensual neoliberal discourse on empathy. They repeatedly assure Three that they know how she feels; their empathy is couched in the jargon of "emotional intelligence" and the "efficient management of emotions"—they "train" through "role-playing," speak of their "clients" and are concerned about "transparency" and "protocol"—and the gestures of habit—including offers of tea, coffee and coat hangers. These are what Deleuze calls the refrains and routines of the affective frame of consumer culture (O'Sullivan [2005] 2010, 277), which were replicated in performance by One and Two's matter-of-fact, business-like body language.[7] In contrast, Marianne Jean-Baptiste's body—as Three—came across as a "site of emotional negativity" (Ngai 2005, 1). This was clearly *perceived* by reviewers of the premiere production, who described her in affective/emotional terms as strikingly refractive: arms folded, hands held together or shaking, "huddled in her coat" (Halliburton 2015), "coiled" (Nathan 2015), "totally inturned" (Clapp 2015). At the same time, I suggest, Jean-Baptiste's embodied opacity functioned in a highly productive, albeit paradoxical way. On the one hand, it created "affective gaps and illegibilities" (Ngai 2005, 1) that repulsed any automatic empathetic reaction on the part of spectators towards Three as victim. On the other, like black holes, those gaps and illegibilities had the potential to powerfully draw spectators in. In other words, rather than gesture towards affect as ineffable, precognitive experience, they allowed spectators to affectively/emotionally sense, and incited them to cognitively process and linguistically articulate, Three's dysphoric or ugly feelings. The clinical set, a sparsely furnished room with reflective black walls and bathed in a cold light from rows of fluorescent tubes that, tunnel-like, vanished into a black hole upstage, functioned as a spatial replica of Three's paradoxical embodied opacity (Fig. 2.1).

The written text also foregrounds Three's emotional refractiveness and negativity. The play's two opening "movements," up to the moment Two hustles back in with hot drinks (tucker green 2015, 9), are a highly resonant sample of its affective/emotional verbal texture and structure. One and Two's prattle about automatic light switches, their offers of tea, coffee or water from the water cooler and their questions about changing the time if it is more convenient for Three's husband or whether Three would like to make a phone call (3–8) are prime examples of what Elisabeth Massana calls "(distr)active silence" in tucker green's work, apparently banal conversations that hint at "the power structures and hierarchies that shape the characters" (2020, 264). In this case, One and Two's (distr)active silences signal to the hierarchical affective frame underpinning their encounter with Three—the fact that, as relatively privileged subjects, they are extending empathy unidirectionally towards her in a coercive exercise of narcissistic affective/emotional identification that occludes the "non-universality of pain" (Berlant 1998, 641).

At the same time, One and Two's (distr)active silences seek to cover up another kind of silence, Three's, which the author's notes, characteristically,

Fig. 2.1 Left to right, Shane Zaza (Two), Claire Rushbrook (One) and Marianne Jean-Baptiste (Three) in *hang*, Royal Court Theatre Downstairs, 11 June-18 July 2015, dir. debbie tucker green. Set design: Jon Bausor; lighting: Tim Mitchell. (Photo: Stephen Cummiskey)

describe as "active" ("*Names without dialogue indicate an active silence*"; tucker green 2015, 2).[8] I read Three's active silences as inseparable from the refractiveness of both her body's affective vocabulary and her use of verbal language. In the play's two opening "movements" alone, Three practices the art of active silence no less than fifteen times. In addition, she "*shakes her head*," "*goes to say something then doesn't*," refuses the offer to sit down, says "No" and makes negative statements around ten times, and simply "*clocks* [*One*]," "*says nothing*" or silently "*watches One*" (3–9). According to Ngai, in addition to being experientially and semantically negative, ugly feelings are "'syntactically' negative, in the sense that they are organized by trajectories of repulsion" (2005, 11). To sum up, Three's active silences and her refractive (body) language collectively work to resist One and Two's narcissistic/coercive offers of empathy. Unsurprisingly, the verbal and embodied trajectories of repulsion that Three initiates culminate in moments where she openly denies One and Two's capacity for empathetic imagination. The spatial metaphor she uses on one of these occasions "You *can't* you couldn't get anywhere near" (25; italics in the original)—was reduplicated in performance by the distance Jean-Baptiste kept from Rushbrook and Zaza at all times, which seemed enormous even by northern European cultural standards (Fig. 2.1). Ahmed's discussion of comfort as "the promise of a 'sinking' feeling" between one's body and the space/world around it reverberates strikingly—and, precisely, *negatively*—with the potent image of Jean-Baptiste's/Three's uncomfortable, refractive body and with the use of stage space in *hang*: "To be comfortable is to be so at ease with one's environment that it is hard to distinguish where one's body ends and the world begins. [...] in feelings of comfort, bodies extend into spaces, and spaces extend into bodies. The sinking feeling involves a seamless space, or a space where you can't see the 'stitches' between bodies" (2004, 148).

A Noncathartic Aesthetic: Temporality and "Lines of Flight"

Structurally, *hang* returns cyclically to the kind of "movement" I have just described. In what follows, I take the play's "repetitive" temporality and "overextended" duration (Maxwell 2015), as well as its "denial of many of the traditional satisfactions of drama" (Billington 2015), to be central to both its aesthetics and its affective texture and significance. For Deleuze as much as Rancière, aesthetics can operate as a rupture in relation to a normative, consensual affective frame. A key way it can do so in the context of the accelerated tempo of neoliberal consumer culture, Deleuze suggests, is by opening up a gap between stimulus and response, slowing down time to create moments of stasis or contemplation. This may generate "lines of flight"—nonhabitual responses, both affective and cognitive, that may produce possibilities for a reconfiguration of our subjectivity, that is, for resingularisation: "the pause between action and reaction is what constitutes the human as a particularly complex brain-body assemblage" (O'Sullivan [2005] 2010, 277). I want to relate this to Ngai's view of "narrative expansion or stretch, in which 'discourse time' becomes considerably longer than 'story time'" (2005, 13) as a key component of what she calls a "noncathartic aesthetic" (2005, 9) of ugly feelings that "interfere[s] with the outpouring" of "potentially ennobling or morally beatific" (2005, 6) emotions, such as empathy—catharsis being, of course, one of the central "traditional satisfactions of drama" (Billington 2015).

I believe *hang* belongs to the noncathartic aesthetic mode identified by Ngai, a kind of art that slows down discourse time and thereby "produces and foregrounds a failure of emotional release," a gesture that is "a kind of politics" (Ngai 2005, 9). Overall, the play's noncathartic aesthetic joins its affective/emotional refractiveness and its withholding of factual detail to create forms of illegibility that dissensually interrupt the dominant affective frame, tugging at and troubling spectators' consensual/habitual affective/cognitive responses, particularly in terms of empathy. Ultimately, the play refuses to offer the affective consolation of empathetic emotional release for the victim, Three. The spectator is left in a state of arrested affective/emotional agency, immersed in the dysphoric meta-affect of disorientation or bewilderment, of being lost in one's "map" of available affects (Ngai 2005, 14). But it is precisely such confusion, I argue, that keeps the "incrementally altering chain" of affective/emotional response and cognitive reflection—feeling *and* thought, thought *and* feeling—potentially "pressing" on us as we leave the theatre. That is, paradoxically, it keeps us, affectively *and* cognitively, on the move. In this respect, Natasha Tripney's "you find yourself, at the final blackout, *holding your breath*" (2015; italics added) and Matt Trueman's "[i]t is a play that *sticks to the throat*" (2015; italics added) are entirely fitting bodily metaphors to describe the effect of *hang* on spectators willing to engage with its "negative" aesthetics.[9] A close reading of the play's final moments will show how this paradoxical blend of affective and cognitive arrest and movement reaches a point of saturation around Three and her aggressor.

At the end of the play, the process of withholding the affective/emotional experience of catharsis from spectators zooms in on the letter the attacker has written to Three. Both the letter itself and its contents have been withheld from Three by One and Two. From the moment One first mentions the letter (tucker green 2015, 33) to the moment Two produces the envelope containing it (42), discourse time is stretched out while the two bureaucrats give conflicting accounts of when the assailant wrote it, until it transpires that they read it "five weeks ago" and he wrote it "[a] couple of months before / then" (43). One and Two, that is, release the letter to Three only when her decision that her aggressor be hanged has been made and confirmed (60). As regards Three, from the moment Two pulls the envelope out (42) to the moment she asks One, "What does it say in the letter?" (61), not only is discourse time slowed down, but her body traces a literal trajectory of attraction and repulsion on stage as, left alone in the room for a few minutes, she first watches the envelope intently from where she is sitting, then gets up and walks towards the water cooler, "*approaches the envelope*," "*touches the tiniest corner of it*," "*backs off*," "*subtly sniffs it*," "*watches it*" and finally returns to her chair (45). Discourse time continues to be stretched out while Three, "*painstakingly slowly*" because of her shaking hand (66), signs the forms testifying to her choice of execution method, asks Two to read the letter and, failing this, turns to One to open it for her (69).

The letter itself is affectively/emotionally saturated with imprints of the aggressor's body. It is handwritten (63, 71) and, in Three's words, it carries "his, tone. His intonations. His accent. His breath, weight of his breath. His spit. His smell. His odour, his sweat, the weight of his sweat, his… / Them fucking blue eyes, his eyes in my… and it will be his voice that I hear, that I hear it in that I read it, that I read it in, because you wouldn't read it—no" (67). The man's affective/emotional presence intensifies when Three pulls the letter from the envelope, "*a small passport-sized photo falls out*" and she "*studies it intently*" (69–70). Although the letter is short, "Not even a page" (70), the assailant's words are withheld from us, since Three's reading of the letter, right at the end of the play, takes place in almost complete silence. In the published text, the sustained focus on Three's trembling hands as she reads silently has the effect of foregrounding the two bits she does read aloud: "Dear" and "(*quietly*) He's… *She continues to read.* … 'Sorry.' *She continues to read. Beat. End*" (71).

As Ahmed observes in "Just Emotions," her conclusion to *The Cultural Politics of Emotion*, an offender's expression of remorse automatically calls for a return by the victim "through an expression of forgiveness" (2004, 198)—a kind of forgiveness that, in the case of *hang*, resonates with Jacques Derrida's aporetic understanding of it: "forgiveness forgives only the unforgivable" (2001, 32–33). Viewed in this way, the end of the published text hints at the possibility of an "'exchange' of emotions" (Ahmed 2004, 198) between assailant and victim that might bring about some kind of restoration. However, crucially, the play becomes arrested at this point. Instead of witnessing the circulation of affects/emotions between aggressor and victim that might enable the cathartic release of the spectators' own feelings—particularly straightforward, uncomplicated empathetic identification with Three—we are stuck in a state of affective/emotional saturation that, paradoxically, presses on us to keep moving, both affectively and cognitively. Interestingly, for the premiere production of the play at the Royal Court, tucker green revised the ending to delete any disclosure of the aggressor's words. This left the contents of the letter completely to "the individual audience member's imagination" (Rabey 2020, 200), which redoubled the saturated pressure on them. For Deleuze and Guattari, saturation is an unstable state of maximum concentration that may produce lines of flight that make the coherence of normative, consensual frames "leak" (Parr [2005] 2010a, 150). The question is, what dissensual affective and cognitive paths does the play seem to invite us to explore?

"Just Emotions": Feeling, Thought and (In)justice in *Hang*

I suggest the arrested, saturated end of the play works as an invitation to spectators to affectively *and* cognitively address the question Ahmed asks at the start of "Just Emotions": "How are emotions bound up with stories of justice and injustice? [...] Is a just response to injustice about having more 'just emotions,'" such as empathy, "or is justice never 'just' about emotions?" (2004, 191). The fourth and last face of my critical prism, Ahmed's reflection on the relationship between emotions and (in)justice, thus ultimately returns to my opening argument about the ongoing mutual implication between affects/emotions/feelings and thought/judgement/cognition—the latter in the shape of the public domain of justice and injustice.

In the field of moral and political philosophy, Ahmed points out, "[j]ustice becomes a form of feeling, which is about 'fellow-feeling'" (2004, 195), a capacity to feel with and for others—namely, empathy and sympathy. However, this view works through occluding power relations: it not only "individuate[s], personalise[s] and privatise[s] the social relation of injustice" (Ahmed 2004, 195), but it can also "repeat the forms of violence it seeks to redress, as it can sustain the distinction between the subject and object of feeling" (Ahmed 2004, 193). Seen in this light, Three's persistent repulsing of One and Two's offers of empathy, the play's making it well-nigh impossible for spectators to turn Three's suffering into empathy for her and its saturated ending work to produce a line of flight that affectively and cognitively motions spectators away from the consensual frame that sees empathy as the solution to every social ill and injustice.

In sum, *hang* resonates strongly with Ahmed's claim that "the terrain of (in)justice cannot be a question of 'having' or 'not having' an emotion" (2004, 195).

Secondly, since "injustice is a question of how bodies come into contact with other bodies" in the context of "particular kinds of affective relations to social norms," "challenging social norms involves having a different affective relation to those norms" (Ahmed 2004, 196). Three's ugly feelings—her anger, rage and resentment, which are exactly the three affects Ahmed identifies as possible effects of injustice (2004, 196) and which underpin Three's call for the most extreme form of retributive justice for her assailant, namely the death penalty—may thus be read as uncomfortably challenging social expectations that position the victimised (black) woman as the abject recipient of pain and suffering. In connection with this, drawing suggestively on contemporary translation studies, Pedwell asks "what it might mean to understand empathy not as affective access to 'foreign' psychic or cultural worlds and/or the production of emotional equivalence" (2014, 37), but rather as a process that requires "surrendering oneself to *being affected by* that what is experienced as 'foreign'" (2014, 38; italics in the original). If anything, it is this reconfigured understanding of empathy as a transformative force that may allow "the violence of an affective experience to truly inform thinking" (Bennett 2005, 55) that spectators are encouraged to experience at the end of *hang*. When viewed in this way, empathy may be described as a "just emotion" in Ahmed's terms—that is, one that "works *with* and *on* rather than *over* the wounds that surface as traces of past injuries in the present" (2004, 202; italics in the original). An emotion that allows us to affectively sense and cognitively understand that, while Three's ugly feelings may be "incomplete form[s] of human knowledge" (Lorde [1984] 2007, 152), they are also legitimate manifestations of the unjust distribution of suffering in a sexist, racist culture.

Thirdly, and relatedly, justice is not simply about healing through overcoming pain or ugly feelings, as this "can involve the erasure of relations of violence" (Ahmed 2004, 197). As Ahmed explains, this is the approach taken within the field of restorative justice, including the truth commissions set up in response to historical injustice of the kind tucker green's *truth and reconciliation* (2011) explores. According to this criminological frame, "justice is about making offenders 'feel' the costs of their crime," thereby "repair[ing] injury for victims" (Ahmed 2004, 197) and restoring "good relationships" (Ahmed 2004, 199). Conversely, in *hang* the foregrounding of Three's ugly feelings and the noncathartic, saturated ending work to interrupt the logic of restorative justice. Instead, the play places spectators on the threshold of an affective and cognitive line of flight sustained by unspoken questions that are, nevertheless, powerfully intimated by its saturated ending. Firstly, the implications of the "personalising of crime" that restorative justice depends on, that is, its occlusion of crime's "public and systematic dimensions" (2004, 198) and of "the injustice of how 'relationships' work" (2004, 199) to begin with. Ultimately, the larger question of how to recognise an injury so that the victim may learn "to live with injuries that threaten to make life impossible" (Ahmed 2004, 201), as is the case with Three and her family.

tucker green's entire dramaturgy engages relentlessly in what Ahmed calls "the work of exposure" (2004, 200). Persistently, as Ahmed instructs, it refuses to cover over the wounds caused by injustice with any "magic" affective solutions such as empathy. It thereby confronts spectators with questions about suffering, forgiveness, healing, restitution and, above all, (in)justice that require that, affectively and cognitively, we "allow more of what is *not* ourselves to transform what we take ourselves to be" (Colebrook [2005] 2010, 4; italics in the original). Hers is a political dramaturgy that renounces neither affect/emotion nor thought/cognition, thereby powerfully demonstrating that "we are not just talking about emotions when we talk about emotions" (Ahmed 2004, 202). Rather, we are talking about past and present, intimate and social "histories of bodies," and we are talking about the future too, as "different orientations to others" (Ahmed 2004, 202) may emerge from dissensually interrogating existing affective, epistemological and political frames.[10]

Notes

1. Like Lauren Berlant, I use the term *neoliberal* to point to "a set of delocalized processes that have played a huge role in transforming postwar political and economic norms of reciprocity and meritocracy since the 1970s," while being aware that it does not constitute "a world-homogenizing system whose forces are played out to the same effect, or affect, everywhere" (2011, 9).
2. President Barack Obama's much-publicised identification of an "empathy deficit" in the US no doubt contributed to the growing visibility of the mainstream narrative in the mid-2000s (Ehrlich and Ornstein 2012, 4; Pedwell 2014, ix).

3. The phrase "complicating empathy" in the second part of this chapter's title is drawn from Jurecic (2011, 18).
4. In a private conversation, Marilena Zaroulia (Royal Central School of Speech and Drama, University of London) also described her reaction to *hang* as "frustrated" or "irritated," on grounds similar to those mentioned in the preceding lines. I cite this with Zaroulia's permission as perhaps indicating that other audience members shared these reviewers' affective responses too.
5. By this, I naturally do not wish to imply an equivalence between the ugly feelings of the dispossessed in real life and those of a privileged audience in the safety of the theatre.
6. These lines form part of Fischer's critique of Massumi's "reductive tendency [...] to equate affect with bodily immanence, and to preclude cognition, culture, and representation" (2016, 811).
7. I saw *hang* at the Royal Court Theatre Downstairs on July 14, 2015.
8. Both Aston (2011, 195) and Lynette Goddard (2013, 193) mention active silences as one of tucker green's important dramaturgical innovations.
9. In an essay published after the present one had been completed, Maggie Inchley uses the phrase "sticking in the throat" to describe, via feminist psychoanalyst Joan Copjec's work on affect, tucker green's "precise yet elusive poetical practice," which in her view enables pain to circulate "through bodies distant in time and place from those which have suffered, causing reflection among audience members on the cultural practices that sustain gendered and racialized economies and institutions" (2020, 172).
10. I am grateful to Massana and Reid for allowing me to read their then still unpublished manuscripts. This chapter has benefitted from the caring, insightful close reading of Rodrigo Andrés (University of Barcelona) and, especially, Katarzyna Paszkiewicz (University of the Balearic Islands). To them both, my warmest thanks.

References

Adiseshiah, Siân and Jacqueline Bolton, eds. 2020. *debbie tucker green: Critical Perspectives*. London: Palgrave Macmillan.

Ahmed, Sara. 2004. *The Cultural Politics of Emotion*. London and New York: Routledge.

———. 2010. *The Promise of Happiness*. Durham, NC and London: Duke UP.

———. 2014. *Willful Subjects*. Durham, NC and London: Duke UP.

Angelaki, Vicky, ed. 2013. *Contemporary British Theatre: Breaking New Ground*. Basingstoke and London: Palgrave Macmillan.

Aragay, Mireia, and Enric Monforte. 2013. "Racial Violence, Witnessing and Emancipated Spectatorship in *The Colour of Justice*, *Fallout* and *random*." In Angelaki 2013, 96–120.

Aston, Elaine. 2011. "debbie tucker green." In Middeke, Schnierer and Sierz 2011, 183–202.

Batson, C. Daniel. (1991) 2014. *The Altruism Question: Toward a Social-Psychological Answer*. New York: Psychology Press.

Bauman, Zygmunt. (2000) 2012. *Liquid Modernity*. Cambridge: Polity.

Beck, Ulrich and Elisabeth Beck-Gernsheim. 2001. *Individualization: Institutionalized Individualism and its Social and Political Consequences*. Thousand Oaks, CA: Sage.

Bennett, Jill. 2005: *Empathic Vision: Affect, Trauma, and Contemporary Art*. Stanford, CA: Stanford UP.

Berlant, Lauren. 1998. "Poor Eliza." *American Literature* 70 (3): 635–68.

———. 2004a. "Compassion (and Withholding)." In Berlant 2004b, 1–14.

———. 2011. *Cruel Optimism*. Durham, NC and London: Duke UP.

———, ed. 2004b. *Compassion: The Culture and Politics of an Emotion*. London and New York: Routledge.

Bharucha, Rustom. 2014. *Terror and Performance*. London and New York: Routledge.

Billington, Michael. 2015. Review of *hang*, by debbie tucker green. *Guardian*, June 18.

Brinkema, Eugenie. 2014. *The Forms of the Affects*. Durham, NC and London: Duke UP.

Brown, Georgina. 2015. Review of *hang*, by debbie tucker green. *Mail on Sunday*, June 28.

Butler, Judith. (2009) 2010. *Frames of War: When Is Life Grievable?* London and New York: Verso.

Cavendish, Dominic. 2015. Review of *hang*, by debbie tucker green. *Daily Telegraph*, June 18.

Clapp, Susannah. 2015. Review of *hang*, by debbie tucker green. *Observer*, June 21.

Clohesy, Anthony. 2014. *Politics of Empathy: Ethics, Solidarity, Recognition*. London and New York: Routledge.

Colebrook, Claire. (2005) 2010. "Introduction." In Parr (2005) 2010b, 1–6.

Corcoran, Steven. (2010) 2015. "Editor's Introduction." In Rancière (2010) 2015, 1–31.

Cvetkovich, Ann. 2012. *Depression: A Public Feeling*. Durham, NC and London: Duke UP.

Derrida, Jacques. 2001. *On Cosmopolitanism and Forgiveness*. Translated by Mark Dooley and Michael Hughes. London and New York: Routledge.

de Waal, Frans B. 2009. *The Age of Empathy: Nature's Lessons for a Kinder Society*. New York: Crown.

Ehrlich, Paul R., and Robert E. Ornstein. (2010) 2012. *Humanity on a Tightrope: Thoughts on Empathy, Family, and Big Changes for a Viable Future*. Lanham, MD: Rowman & Littlefield.

Fischer, Clara. 2016. "Feminist Philosophy, Pragmatism, and the 'Turn to Affect': A Genealogical Critique." *Hypatia* 31 (4): 810–26.

Fragkou, Marissia. 2012. "Precarious Subjects: Ethics of Witnessing and Responsibility in the Plays of debbie tucker green." *Performing Ethos* 3 (1): 23–39.

Goddard, Lynette. 2013. "debbie tucker green." In Rebellato 2013, 190–212.

Gorman, Sarah, Geraldine Harris and Jen Harvie. 2018. "Feminisms Now." *Contemporary Theatre Review* 28 (3): 278–84.

Halliburton, Rachel. 2015. Review of *hang*, by debbie tucker green. *Time Out London*, June 18.

Hemming, Sarah. 2015. Review of *hang*, by debbie tucker green. *Financial Times*, June 19.

Hemmings, Clare. 2005. "Invoking Affect: Cultural Theory and the Ontological Turn." *Cultural Studies* 19 (5): 548–67.

Inchley, Maggie. 2020. "Sticking in the Throat/Keyword Bitch: Aesthetic Discharge in debbie tucker green's *stoning mary* and *hang*." In Adiseshiah and Bolton 2020, 171–89.

Jurecic, Ann. 2011. "Empathy and the Critic." *College English* 71 (1): 10–27.

Krznaric, Roman. 2014. *Empathy: A Handbook for Revolution*. London: Rider.

Letts, Quentin. 2015. Review of *hang*, by debbie tucker green. *Daily Mail*, June 17.

Lorde, Audre. (1984) 2007. *Sister Outsider: Essays and Speeches*. Berkeley, CA: Crossing Press.

Massana, Elisabeth. 2020. "Cartographies of Silence in debbie tucker green's *truth and reconciliation*." In Adiseshiah and Bolton 2020, 257–75.

Massumi, Brian. 1995. "The Autonomy of Affect." *Cultural Critique* 31: 83–109.

———. 2002. *Parables for the Virtual: Movement, Affect, Sensation*. Durham, NC and London: Duke UP.

Maxwell, Dominic. 2015. Review of *hang*, by debbie tucker green. *Times*, June 18.

Middeke, Martin, Peter Paul Schnierer and Aleks Sierz, eds. 2011. *The Methuen Drama Guide to Contemporary British Playwrights*. London: Bloomsbury.

Nathan, John. 2015. Review of *hang*, by debbie tucker green. *Jewish Chronicle*, June 18.

Ngai, Sianne. 2005. *Ugly Feelings*. Cambridge, MA: Harvard UP.

O'Sullivan, Simon. (2005) 2010. "Subjectivity + Art." In Parr (2005) 2010b, 276–78.

Olson, Gary. 2012. *Empathy Imperiled: Capitalism, Culture, and the Brain*. Berlin and New York: Springer.

Parr, Adrian (2005) 2010a. "Lines of Flight + Art + Politics." In Parr (2005) 2010b, 149–51.

———, ed. (2005) 2010b. *The Deleuze Dictionary*. Edinburgh: Edinburgh UP.

Pedwell, Carolyn. 2014. *Affective Relations: The Transnational Politics of Empathy*. Basingstoke and New York: Palgrave Macmillan.

Rabey, David Ian. 2020. "Jumping to (and Away from) Conclusions: Rhythm and Temporality in debbie tucker green's drama." In Adiseshiah and Bolton 2020, 191–213.

Rancière, Jacques. (2010) 2015. *Dissensus: Politics and Aesthetics*. Translated and edited by Steven Corcoran. London: Bloomsbury.

Rebellato, Dan, ed. 2013. *Modern British Playwriting 2000–2009*. London: Bloomsbury.

Reid, Trish. 2018. "'Killing Joy as a World Making Project': Anger in the work of debbie tucker green." *Contemporary Theatre Review* 28 (3): 390–400.

———. 2020. "'What about the burn their bra bitches?': debbie tucker green as the Willfully Emotional Suject." In Adiseshiah and Bolton 2020, 45–65.

Rifkin, Jeremy. 2009. *The Empathic Civilization: The Race to Global Consciousness in a World in Crisis*. London: Penguin.

Sierz, Aleks. 2015. Review of *hang*, by debbie tucker green. *Arts Desk*, June 17. Accessed March 23, 2018.

Standing, Guy. (2011) 2014. *The Precariat: The New Dangerous Class*. London: Bloomsbury.

Tripney, Natasha. 2015. Review of *hang*, by debbie tucker green. *Stage*, June 17. Accessed March 23, 2018.

Trueman, Matt. 2015. Review of *hang*, by debbie tucker green. *WhatsOnStage*, June 17. Accessed March 23, 2018.

tucker green, debbie. 2003. *born bad*. London: Nick Hern Books.

———. 2008. *random*. London: Nick Hern Books.

———. 2011. *truth and reconciliation*. London: Nick Hern Books.

———. 2015. *hang*. London: Nick Hern Books.

———. 2018. *ear for eye*. London: Nick Hern Books.

Winerman, Lea. 2005. "The Mind's Mirror." *Monitor on Psychology* 36 (9): 48.

CHAPTER 3

Moving Parts: Emotion, Intention and Ambivalent Attachments

Clare Wallace

Caryl Churchill's *Love and Information* (2012) is a permutation of micro scenes that generate a disquieting sense of informational overload and imminent collapse. Tim Crouch and Andy Smith's *what happens to the hope at the end of the evening* (2013; published in Crouch and Smith 2014, 1–63) apparently naively invites emotional engagement as it navigates the ambivalent demands of friendship, political activism, professional and amateur acting and theatrical value. Lucy Kirkwood's *The Children* (2016) naturalistically presents three older characters in the wake of a nuclear disaster wrestling with mortality and their ethical and emotional responsibilities to the next generation and the environment. James Fritz's *Parliament Square* (2017) probes the nature and efficacy of suicidal protest in a contemporary milieu that combines domestic comfort with a profound, yet vague sense of powerlessness and frustration and an acute attention to the body in pain. What becomes visible when we look at

C. Wallace (✉)
Charles University, Prague, Czech Republic
e-mail: clare.wallace@ff.cuni.cz

M. Aragay et al. (eds.), *Affects in 21st-Century British Theatre*,
https://doi.org/10.1007/978-3-030-58486-3_3

contemporary British theatre through the lens of affect? What assumptions accompany this question? After all, it is no news that feelings and emotions matter to and are the matter of theatre. This chapter sets out to examine the ways attending to affect in recent works of British theatre opens up certain lines of flight in considering issues of aesthetic form, ethics and power. Despite their formal diversity, the four plays mentioned above share a particular concern with the modulations of the (im)personal, bodily capacity to affect and be affected alongside a deep ambivalence about the future that feels urgently contemporary. My exploration will revolve around a fluid notion of moving parts as a means of connecting theatre's structure as "affect machine" (Read 2008, 13) with the philosophical and cultural discourse around affect, emotion and agency. Like Sara Ahmed (2004a, b) and Martin Welton (2012) among others, I am going to treat affect, emotions and feelings as reciprocally entangled, and something that in theatre happens as a matter of course. In his theorising of the virtual, Brian Massumi describes the imagination as "thinking feeling" (2002, 135), a phrase he later fuses with a hyphen as "thinking-feeling" to express what he terms "enactive understanding" (2015, 94). In what follows, I want to suggest how it is in the multidirectional processes of moving-acting produced in and by these plays that we can start to unpack the forms of understanding they enact in the ebb and flow of a more general "structure of feeling" (Williams 1977).

Turning?

At an epistemological level, there is a strong investment in movement as a way of differentiating the methods and theoretical bases of what Patricia T. Clough has labelled the affective turn; a turn that, in her words, "expresses a new configuration of bodies, technology, and matter instigating a shift in thought in critical theory" (2007, 2). As Greg Seigworth and Melissa Gregg and stress in their introduction to *The Affect Theory Reader*, "approaches to affect would feel a great deal less like a free fall if our most familiar modes of inquiry had begun with movement rather than stasis, with process always underway rather than position taken" (2010, 4). Yet there is considerable disagreement as to what ideas and concepts underwrite such a shift or, indeed, to what extent labelling it a "turn" at all is accurate or justified. Ahmed's work views emotion and feeling not as states or "dispositions," but as mediating "the relationship between the psychic and the social and between the individual and the collective" in an affective economy (2004b, 119). In contrast, when considering affect theory's usefulness for thinking about performance, Erin Hurley and Sara Warner propose that "[t]his paradigm shift represents the desire to carve out some conceptual space for aspects of human motivation and behavior that are not tethered to consciousness, cognitive processes, and rationality, to validate physical and social dynamics that are inchoate and unpredictable, and to explore impulses and responses that social conventions shape but do not circumscribe" (2012, 99–100). Such an approach proposes a rebalancing of priorities—though not always along the most logically consistent lines—through a focus on lived experience and embodiment that is both potentially productive and generative of keen ambivalences—that sense of free fall—in particular in relation to agency, determinism and the political outcomes of validating such apparently "inchoate and unpredictable" dynamics.

Power Flux: Defining Affect

To clarify somewhat the forms of these ambivalences, I want to touch two points on the continuum of a particular genealogy of affect theory. The first is the thought of Baruch Spinoza, the second is that of Brian Massumi. In *The Ethics*, originally published in 1677, Spinoza delineates the causes and consequences of human action. Spinoza's thesis rests on the assertion that mind and body are not distinct substances; man is subject to the "common laws of Nature," not "a dominion within a dominion" (1994, 152). His definition of affects—in the plural—as "affections of the body by which the body's power of acting is increased or diminished, aided or restrained, and at the same time, the ideas of these affections" (1994, 154) is echoed, with varying degrees of explicitness, in a great deal of contemporary work on affect in the humanities and social sciences. Michael Hardt succinctly paraphrases Spinoza's premises: first, "the mind's power to think and its developments are [...] parallel to the body's power to act" and "the mind's power to think corresponds to its receptivity to external ideas; the body's power to act corresponds to its sensitivity to other bodies"; second, there is "a correspondence between the power to act and the power to be affected" (2007, xi–x). Less often quoted are the latter parts of *The Ethics*, in which "man's lack of power to moderate and restrain the affects" is characterised as "bondage," or indeed part V, where Spinoza elaborates on the capacity of the mind or reason to mitigate affects (1994, 197). Spinoza's concern is, after all, *ethical* and is directed toward the complex problem of how to live a good life given the limitations of human understanding and power. As Hardt acknowledges, Spinoza "requires us constantly to pose as a problem the relation between actions and passions, between reason and the emotions" (2007, x).

Bringing together ideas from Spinoza and Gilles Deleuze, and as noted in the introduction to this volume, Massumi's early work provocatively hones a concept of affect as prepersonal and asocial intensity (2002, 30) and, later, as a "threshold of potential" (2015, 3). Massumi's influential early thinking on affect is founded on its autonomy. Accordingly, he sharply distinguishes affect from emotion: "Emotion is qualified intensity, the conventional, consensual point of insertion of intensity into semantically and semiotically formed progressions, into narrativisable action-reaction circuits, into function and meaning. It is intensity owned and recognized," whereas affect is "irreducibly bodily and autonomic" (2002, 28). Emotion, he writes "is contextual. Affect is situational [or better said] trans-situational [...]. It is pre- and postcontextual, pre- and postpersonal, an excess of continuity invested only in the ongoing: its own" (2002, 217).

The consequences of identifying affect as autonomous in this manner are extensive and have been challenged from many quarters, not least by the work of Ahmed already mentioned. Likewise, Clare Hemmings critically traced the emancipatory manoeuvres assumed by a turn to affect, illuminating how an insistence of its independence of social frameworks hampers critical reflection on the nature of power and the social (2005, 565). Ruth Leys also opened a heated dispute over the "shared anti-intentionalism" of "Deleuze-inspired affect theorists" (2011, 443). She warned that "one price their views exact is to imply such a radical separation between affect and reason as to make disagreement about meaning, or ideological dispute, irrelevant to cultural analysis" (2011, 472). And further considering the problem of judgement, Linda Zerilli has provided a perceptive synthesis of the issues raised by Hemmings, Leys and others to dispute the notion that "affect and cognition are two entirely different systems," a move that merely reinstalls mind/body dualism (2015, 281). The differences between them notwithstanding, each of these critical responses are important problematisations of an idea of affect moving (through) the body in ways that are beyond signification or unimpeded by social conditions, and their reservations flow beneath the surface of my analysis.

Dynamic Structures, Affective Scenarios

These debates, I propose, are themselves part of an evolving contemporary "structure of feeling" about feeling. This phrase, used by Raymond Williams to describe "a particular quality of social experience and relationship, historically distinct from other particular qualities, which gives the sense of a generation or a period" (1977, 131), enables an appreciation of the interaction between currents of feeling and sensibility in a general social sense and the ways these feelings are performed and reproduced culturally and in individual behaviours. As a structure, it is dynamic and perceptible as emergent, that is, socially experienced "in solution" (Williams 1977, 134). Above all, its conceptual value lies in its transversal potential to link otherwise diverse practices within a cultural and social space and time. In the context that concerns me here, a hyperawareness of the varied forces and valences of affect is an integral feature of what Jim McGuigan terms the neoliberal imaginary, in which notions of being in the world are tightly plaited with economies of exchange and the commodification of human experience (2016, 27). Clough, too, links the development of a discourse of affect with the political economy of the late 1990s and early twenty-first century. Significantly, she observes how "[i]n this context, the circuit from affect to emotion is attached to a circulation of images meant to simulate desire already satisfied, demand already met, as capital extracts value from affect—around consumer confidence, political fears, and so forth, such that the difference between commodification and labor, production and reproduction are collapsed in the modulation of the capacity to circulate affect" (2010, 220–21). Ahmed's work on emotional circulation and exchange, which understands emotions as a "form of capital: affect does not reside positively in the sign or commodity, but is produced only as an effect of its circulation" (2004b, 120), clearly anticipates many of Clough's points.

Creative work participates in the thinking-feeling of the sensorium of a given time. How it does this is lucidly explored by Lauren Berlant in *Cruel Optimism*, and it is through some of her observations that my analysis of plays is diffracted. Berlant proposes that "[t]he key [...] is not to see what happens to aesthetically mediated *characters* as equivalent to what happens to people but to see that in the affective *scenarios* of these works and discourses, we can discern claims about the situation of contemporary life" (2011, 9; italics in the original). Like Berlant, I am interested in the reciprocity of affect and form, how "[a]ffect's saturation of form can communicate the conditions under which a historical moment appears as a visceral moment, assessing the way a thing that is happening finds its genre" (2011, 16). The formal diversity of the four plays to which I now turn is indicative of the transitive capacity of the affective to attach to or be magnetised by various modes of representation, be it a revitalised realism (Aston 2016), postdramatic forms or what Dan Rebellato has called an "apocalyptic tone" (2017).

Affect Algorithm: *Love and Information*

In his 2017 essay "Of an Apocalyptic Tone Recently Adopted in Theatre," Rebellato considers the ways contemporary British theatre has embraced strategies of negation in the face of totalising capitalist realism. He takes a poststructuralist tack to argue persuasively that Churchill's *Far Away* (2000) and *Escaped Alone* (2016) are "fully apocalyptic" in a Derridean sense, in which the "apocalyptic disrupts [...] the assuredness of language, the unity of meaning, the clarity of expression" (par. 54). Rebellato isolates a tendency in Churchill's later work, "a kind of anti-authorial quality, a blank quality that is freed from affect, that imposes itself as cleanly and lightly as possible on the actor: writing that is freed from tone," and argues this "toneless tone" (par. 57) *is* Churchill's tone. While appreciative of the political direction of Rebellato's argument, I want to contest the suggestion that her work is free(d) from affect. Instead, I see Churchill's recent work as increasingly involved with affect and its politics—in the circulation of emotions, the capacity to affect and be affected, the improbable and transversal connections opened by these movements and the warping of cause and effect, power surges and deficits are integral to its aesthetics. The flatness of the dramatic writing is persistently distorted by scene splicing and jolting alterations of mood and subject that invite thinking-feeling hinged to moving-acting.

Love and Information in many respects seems to exemplify the "toneless tone" Rebellato observes. There is something deliberately programmatic in the ways it handles feeling and emotion to generate impressions that loop between intense and diffuse, obvious and obscure. It is structured in seven titled sections comprising of numerous short scenes—fifty-one in all, plus more than twelve optional extra fragments or effects, so the final number and arrangement may shift in different productions. Stage directions indicate that the sequence of sections should remain fixed, while the order of the scenes within each section—apart from the final scene—and the inclusion of the random ones is left to the director. This background operational code governs the sequence determining the shape of the performance and the affects it produces, yet remains invisible to a spectator who is unfamiliar with the script.

The play's flow of data, communicated in micro scenes, is arranged in various nonsequential encounters and fragments. Conventional dramatic elements within this system have been reduced to minimal units. There are no named characters and little sense of development, plot or causality; instead, what appears are accumulating units of semiautonomous information that build a feeling of exacerbated contingency. Following its somewhat self-explanatory title, the motif pulsing through the play is diverse forms of information, from secrets, messages, recordings, research, biological data, memory work, sign language and forms of visual code to, inevitably, love. The abrupt cuts from scene to scene actively prevent reflection on, or development of, this information and foster an "intimately impersonal" attitude (Seigworth and Gregg 2010, 3) to the figures and material involved in each scene.

Flickering attention is drawn to failures in feeling, misplaced/misdirected emotion or neurological experiments that aim to materially pin down brain functions: the exhausted torturer/interrogator, the melancholy amnesiac who cannot recognise his own wife, obsessive adolescent celebrity worship, autism, ex-lovers' fond reminiscences, the depressive, the scientist slicing up chickens' brains and so on. Forms of affective dysfunction proliferate, from hypersensitivity to insensitivity. These intermittently attach to the figure of the child. Scenes titled "The Child Who Didn't Know Fear," "The Child Who Didn't Know Sorry" or "The Child Who Didn't Know Pain" gesture toward dilemmas about the nature of feelings, emotions and affects—whether they are innate and biologically determined or learned socioculturally—that may be traced in much scholarly work, from William James (1890) through to Ahmed (2004a, 8), as well as in the work of Silvan Tomkins, whose influence on the thinking of Eve Kosofsky Sedgwick (2002) and Massumi (2002) is so salient. Vital here is the resonance of the child's innocence, the ways the "not-yet-subject" (Ahmed 2004a, 17) is a space of potential or affective futurity. These scenes also ominously seem to propose the transmission of such dysfunctional patterns to an indeterminate future, a recurrent theme in Churchill's work.

All this is very much contiguous with Churchill's sustained theatrical critique of the sensorium of contemporary capitalism. As Mary Luckhurst notes, the play offers an image of "the increasing anatomisation of human life, and the loss of compassion and connection" (2015, 180). Elin Diamond and Vicky Angelaki are among those who also have dwelt upon the play's political import. Diamond asserts that *Love and Information* "takes the emotional temperature of information overload and asks how we live and love among the sound bites" (2014, 463). Similarly, Angelaki uses the ideas of Richard Sennett to elaborate how "intimacy is [...] played out on the terms of market exchange, where individuals merely offer up a construct of themselves for consumption" (2017, 35). She argues that the fragmentariness of the play disturbs the hermeneutic process: "we are not given the security of peering inside; we must fill the gaps of that which we do not see and the affect is disquieting" (2017, 31).

However, I would argue that the disturbance primarily lies in the way the meticulous algorithm of the play rebuffs understanding as a narrative puzzle that might, somehow, be assembled in order to reinstall a reassuring "life-affirming" message. It is purposefully flat and impersonal; there is no vantage point outside its workings from which to supplement it. The result is a somewhat enervating, durational experience that runs to around two hours without pause. It is a system of encounters that is affective as aggregation and contingent relation, not stabilised in characters as individual subjects. Rather, what we see in the multiplying of scenes, of moving parts, is an emergent deindividualisation and a sense of being at the mercy of something ineffable that is inexorably moving on—and this is what is so unsettling about it.

If the play's beginning may vary, it is significant that the end of its permutations is fixed, a foregone conclusion, which is why I have referred to the play as an algorithm since there is an endpoint to its processes. The last scene, titled "Facts," is a series of apparently arbitrary gameshow-style questions, answered with facts; threaded into this sequence a speaker asks, "Do you love me?" and after several other questions and answers, the response, "I do yes I do," bounces back (71), but entangled with the answer to another question. The affirmative gesture is so deliberately weak, it seems Churchill herself is not convinced that a declaration of love might save the day. The bodily capacity to affect and be affected is configured anxiously in *Love and Information*, played and replayed to the point of exhaustion. But this is its point, the whole being greater than the sum of its parts.

Good Life/Half-Life: *The Children*

In *Cruel Optimism*, Berlant dwells upon the affective charge of genres of good-life fantasy, and how under present environmental, political and economic conditions such optimistic attachments seem increasingly unfeasible. She asks, "[w]hy do people stay attached to conventional good-life fantasies—say, of enduring reciprocity in couples, families, political systems, institutions, markets and at work—when the evidence of their instability, fragility, and dear cost abounds? Fantasy is the means by which people hoard idealising theories and tableaux about how they and the world 'add up to something.' What happens when those fantasies start to fray [...]?" (2011, 2). Kirkwood's 2016 play *The Children* deftly places the persistence of such attachments alongside the hazards of nuclear catastrophe and a crisis of and in the ordinary.

Formally, *The Children* contrasts so sharply with *Love and Information* that it is tempting to say that they are diametrically opposed. The familiar aesthetic contours of the play—its small cast of psychologically developed characters, in a single domestic setting engaged in plot-driven dialogue and temporally coherent action—inevitably produce a very different texture of feeling and affective rhythm. The movement of the play's plot is also familiar—from context to complication to crisis and resolution. An impression of carefully maintained stability is transmitted in the stage picture—or to echo Berlant's word, tableau—that is revealed in a painterly manner as the lights slowly come up. Whereas *Love and Information* never allows attention to rest, the static quality of this scene is remarkable. The cottage kitchen with its array of homely objects is "*at a slight tilt. The land beneath it is being eroded*" (Kirkwood 2016, 4). The mundane at a slight angle is crucial to the affective scenario Kirkwood develops here.

The action of the play is simultaneously slight and seismic. Its protagonists Hazel and Robin, who ironically describe themselves as "simple retired nuclear engineers slash farmers" (30), are visited by a former colleague, whom they apparently have not seen in thirty-eight years—we learn later that Robin had for many years continued an intermittent affair with Rose. Hazel and Robin are model middle-class citizens, ageing gracefully, if slightly anxiously, attentive to the needs of their adult children and grandchildren, now stoically living through the aftermath of an environmental catastrophe in which they are professionally complicit. Their good-life retirement project as organic farmers within view of the nuclear power station they helped to develop has been dramatically "compromised" (54) by an accident that has left the surrounding area contaminated by radiation and the power plant in a volatile state. In consequence, they abandoned their home and farm for a cottage which is further away from the exclusion zone, but still suffers extreme energy rationing.

Hazel is quickly established as the character with a powerful attachment to eudaimonic well-being, expressed as a desire to maximise her life experience and expectancy in various mundane and predictable ways. Healthy eating, yoga, plucking the hairs that occasionally sprout on her chin are part of her conscious resistance to ageing—"This is not the end of our lives but a new and exciting chapter" (16), she insists. Yet despite the comedy of conscious resistance and self-regulation, the unpredictability of bodies and their material realities cannot be totally contained by sheer common sense and mindfulness. Rose's sudden appearance produces a physical rather than verbal greeting: Hazel is so shocked that she gives her old colleague a bloody nose. And this is the first of numerous reminders of the instability of bodily capacity that permeate the play, including, in addition to unwanted facial hair and leaking blood, cancer, unpredictable libido or mere slowing down.

Hazel's perfectionism is expressed in a life lived according to plan—always looking after her skin, a successful career, an enduring marriage, home, children, retirement. Her confident mantra, "if you're not going to grow, don't live" (16), suggests a sense of somewhat ruthless clear-sightedness, but it is all too easy to overlook the extent and duration of Hazel's emotional labour in living well. Of course, it becomes clear that Hazel's risk-averse habits and meticulous concern for healthy eating and regular exercise are catalysed by a terror of precarity, of losing control of the body and of death. Rose, by contrast, is everything Hazel is not: rootless, a risk-taker, unmarried, childless, disorganised, a cancer survivor. Following the meltdown at the power station, the flooding of their family home and contamination of the farm, Hazel decides that they have earned the right to abandon the mess, to be self-centred: "We'd earned the right, on this one occasion, just to say: at our time of life, we simply cannot deal with this shit" (21). As a result, they have downsized from an exemplary good-life scene to the modest confines of the present one, where Hazel labours to shore up its obvious limitations through sheer will power.

Rose's reentry into their space destabilises their equilibrium and exposes the unsustainability of presupposed individualistic containment. As the play's title already promises, notions of self-fulfilment, self-extension and species continuity orbit around the collective figure of children.

Throughout the play, conversation keeps returning to the topic as one's genetic legacy, the rearing of children as a duty, as sources of (dis)satisfaction and, ultimately, guarantors of futurity. There is an insidious complacency to Hazel and Robin's reproductive success. Yet it is an obvious, understandable attachment. With their four adult children and cohort of grandchildren, it is clear that they feel their experience is naturally superior to Rose's childless existence. Rose disturbs the surface of the ordinary with an ethical challenge, one that attends impersonally to relationality and reciprocity, that dispassionately surveys the finitude of natural resources and the irrefutable threat of nuclear catastrophe. By asking them to join her in shutting down the power plant with a team of similarly retired scientists, Rose invites them to exchange self-centredness for self-sacrifice in aid of a potential future—not their children specifically, but children, as subsequent generations, generally. What Rose's interpellation produces is a recognition of the precariousness of the good-life fantasy exclusion zone of middle-class individualism. Rose, quite literally, brings the shit back—by using the wrong toilet, which then overflows into the kitchen.

The Children returns attention to the workings of passive and active affects and ethical agency. Its naturalism is key to the thinking-feeling it solicits. This genre, with its investment in individual character, rational causality and environmental determinism, has, amid the ubiquitous precarities of the present, the capacity to transmit what Berlant refers to as "crisis ordinariness" (2011, 10). And yet, while deploying the conventions of naturalism, the play underscores the inadequacy of the values that underpin it. This impasse renders palpable the affective charge of the good-life fantasy and the adjustments required to maintain it. *The Children* suggests that the fantasy is unsustainable; its foundations are unstable, as is scenographically insinuated. Through an "interruption the personal, and the work of normativity to create conventions of the personal" (Berlant 2011, 159), Kirkwood extends an image of unpredictable relationality. The play thus disturbs the contours of its generic predispositions—the environment will not be relegated to an underlying or background force that merely contributes to character, rather it will overwhelm them. Something more than the personal or individual self-interest is required, but this is as fragile as Rose's ethical appeal or the play's closing image, when Hazel and Rose move through a sequence of Yoga sun salutations.

Moving the (Im)material: *What happens to the hope at the end of the evening*

A central term in understanding the impetus of Crouch and Smith's work is the notion of dematerialisation. The source of this idea and some of its outcomes in their theatre practice have been lucidly discussed by various scholars, including Stephen Bottoms (2009), Cristina Delgado-García (2014) and Karen Jürs-Munby (2016). As Smith notes in his PhD thesis, "[t]he practice [he calls] dematerialised theatre was initially inspired by Lucy Lippard's monograph *Six Years: The Dematerialization of The Art Object from 1966 to 1972* (1973)," which he came across in 2003 (2014, 18). The processes of dematerialisation purportedly serve to activate a heightened awareness of the metaphorical and metonymical work of the imagination in the realisation of the art work—ostensibly very cerebral activities—as well as an attention to where, or better said, in whom that work takes place (Rebellato 2009). In effect, Crouch's impatience with "literalism" (Crouch and James 2009) and Smith's commitment to "actually re-materialise an act of theatre, returning to and readdressing what its basic properties may be" (2014, 25) are reactions to conventional aspects of mimesis in theatre performance and signal a dissatisfaction with the artistic or political potency of those conventions of representation. In what follows, I will suggest that an integral element within their practice, hyperconceptual as it may seem, is affective—theatrical performance's capacity to shape and move feelings.

Spinoza describes hope as "an inconstant joy, born of the idea of a future or past thing whose outcome we to some extent doubt" (1994, 190). Crouch and Smith's *what happens to the hope at the end of the evening* (henceforth *what happens to the hope*), first presented in London in July 2013, elaborates a multivalent reflection on concepts and affects, the performance and performativity of emotions. The play splices different worldviews, attitudes to theatre space, modes of address and what Michael Kirby called matrixed and nonmatrixed acting (1972). Two characters, Andy and Friend, enter a brightly lit stage space that contains a chair and music stand with a script. Andy begins by welcoming the audience, sharing his passion for theatre: "being together with some people in a room like this [...] a space where we can really be together, sit together and listen to a story" (Crouch and Smith 2014, 2). He begins a simple story about waiting for a friend whom he has not seen for years, interrupts it with another, and then invites everyone to shake hands. Having fostered a particular, friendly, unassuming feeling and a set of expectations about the shape of the show, Andy and Friend "begin" their performance, in which they enact their reunion.

This double beginning is indicative of the structure of the piece as a whole, a structure that produces its emotive force. Dramatic scenes between the two are paused and interrupted by Andy's ponderings on their friendship, communication and ideas about the nature of theatre. *what happens to the hope* works along the lines of an alternating-current dynamo. Smith and Crouch switch between forms of presentation and genres of address: one tentatively postdramatic and diegetic, the other more conventionally dramatic and mimetic. This directs how the two bodies on stage are scripted: one as a "fictional" character acting, the other as a "real" person reading. Their personas continue the opposition: Friend is impulsive, angry, libidinal, while Andy is reflective, loving, controlled. Friend is an activist, Andy an academic. Aggression vs. pacifism, confusion vs. comprehension, anger vs. acceptance, action vs. thought, pessimism vs. optimism, failure vs. success, body vs. mind—the oppositions between the two repeat at all levels throughout.

The play's metatheatrical structure multiplies ironic disjunction between concepts and sensation, and that is both humorous and uneasy. The idea of friendship seems mismatched to the practice of it; the ideal notions of theatre clash with how it is experienced. Andy criticises his friend's inability to control himself, while Friend pushes back against the beautiful theories—when Andy mentions Jill Dolan's oft-cited claim that "theatre is capable of [...] utopian performatives," Friend's response is "Fuck sake" (48). As Smith explains,

> Crudely, I represent an idea of autobiographical performance, and Tim (who is not Tim, but Friend in the text) is a kind of attempt at naturalism, or in-yer-face theatre, even. He wants to have a set on stage. He wants to represent my living room. I just sit on one side of the stage and read my lines, a bit like Spalding Gray or someone like that might do. My hope is that the two forms meeting and clashing like this might mean that they illuminate each other for what they are. Both authentic and inauthentic. Both real and not real. Just different methods of representation. (e-mail message to author, September 29, 2016)

And yet there is something more to *what happens to the hope* than illuminating dialectical jousting. The alternating mechanism produces not a synthesis, but an affective relational capacity grounded in a mobile mutuality. Arguably, this bypasses the art/life disjunction impasse with all its disappointingly unfulfillable promises. Andy's anecdote about the Living Theatre performance that led its audience "out into the street [...] to shout 'Paradise Now!'" (46) seems emblematic of the impossible attachment to collapsing art into life. Paradise is, inevitably, always elsewhere—in the past, the future, not in the now. Crouch and Smith's play, however, strives to keep hope in circulation by accepting its uncertainty. It does so by allowing the poles to switch. At the end of the evening, Andy and Friend have swapped places as the latter takes over the former's part, amplifying a sense of moving-acting as processual:

> FRIEND: We arrive here from some other place, but this is also a place. We listen and watch and we make. We do all of these things together. And at the end we get up and we leave and we do something else. We move somewhere else. To someone or something else. We start again.
> My friend is here.
> Paradise now. Paradise now. Paradise now. (63)

INCENDIARY ACTS: *PARLIAMENT SQUARE*

On January 16, 1969, twenty-year-old student Jan Palach set himself alight to protest the demoralisation of Czechoslovaks following the Soviet occupation of 1968. Though certainly not the only one, he is perhaps the most widely known of the "living torches" in Central and Eastern Europe at that time (Jan Palach–Charles University Multimedia Project 2007). Fifty years later, on January 18, 2019, a fifty-four-year-old man set himself alight in the middle of the day in roughly the same spot with the declared intention of "going out like Palach." There is something of a grim irony in the fact that his life was saved by an employee from a nearby Starbucks, who ran to his aid with a fire extinguisher as largely unaware crowds of shoppers and tourists wandered in the vicinity. Both acts are gut-wrenching, deliberate public performances that seize our attention, work on our feelings and demand reaction to what is transmitted. If Palach's act is now understood as political, commemorated in a poster exhibition just steps away from the site of the incident, the horror of this recent attempted self-immolation is swiftly explained (away) as mental illness. Self-immolation as protest moves contradictorily, as the horror of pain offered to a witnessing public attaches unpredictably to anger, disgust or despair.

There is something quite uncanny in the way the confluence of these events echoes the subject of Fritz's ***Parliament Square***, a play about the limits of protest that begs attention in terms of the affective economy it presents. At the play's centre is Kat, a young mother who decides to immolate herself in Parliament Square in London. The piece is organised in three sections: fifteen seconds, reportedly the time it takes for nerve endings to cease registering the pain of burning; fifteen steps, Kat's rehabilitation goal; and fifteen years, the time elapsing since Kat's action and the present moment. Kat is accompanied by an inner voice, physically represented in the opening production at Manchester's Royal Exchange Theatre and the Bush Theatre in London by another actor, who coaches and cajoles her towards her self-destructive goal. The second section unfolds the immediate aftermath of Kat's suicide attempt on those around her—her mother, husband and the young woman, Catherine, who saved her life. In the third, abbreviated phrases chart the passing of years—the growing up of Kat's daughter Joe, Kat and her husband Tommy's life together, her mother's illness and finally Catherine's decision, inspired by Kat's example, to immolate herself in the same spot. This jagged flash forward is punctuated by the refrain, "The world gets worse," repeated seventy-three times in the printed text.

The cast of seven actors performed on a bare stage, using minimal props: some stools, a bed and bands of yellow cloth that restrained Kat's body and signalled its changed capacity after her traumatic injuries. Fire was evoked using smoke, light and, in the final scene, confetti-like strips of paper. The elasticity of time is yoked to the play's affective charge and the ways experience is communicated—the stretching of each fraught moment of doubt, fear and determination in the first section, the overflow of emotions into the slow recovery of the second, and then the telescoping of time in the third as we skip across truncated impressions of the intervening years.

The header on the page for the show on the Bush Theatre's website poses the question of the play: "How far would you go for what you believe in?" At a time of ideologically motivated suicide events and terrorist attacks, it is not a question posed lightly. The education pack provided by the Bush Theatre for secondary school students (Key Stages 4 and 5) carefully situates and domesticates the play's concerns. One of the student exercises proposed is to write a manifesto, the goal of which is to "make your audience 'feel' something" (Bush Theatre 2017, 6). This cerebral exercise in making something emotive is ill matched to the visceral catching of the flames on the skin and the potentially uncontrollable (political) conflagration that is desired and anticipated.

Pain, according to Elaine Scarry, is an affect without object, experienced within a body. It contracts. It is resistant to description; its sense is only transmitted to other bodies via the imagination (1985, 161–62). Ahmed also probes the workings of pain and how it accrues social and political meaning through contingency. "Pain," she contends, "is not simply the feeling that corresponds to bodily damage. Whilst pain might seem self-evident […] the experience and indeed recognition of pain *as pain* involves complex forms of association between sensations and other kinds of 'feeling states'" (2004a, 23; italics in the original). She goes on to propose that "an ethics of responding to pain involves being open to being affected by that which one cannot know or feel. Such an ethics is, in this sense, bound up with the sociality or the 'contingent attachment' of pain itself" (2004a, 30). And it is this capacity to be affected that may flow forward into anger at injustice.

In the compelling oscillation between the two voices of Kat's consciousness in the first section, *Parliament Square* builds a palpable feeling of anxious anticipation that finally erupts aurally in "the worst scream we've ever heard" (42) as Kat burns. The scream is a visceral marker of a "threshold of potential" (Massumi 2015, 3) that rips though the character's rationalisations of her planned intervention. The threshold passed is less an expression point of political efficacy, as is imagined by Kat, than a trigger for the play's recirculation of a profound ambivalence around power and empowerment. What prompts her decision and what does it give rise to? If pain may be thought to be objectless, then protest cannot. Kat seems angry with the state of society. She is determined to do something to "stop the rot" (40). She conceives of her public suicide as a necessary and productive act of political agency—"I can do something" (40). As such, she anticipates a future affected and radically altered by her pain. A revolutionary politics is to be catalysed by her death—"Everyone who sees this is going to be changed and they're going to see that when we don't like what's going on we can get up out of our chairs and do something about it. […] they'll think if that woman can do that I can do something" (40). At the same time, Kat's motivation is frustratingly vague and inchoate. The projected contagious political effect seems irredeemably entangled with an egoistic desire to be recognised and an impressionability that insinuates mental fragility. It is an impetus that paradoxically envisions death as a means of transcendence, a fantasy of unbounded capacity—her face will be on the news, she will be universally known, she will *move* the world.

Significantly, after Kat's resentment at being saved ebbs away, her activist sentiments slide seamlessly into an acceptance of the middle-class status quo with all its consumerist trappings. All that is left are the marks on her body. A dangerous fatalism seeps through *Parliament Square* that stands unchallenged within its dramatic arc. The world degenerates with bland ubiquitous inevitability as ordinary life continues—children grow up, new jobs are found, houses bought and so on. And yet Kat's long repudiated action still has contagious affect. Catherine's resolution to kill herself in Parliament Square, allegedly to fight for the good in the world (94), is inspired by Kat's attempt, and Kat acquiesces to her death at the play's conclusion. Radical acts of public self-annihilation have undeniable affective anticipatory force, but their political efficacy is dubious at best. What they signal most powerfully is a despair that "absorbs genuine energy for social change" (Berlant 2011, 259). Fritz's play, with its concluding quandary about power and feeling powerless, communicates a sense of profound impasse viscerally felt in the political ecology of the present, where despair is never far away.

Moving Parts

Thinking about theatre through the lens of affect solicits a consciousness of the forms and objects of emotion, the circulation of feelings and their outcomes, what they do and how they move us. The anxious aggregation of fragments in *Love and Information*, the cruelly optimistic scene and ethical confrontation in *The Children*, the alternating currents of *what happens to the hope* and the tripartite probing of pain and protest in *Parliament Square* are admittedly diverse affective scenarios, but they tend in a direction. They enact an understanding of the flows and sticking places of affect—specifically, ambivalent attachments to ideas of agency and efficacy, be they personal, political or theatrical—within a messy relational system. Creatively, they converge in intervening in the sensorium of a present in which disempowerment is strongly felt by tracing mixed feelings about intention and, to borrow from Spinoza, what a body can do.[1]

Note

1. This work was supported by the European Regional Development Fund (ERDF) project "Creativity and Adaptability as Conditions of the Success of Europe in an Interrelated World" (No. CZ.02.1.01/0.0/0.0/16_019/0000734).

References

Adiseshiah, Siân and Louise LePage, eds. 2016. *Twenty-First Century Drama: What Happens Now*. London: Palgrave Macmillan.

Ahmed, Sara. 2004a. *The Cultural Politics of Emotion*. London and New York: Routledge.

——— 2004b. "Affective Economies." *Social Text* 22 (2): 117–39.

Angelaki, Vicky. 2017. *Social and Political Theatre in 21st-Century Britain: Staging Crisis*. London: Bloomsbury.

Aston, Elaine. 2016. "Room for Realism." In Adiseshiah and LePage 2016, 17–35.

Berlant, Lauren. 2011. *Cruel Optimism*. Durham, NC and London: Duke UP.

Bottoms, Stephen. 2009. "Authorising the Audience: The Conceptual Drama of Tim Crouch." *Performance Research* 14 (1): 65–76.

Bush Theatre. 2017. *Parliament Square Education Pack*. Accessed February 10, 2019.

Churchill, Caryl. 2012. *Love and Information*. London: Nick Hern Books.

Clough, Patricia T. 2007. "Introduction." In Clough with Halley 2007, 1–33.

———. 2010. "The Affective Turn: Political Economy, Biomedia, and Bodies." In Gregg and Seigworth 2010, 206–25.

Clough, Patricia T., Jean Halley, eds. 2007. *The Affective Turn: Theorizing the Social*. Durham, NC and London: Duke UP.

Crouch, Tim, and Karl James. 2009. Conversations on Making. *siobhandaviesdance*. Accessed February 9, 2019.

Crouch, Tim and Andy Smith. 2014. *Adler & Gibb/what happens to the hope at the end of the evening*. London: Oberon.

Delgado-García, Cristina. 2014. "Dematerialised Political and Theatrical Legacies: Rethinking the Roots and Influences of Tim Crouch's Work." *Platform: Journal of Theatre and Performing Arts* 8 (1): 69–85.

Diamond, Elin. 2014. Review of *Love and Information*, by Caryl Churchill. *Theatre Journal* 66 (3): 462–65.

Fritz, James. 2017. *Parliament Square*. London: Nick Hern Books.

Gregg, Melissa and Gregory J. Seigworth, eds. 2010. *The Affect Theory Reader*. Durham, NC and London: Duke UP.

Hardt, Michael. 2007. "Foreword: What Are Affects Good For?" In Clough with Halley 2007, ix–xiii.

Hemmings, Clare. 2005. "Invoking Affect: Cultural Theory and the Ontological Turn." *Cultural Studies* 19 (5): 548–67.

Hurley, Erin and Sara Warner. 2012. "Affect/Performance/Politics." *Journal of Dramatic Theory and Criticism* 26 (2): 99–107.

James, William. 1890. *Principles of Psychology*. New York: Henry Holt.

Jan Palach–Charles University Multimedia Project. 2007. Accessed February 10, 2019.

Jürs-Munby, Karen. 2016. The Politics of 'Dematerialised Theatre' by Tim Crouch and Andy Smith. Lecture given at Studies in Performing Arts and Media, Ghent University, February 23.

Kirby, Michael. 1972. "On Acting and Not Acting." *TDR* 16 (1): 3–15.

Kirkwood, Lucy. 2016. *The Children*. London: Nick Hern Books.

Leys, Ruth. 2011. "The Turn to Affect: A Critique." *Critical Inquiry* 37 (3): 434–72.

Luckhurst, Mary. 2015. *Caryl Churchill*. London and New York: Routledge.

Massumi, Brian. 2002. *Parables for the Virtual: Movement, Affect, Sensation*. Durham, NC and London: Duke UP.

———. 2015. *Politics of Affect*. Cambridge: Polity.

McGuigan, Jim. 2016. *Neoliberal Culture*. London: Palgrave Macmillan.

Read, Alan. 2008. *Theatre, Intimacy & Engagement*. Basingstoke and New York: Palgrave Macmillan.

Rebellato, Dan. 2009. "When We Talk of Horses: Or, What Do We See When We See a Play?" *Performance Research* 14 (1): 17–28.

———. 2017. "Of an Apocalyptic Tone Recently Adopted in Theatre: British Drama, Violence and Writing." *Sillages Critiques* 22. Accessed February 1, 2018.

Scarry, Elaine. 1985. *The Body in Pain: The Making and Unmaking of the World*. New York and Oxford: Oxford UP.

Sedgwick, Eve Kosofsky. 2002. *Touching Feeling*. Durham, NC and London: Duke UP.

Seigworth, Gregory J. and Melissa Gregg. 2010. "An Inventory of Shimmers." In Gregg and Seigworth 2010, 1–25.

Smith, Andy. 2014. What We Can Do with What We Have Got: A Dematerialised Theatre and Social and Political Change. PhD diss., University of Lancaster.

Spinoza, Baruch. 1994. *A Spinoza Reader: The Ethics and Other Works*. Translated and edited by Edwin Curley. Princeton, NJ: Princeton UP.

Welton, Martin. 2012. *Feeling Theatre*. Basingstoke and New York: Palgrave Macmillan.

Williams, Raymond. 1977. *Marxism and Literature*. Oxford: Oxford UP.

Zerilli, Linda M.G. 2015. "The Turn to Affect and the Problem of Judgment." *New Literary History* 46 (2): 261–86.

CHAPTER 4

Love and the Intentionality of Affect in Lucy Prebble's *The Effect* and debbie tucker green's *a profoundly affectionate, passionate devotion to someone (-noun)*

Korbinian Stöckl

In "The Turn to Affect: A Critique," Ruth Leys explains the affective turn as a reaction against the strong academic preference for individual and collective workings of the mind in the wake of structuralism, poststructuralism, constructionism and psychoanalysis, which had largely disregarded the materiality of bodies, affects and emotions (2011, 440–41; see also Wetherell 2012, 19). At present, however, the turn to affects and the new interest in the findings of biology, psychology and neuroscience run the risk of replacing the previous neglect of human corporeality with an equally lopsided view of affects as purely bodily phenomena sharply disengaged from all kinds of mental, cognitive or discursive processes. The idea put forward by scholars like Brian Massumi, Eric Shouse or Nigel Thrift that affects are "nonsignifying, autonomic processes that take place below

K. Stöckl (✉)
University of Augsburg, Augsburg, Germany
e-mail: korbinian.stoeckl@uni-a.de

M. Aragay et al. (eds.), *Affects in 21st-Century British Theatre*,
https://doi.org/10.1007/978-3-030-58486-3_4

the threshold of conscious awareness and meaning" and are thus "prior to intentions, meanings, reasons, and beliefs" (Leys 2011, 437) relegates them to a realm of human experience that is exclusively bodily and clearly separable from consciousness. This conception depends, as Leys argues, on a "highly idealized or metaphysical picture of the mind as completely separate from the body and brain" (2011, 455). It is a hallmark of this view that affect is nonintentional, namely, that it is not *about* something, since "there is a gap between the subject's affects and its cognition or appraisal of the affective situation or object" (Leys 2011, 443). There are reasons to doubt the experiments and positions in psychology and neuroscience on which this view is often based (Leys 2011, 444–63; Wehrs 2017, 2; Wetherell 2012, 43), but this is not the place to discuss its scientific value. What I will argue instead is that a sharply anti-intentionalist view of affects sits uneasily alongside the apparent fact that in the reception of art and literature cognitive and corporeal processes are inextricably connected. As Donald R. Wehrs argues with regard to literary texts, they "elicit and explore 'mind/body' interactivity" (2017, 2). Their depiction of emotionally stimulating content, in other words, provokes affects as "conjoined physical and mental activity" (Wehrs 2017, 2). Theatre, given its materiality, is perhaps particularly adept at stimulating the bodily dimension of this conjoined activity. But the response elicited by a performance still involves intentional mind/body interactivity—an affective reaction that is about the performance.

The anti-intentionalist view of affect is certainly compelling, not least due to certain seductive notions—including indeterminacy, pure potential and autonomy—that supposedly distinguish it from emotions, considered derivative forms of pure affect, already limited and explained by the conscious mind (Wehrs 2017, 39–40; Leys 2011, 442). In Shouse's words, "affect is a non-conscious experience of intensity; it is a moment of unformed and unstructured potential" which "cannot be fully realised in language" and which "is always prior to and/or outside of consciousness" (2005, par. 5). Alluring as this notion of affect may be, paradoxically it also comes close to turning affect—supposedly, as noted above, encompassing purely physical phenomena—into a metaphysical concept that defies empirical observation and description. It also raises the question what is to be understood by "nonconscious experience." How can something that is experienced remain unconscious? Does "nonconscious" here mean that the experience is not cognitively or rationally processed—which implies a mind/body dualism in which the mind is completely disembodied?

Moreover, a question that is particularly relevant for drama and theatre studies concerns the elicitation of affects through texts and performances. As Leys observes, for anti-intentionalist affect theorists "political campaigns, advertising, literature, visual images, and the mass media are all mechanisms for producing [...] effects below the threshold of meaning and ideology" (2011, 451). But how is the production of e/affects to be understood if it is not as the reaction of an embodied mind to the perception of some content or "message"? Can the affective effect of a text or performance be seen as independent from its content or meaning? Furthermore, if affect, as soon as it becomes conscious, observable experience, ceases to be affect, are we not then dealing with a metaphysical idea that has no presence in lived reality? If, on the other hand, affect is more than an elusive metaphysical idea, are then not its production, transmission and reception always bound up with a concrete situation or context that is present to the conscious mind?

I have addressed these questions because they lead to a conclusion that will guide the following analyses of dramatic texts: I suggest that it is neither practicable nor reasonable to separate affects from their context, that is, from their eliciting conditions, the various modes of their cognitive processing and the discourses in which all this is embedded. In this regard, I will follow Margaret Wetherell's argument that "human affect is inextricably linked with meaning-making and with the semiotic (broadly defined) and the discursive. It is futile to try to pull them apart" (2012, 20). According to Wetherell, the majority position in contemporary affective sciences is that "[a]ffect has conscious and non-conscious, bodily and cognitive, elements linked in highly complex ways" so that "cognition and brain/body activity are seamlessly intertwined" (2012, 61–62). She sums up the current state of research as follows:

> The picture that psychology and neuroscience typically now paints [*sic*] of affect is of a highly dynamic, interacting *composite* or *assemblage* of autonomic bodily responses (e.g. sweating, trembling, blushing), other body actions (approaching or avoiding), subjective feelings and other *qualia*, cognitive processing (e.g. perception, attention, memory, decision-making), the firing and projecting of neural circuits (e.g. from the thalamus to the cortex and the amygdala), verbal reports (from exclamations to narratives) and communicative signals such as facial expressions. An emotional episode, such as a burst of affect like rage or grief, integrates and brings together all of these things in the same general moment. (2012, 62; italics in the original)

In view of this, Wetherell sees "little point in trying to decompose affective activity into its bodily and discursive constituents" (2012, 53). She shares this conviction with Sara Ahmed, who holds that "the distinction between sensation and emotion can only be analytic" and argues for an approach that seeks "to avoid making analytical distinctions between bodily sensation, emotion and thought as if they could be 'experienced' as distinct realms of human 'experience'" (2004, 6). My own stance also turns away from a view of affects as nonintentional, preconscious, autonomous and indeterminate forms of pure potential or energy. Affects do not occur in isolation and are not experienced independently from the form in which they manifest themselves to awareness, and it is only in this form that they are observable and thus suitable objects of interest. In experience, affect and cognition are radically entwined. In what follows, I contend that this is the very argument Lucy Prebble's *The Effect* (2012) and debbie tucker green's *a profoundly affectionate, passionate devotion to someone (-noun)* (2017; henceforth *a profoundly affectionate, passionate devotion*) make, respectively on a thematic and on an aesthetic level.

"A Viagra for the Heart": Love Chemistry in *The Effect*

Prebble's third play, *The Effect*, was met with less enthusiasm from critics than her extremely successful *Enron* (2009). The love story of two subjects undergoing a medical trial for antidepressants did not fully live up to the expectations created by her neo-Brechtian unravelling of the Enron crisis. Nevertheless, the vast majority of reviews were favourable, often praising the play for its depth and intelligence. Conspicuously, whenever the play was criticised, the negative assessment displayed a sense of disappointment that Prebble had marred its promisingly critical, ethico-political potential by overemphasising the love plot around which it is constructed (Letts 2012; Nathan 2012; Purves 2012; Szlawinska 2012). In the favourable reviews, on the other hand, the love plot is not seen as undermining a critical examination of the ethical complications of neuroscience and the pharma industry. Rather, the combination of the two components is appreciated as creating a play that is both intellectually and emotionally appealing. None of the reviews, however, puts its main focus on the play's enquiry into the nature of love, which is precisely what I intend to do in what follows. Rather than assuming *The Effect* to be a political play embellished or, alternatively, somewhat weakened by a trivial romance plot, I regard the love story and the troubling questions prompted by recent neuroscience about the chemistry of love as lying at the play's core.

In fact, by exploring what happens when two people are falling in love, the play tackles the very problems of mind/body dualism I have broached above. Characters and spectators alike are confronted with the question whether falling in love can be understood as a purely bodily process. Is love reducible to a series of chemical and neuronal activities that are then, retrospectively, explained by the conscious mind as love? Or are the chemical and neuronal processes that can be made visible by modern neuroscience the symptoms that signal a conscious experience of love? In the end, the underlying question really is whether the phenomenon of love can be separated into a bodily and a mental sphere at all.

The Effect is set in a medical research institute where two neuroscientists, Dr Lorna James and Dr Toby Sealey, are testing a new antidepressant agent with an unspecified number of participants, only two of whom appear on stage. Connie, a pragmatic psychology student stuck in an apparently unsatisfactory relationship, and Tristan, a flirty, romantic drifter, hit it off almost immediately. When it is revealed that the antidepressant they are testing is supposed to increase levels of dopamine—the substance held responsible, among other effects, for falling in love—the developing romance between Connie and Tristan is shadowed by doubts as to whether it is an effect of the drug or, as Dr James presumes, "entirely natural" (Prebble 2012, 48). Connie mistrusts her growing infatuation, ascribing it to the antidepressant and thus denying its authenticity. Tristan, on the other hand, eagerly gives in to his increasing passion and refuses to believe love may be a purely organic, chemical reaction. When Connie claims that their love is "fake" (32) because it is caused by the drug-induced dopamine, Tristan's reply is simple: "People meet each other and fall in love all sorts of ways, doesn't matter what starts it. I'm sure there's a rush of something chemical if you meet on holiday or on a bus with a bomb on it, doesn't mean Keanu Reeves and Sandra Bullock [in *Speed* (1994)] aren't really in love" (35). For him, the involuntary, unconscious chemistry love involves does not explain away love as if it stopped being (experienced as) an intentional affection for a particular person.

As the play proceeds, Connie's sceptical position is undermined by inherent contradictions. Although she has seemingly adopted the materialist view that "[e]verything we do is just about what's pumping round inside us" because "[w]e *are* our bodies, our bodies are us … there's not something *more*" (34; italics in the original), she is unwilling to accept her love for Tristan as the "real thing" because it might be drug induced. While for Tristan, "[i]t is what it is. Doesn't matter why," for Connie, "[i]t's all that matters" (35) because, despite her alleged materialism, she seems to believe that love is more than a purely chemical bodily function—namely, that it originates in intentional affect caused by and directed at a particular person. The fact that she doubts her feelings because there might be "something else, something else controlling me" (54) reveals that, in fact, she has not fully incorporated the view that she *is* her body. Rather, she still distinguishes between "herself" and the neurochemical activities in her body.

Throughout the play, Tristan's strong belief in the power and the mystery of love resists any attempt at demystification or disenchantment, whereas Connie remains dubious. Her disbelief, however, is counteracted by her uncontrollably intensifying passion. "I can't help the way I feel!" (60), she complains to Dr James, admitting to the incapacity of her cognitive will to interfere with an affect that is consciously experienced as intentional but resists any wilful guidance and control. And yet, even towards the end of the experiment, with both lovers at the height of passion, Connie does not entirely abandon her rational scepticism for the sake of feeling:

> TRISTAN: I'll tell you what I want. I don't want to *reason* with you. I want to know right now, in this moment, what you *feel*.
>
> *Beat.*
>
> CONNIE: I. I feel. Oh god. I think I don't love you the way that you love me. (73; italics in the original)

Connie's reply is not the hackneyed cliché it sounds. It expresses her conviction that their experiences of love are of an essentially different nature since, based on erroneous information, she believes at this point that, unlike herself, Tristan is not on the drug but has been administered placebos. It is indeed her pragmatic reasoning that prevents her from embracing the love she feels for Tristan, a reasoning that depends paradoxically on the romantic conviction that genuine love has to be intentional from the start. It has to be like Tristan's, in other words, who, she believes, has "naturally" fallen in love with her, while she regards her own feelings as inauthentic because they are induced chemically and independently from any form of consciousness.

A similar discussion arises between the two doctors observing the drug test. The symptoms of the participants are perfectly in accordance with the symptoms of infatuation observed and described in biological anthropologist Helen Fisher's widely read *Why We Love: The Nature and Chemistry of Romantic Love*. Fisher reports on an experiment she conducted to prove her thesis "that romantic love is a universal human feeling, produced by specific chemicals and networks in the brain" (2004, 51), especially by increased levels of dopamine and norepinephrine. The test subjects "were so intensely in love that they could hardly eat or sleep" (2004, 58), while "candidates taking any kind of antidepressant medication were weeded out from the ensuing brain-scanning experiment" (2004, 61) to ensure that increased levels of dopamine and norepinephrine were not caused by medication. Fisher's research focused on the phase of passionate infatuation, to which she ascribes a series of symptoms that an earlier questionnaire-based research had shown to be shared across boundaries of age, gender, sexual orientation, religious affiliation and ethnic group without significant differences (2004, 4–5). The symptoms include a "special meaning" of the beloved, "focused attention," "obsessive meditation about the beloved," "loss of appetite and sleeplessness," "tremendous energy," "mood swings," a "craving to merge with the beloved," "changing priorities," "emotional dependence," "separation anxiety," an intensification of romantic passion through "[s]ocial or physical barriers," a "sexual connection," "jealousy" and a feeling that love is "involuntary," "uncontrollable" and a "transient state" (2004, 6–23). In the end, Fisher's experiment corroborated her assumption that romantic love is a basic human drive and, as such, is associated with the brain's reward system and with increased levels of dopamine (2004, 75).

Connie and Tristan show all these symptoms. After the first dose of the antidepressant agent, they display "[e]levated mood," "[i]ncreased energy levels" and "[w]eight loss" (Prebble 2012, 23). The barrier that kindles their romance is provided by the fact that sexual activity between participants in the test is forbidden, which renders sneaking out at night to a nearby abandoned asylum and, later in the play, secretly making love, outright romantic adventures. When asked to think of something positive during a brain scan, "[*t*]*hey think of one another*" (42), demonstrating the beloved's special meaning and their obsessive meditation about one another. After the second dose increase, Connie and Tristan describe themselves in conversation with Dr James as anxious, alive, alert, vivid, sleepless and sexually aroused (49–52). They both express lack of control over their feelings (54, 60) and they both display jealousy—Tristan whenever Connie's boyfriend is mentioned (65) and Connie when she has the impression that Tristan is flirting with Dr James (69). They change their priorities, at least temporarily, to accommodate the beloved—thus Connie, who previously would not agree to go travelling with Tristan, offers to live with him in "Paris, New York. A farm. Anywhere," and the notorious drifter Tristan speculates about settling down and "opening a dry cleaners" (56). Finally, that love might be only a transient state is a problem at least for Connie, who fears that it will not outlast the period of the experiment.

While there is no dissent between the two doctors about these observable symptoms, the role played by dopamine in the neurochemical phenomenon of romantic love provides the basis for heated debate. Examining brain scans of Connie and Tristan, they notice "[s]trong activity in the dopaminergic pathways and the reward centres of the brain in general," which they both agree corresponds to an "anti-depressant effect" (43). They disagree, however, about the cause of the effect—in other words, whether they show the symptoms because they are in love or think they are in love because they experience the symptoms. Dr James, although she subscribes to the view that "everything's physical in the end" (23), tries to preserve an element of the conscious or intentional and argues that the observable neural symptoms of love are not caused by the drug but by the participants' "intense and protracted flirtation" (44). Unlike Toby, therefore, she is not prepared to reduce human emotional life to neurochemical mechanics:

TOBY: If the agent is causing all these symptoms, why on earth *wouldn't* they assume they were infatuated?
DR JAMES: You think because they feel all the things one would associate with infatuation they are just ... assuming that's what they are.
TOBY: Assuming, exactly. The body responds a certain way to what it's being given, they can't sleep, they can't eat, they're in a constant state of neural excitement ever since they met, what's the brain going to conclude?
DR JAMES: You think it mistakes that for love?
TOBY: Not even mistakes it, creates it, after. To make sense of the response. (44–45; italics in the original)

For Toby, love is not the cause of anything. It is only the conscious mind's retrospective explanation for a certain form of chemical imbalance—an imbalance that may as well be drug induced as not.

Toby and Dr James are in a similar dispute concerning the nature of depression. As it turns out, Dr James suffers from "profound depressive episodes which she refuses to medicate" (79) because she does not believe in the effectiveness of antidepressants—or indeed, in Toby's explanation of depression as a curable illness caused by chemical imbalance. Against this position, she insists that depression "doesn't just appear" (47) but is a reaction to external events such as sudden unemployment or the loss of a beloved person. Just like love, she sees depression not as a spontaneous, inexplicable chemical imbalance but as the result of "an interaction with the world" (47) and hence as irreducibly intentional.

It is no coincidence that the practitioners' debates about love and depression are so similar. As Susannah Clapp rightly remarks, the two states are presented as each other's opposite in the play (2012). Not only are they caused, respectively, by elevated or lowered levels of dopamine, but their symptoms are described in terms that form a binary opposition. As Toby argues, "[d]epression's characterised by deadness of emotion, right? Insularity, lack of engagement with the world and those around you," whereas he locates the "extreme emotion, excess engagement, overwhelming purpose and feeling" displayed by the participants in the test at "the other end of the spectrum" (46). It is for this reason that he thinks he might have discovered what Dr James sneeringly calls "a Viagra for the heart" (46)—an agent that cures depression and elevates healthy or "normal" persons into a mood they might experience as love. The following dialogue about depression is thus also an expression of the doctors' views on love:

> TOBY: In ten years we'll have a blood test for depression. We'll have a biomarker and a cure. The stigma will be over.
> DR JAMES: You'll never have your biomarker. It isn't like that.
> TOBY: This is why I get annoyed, Lorna. You cling to the mystery. You celebrate it, almost.
> DR JAMES: I do what?
> TOBY: You don't want it to be curable, you want to make it grand and tragic, it doesn't have to be.
> [...] It doesn't make it less to accept it's chemical. (81)

Indeed, whether for love or depression, the fact that there is chemistry involved does not “make it less.” All four characters accept that the symptoms of love Connie and Tristan experience stand in relation to raised levels of dopamine, yet only for Toby does this mean that the secret of love is disclosed. For Connie, it makes a difference whether the dopamine level has been raised by medication or in a “natural” way—the magic of love, for her, is what starts the chemical imbalance in the second case. Similarly, the mystery to which Dr James clings is the unanswered question of what exactly, and in what ways, regulates the lack or surplus of dopamine in states of depression or love. For her, the source of the enigma lies in the human brain, which is too complex to be fully understood. No matter what external event sets off the chemical imbalance of either depression or love, the workings of the brain in causing, processing and interpreting this imbalance remain inexplicable. As she says to Toby during their argument:

> We’re all just walking examples of a biological fact, Toby. Everything you feel and think you feel is just your brain explaining away the awful simplicity of your body. But you’ll be forever safe from realising that because if your brain were simple enough for you to understand. You would be too simple to understand it. Do you understand?
> […]
> All this looking at brains with other brains, like a camera trying to take a photo of itself. (84)

Tristan, finally, hardly ever doubts the authenticity of his love for Connie, and though this is linked to the fact that he is the only character without any knowledge of psychology and/or neuroscience, the play seems to prove him right in the end. When Connie falsely assumes that Tristan is not on the drug but has only received placebos, she makes him swallow her pill so as to make sure they both feel the same. This causes Tristan to overdose and experience a breakdown, so that the experiment has to be abandoned.

The play ends with a series of short alternating scenes. Connie, now certainly clear of the drug, routinely but affectionately cares for an amnesiac Tristan, slowly preparing him to leave hospital and live at her place, while Toby entreats Dr James to allow the severe depression that has overtaken her to be treated medically. The final stage direction provides some form of closure and, importantly, again stresses the significance of love as the play’s major theme:

> CONNIE *and* TRISTAN, *together, walk out into the real world for the first time.*
> DR JAMES, *alone, looks at the door, looks at the cup/pills beside her, decides, and takes them.*
> *Underneath this, we hear the sound of an EEG; electrical activity in the brain produced by neurons firing. Underpinning this is the bass of a heart beat from an ECG. These are the sounds of human love.*
> *End experiment.* (101)

Sarah Hemming describes this as "a healing ending in which, whatever causes love, we see its effects" (2012), an interpretation that ties in with Tristan's view that the protagonists of *Speed* are, at the end of the film, genuinely in love with one another even though it may have been the neurochemical imbalance caused by an extreme situation that started it. I would, in fact, go one step further and agree with Michael Billington that Prebble's play favours the idea that both love and depression are triggered by external factors and "that the love between Tristan and Connie depends on something deeper than artificial stimulants" (2012). Raised levels of dopamine, Billington implies, are not sufficient to make people fall in love with each other, although they may certainly help. Regarding the question whether the chemical imbalance observable in lovers is either the *same* as love, its *cause* or its *effect*, the play does not provide a definite answer but leans towards the third possibility. That love is not reducible to chemistry—that is, to completely nonintentional processes—is, again, supported by Fisher's study: "Even taking pills (or street drugs like cocaine or amphetamines) that raise levels of dopamine in the brain won't make someone fall in love with you if he or she is not ready or is looking for an entirely different kind of partner" (2004, 199). Understanding the chemistry of love does not amount to understanding love, as Fisher states at the end of her book: "no matter how well scientists map the brain and uncover the biology of romantic love, they will never destroy the mystery or ecstasy of this passion. […] Regardless of what one knows about this subject, we all feel the magic" (219).

Ultimately, and not surprisingly, the play brings up more questions than it answers. Whether "[w]e *are* our bodies" (34; italics in the original) or our brains, as Connie and Dr James temporarily think, or whether self and identity transcend body/brain materiality, as they presume at other times, remains open. So does the question whether neurochemical activities are causes or effects, symptoms or explanations. But the play offers a way out of the philosophical and neuroscientific problems it cannot solve.

Its argument that raised levels of dopamine, which can be caused by drugs or by exciting situations alike, *can* be but are not necessarily experienced as love, implies that it makes little sense to call a neurophysiological state "love" unless it is experienced as such. In other words, whatever its chemical basis, love becomes what it is only if it is consciously experienced as an intentional affective state. The play seems to agree with Tristan, who shows little interest in the compartmentalisation of love into bodily and mental, unconscious and cognitive elements, but accepts his experience as what it is. He is apparently confirmed in his belief by Connie's protracted affection for him long after the experiment is over. This position is reminiscent of Wetherell's:

> Overall, I doubt the pragmatic value of violently severing parts of the assemblages recruited in bursts of affect and using a verbal scalpel to extract just the body/brain responses. It is a mistake to try to remove pre-conscious visceral perception from its usual and habitual world/brain/body/mind contexts, and to artificially freeze and isolate affect as a separate element from the dynamically integrated sequences in which these things normally operate. No easy distinction can be made between visceral and cultural meaning-making, and why should we make one—where is the advantage? (2012, 67)

Much in this vein, Tristan sees no advantage in demarcating the bodily and mental components that together add up to his affective experience. Similarly, he sees no advantage in speculating about the affective stimuli responsible for this experience in isolation. In his nonacademic naivety, he is the only character in the play who makes no attempt at separating analytically what only occurs and "makes sense" together. For him, it "doesn't matter what starts [love]" (35) because it only takes on relevance in its entirety, in its entwinement of unconscious neurochemistry with conscious awareness and intentionality. Just like the love between his mythical namesake Tristan and Isolde—which may or may not have been started by a magic love potion according to different sources (Singer [1984] 2009, 104)—or that between the protagonists of *Speed*—which may or may not build upon the "rush of something chemical" (35) following their exposure to extreme danger—the love between him and Connie may or may not be elicited by an antidepressant agent. This simply does not bother him because it is only his conscious experience of it as an intentional affect that makes it what it is.

Recognising Precariousness: Responding to *a profoundly affectionate, passionate devotion to someone (-noun)*

At the beginning of this chapter, I have argued that theatre, as an embodied practice, has a heightened potential to elicit and explore mind/body interactivity. In my analysis of Prebble's *The Effect*, I have confined myself to the play's thematic *exploration* of this interactivity. In what follows, instead, I approach tucker green's *a profoundly affectionate, passionate devotion* from the perspective of how it *elicits* affects. Thematically, the play is as much about love as its title suggests, exploring in particular the precarious dynamism of want and desire and the difficult interplay of feeling, knowing and expressing love. However, I will focus mostly on the play's aesthetics rather than on its thematic problematisation of affects/love, and will only provide a brief synopsis before elaborating on its strategies for provoking affective audience responses. Yet, as I will argue, these responses are not fully separable from the perception of the thematic content but are, indeed, instances of mind/body interactivity.

The play consists of three parts, each figuring two nameless male and female characters in troubled love relationships. While the couple in part one are presented in a series of fragmentary episodes that show them being deeply in love at one time and having a heated argument at another, parts two and three each present one longer scene of domestic life. The couple in part one quarrel about their unwillingness or inability to understand each other, express their feelings for one another or effectively support the other in times of need; they argue about the other's annoying habits, the possibility of having another child, their sexual desirability and their fear of being "useless" or replaceable—until it transpires that the woman died some time ago while her widowed husband is unable to cope with the loss and care for their traumatised daughter. The only obvious connections to part two are the similarity of the mutual accusations of inattentiveness and the acerbic tone of the second couple's argument, which culminates in a verbal fight for power and attempts to force the other to apologise for past failures. The third part loosely connects the whole play as it presents the male character of part two, who is now in a relationship with the daughter mentioned in part one—a fact that can only be guessed at from the sparse hints given in the dialogue but is explained in the list of characters. Again, the conversation is marked by mutual accusations of miscommunication. In addition, the two characters display forms of jealousy. The young woman objects to her partner's sickbed visits to another woman, probably his former partner from part two. The male character, on his part, resents his girlfriend's emotional suffering caused by her broken relationship with her father, as it reminds him of his inability to make her happy. They both, in other words, experience themselves as insufficient in their desired roles as the other's sole object of love and source of happiness, an experience that had already dominated several episodes in part one and surfaces as one of the main reasons for love's precariousness in the play. This feeling of insufficiency reinforces the sense of vulnerability and dependence inevitably entailed in love towards an uncontrollable other who is deemed indispensable for one's well-being.

While the subtle connections between the three parts seem to call for a cognitive processing of the plot, the play's aesthetics entails a distinctly affective reception. In fact, how the different parts relate to one another is hardly significant for the main impact of the play, as it neither develops a storyline moving towards an ending nor seeks to create suspense through a progression of plot. It basically does without properly dramatic action and instead presents fragmentary scenes of dialogue that grant the spectator episodic insights into domestic life. That these glimpses nevertheless have the potential to evoke strong affective audience responses depends on various strategies that seem aimed at making precariousness experienceable. The fragmentary composition of the play encourages the audience to focus their attention on each single scene for itself rather than perceiving them only as parts of a more significant whole. The spectator need not concentrate on how the scene relates or contributes to a coherent story and can thus fully take in its emotional intensity. In addition, the quick scene changes, which often come along with complete changes of mood between the characters and are not logically motivated in terms of cause/effect but happen abruptly and unexpectedly, accentuate the precariousness and incalculability of love. Love, anger, jealousy, disappointment, affection and neediness characterise the couples' dialogues in swift and unpredictable alternation, emphasising the insecurity inherent in human relationships.

On another level, the specific stage design of the original production may have reinforced affective responses from audience members. In the small Jerwood Upstairs studio space at the Royal Court, the audience was placed on swivel chairs and surrounded on three sides by a narrow catwalk that served as the stage. The completely empty stage was limited by bare back walls without any doors or windows. In scenes of heavy arguments, there was no space for the characters to retreat, escape or take shelter—nor for the audience, whose sense of confinement and vulnerability in relation to more conventional spatial and seating arrangements was intensified. Often, in scenes expressing the characters' emotional or communicative separateness, the actors would take up positions at the two strips of the stage that faced each other, making it impossible for spectators to see them both at the same time. This induced spectators to either decide for one of them or turn from one side to the other on their swivel chairs. Emotional distance was thus translated into physical distance, with the audience as the separating factor between the partners. Different individual reactions notwithstanding, it was arguably impossible for spectators to remain "unaffected" at these points that either required active movement or a decision to "side" with one of the characters and in any case put them in the uncomfortable position of having come in between the two lovers. Especially during the scenes of verbal fighting, the uneasy feeling of enduring an argument over one's head was inevitable. In moments of consensual affection, on the other hand, the actors would meet somewhere on stage, thus coming into view together and creating images that were in stark contrast to the moments of strife and crisis. In general, the production made much use of the effects of proximity and distance, both between the actors and between actors and audience. In the small and fully lit Upstairs studio, all present were "exposed" to each other throughout the performance, emphasising the vulnerability of the characters within their love relationships but also imposing on the audience an anxious feeling of eavesdropping and excessive closeness. Moreover, during emotionally intense scenes, audience members and their visible reactions to the performance were exposed to their fellow spectators. This reinforced the atmosphere of vulnerability and lack of privacy produced by a play dominated by scenes of lovers who know and relentlessly attack each other's most intimate weaknesses and soft spots.

The play's most important means to provoke affective responses, however, is a feature that is best described as "recognisability" and was repeatedly mentioned in reviews. Dominic Cavendish, for instance, applauded tucker green's "achievement [...] to stir a visceral recognition of life and love at its most coolly recriminatory" (2017), and Joe Vesey-Byrne wrote that "the evening feels like a privileged peep inside the lives of three recognisable love stories" (2017). Even Billington, otherwise frustrated by the play's "lack of specificity," could at least appreciate the "passages any long-term couple will recognise" (2017). What they all refer to are the many scenes in the play that are unambiguously identifiable as episodes from a domestic relationship, be it specific daily nuisances like being disturbed while watching TV or sitting on the toilet, moments of deliberate or unintentional inattentiveness towards the other, or the very vague argument about "that (thing), that you do—did. With your Thing. To me— [...] Thinking I liked it" (13), which, whatever it was, the other now claims to never have liked. The spectator's recognition of these episodes has the potential to provoke what Patrick Colm Hogan refers to as "empathic emotions," the affective responses that, in his view, are most typically produced by literature and are "directly parallel to the emotions we have when hearing about someone who experienced some joy or sorrow at a distance from us, someone we can neither help nor harm" (2011, 23). As noted earlier, the theatrical situation can arguably reinforce this empathic reaction as the physical presence of the actors reduces the sense of distance while their movements and facial expressions may trigger affective responses on their own. After all, as Wetherell argues, "[t]he individual is a site in which multiple sources of activation and information about body states, situations, past experiences, linguistic forms, flowering thoughts, etc. become woven together" (2012, 21), so that recognition refers not only to the rational comprehension of the characters' situation but also to the spectator's perception and processing of the emotional states conveyed by the actors' bodily behaviour.

In addition, recognition may also occur on a different level—one that involves "egocentric emotions" (Hogan 2011, 22) in the sense that the affective response is not (just) empathy but is bound up with one's own situation. In this respect, what Philip Watkinson describes in this volume as the "abstract" aesthetics of tucker green's play takes on a special function. It remains unclear what exactly the verbal arguments between the three couples are about. The reported illnesses from which one of the partners in parts one and two had been suffering are never specified. In part two, both partners are frequently described as "*busy*" in the stage directions—an excuse they turn to in order to avoid conversation but that is never specified as a concrete activity and was indicated in the performance by the characters scribbling meaningless doodles on the walls surrounding the stage. Moreover, it is never clarified what the apology one partner is demanding from the other is due for. In all three parts, it transpires that each character is urged by unfulfilled needs and wants—and also by a desire to satisfy those of the other—but their exact nature remains largely unspoken. Most notably, the characters have no proper names but are referred to as A and B in the first part, Woman and Man in part two, and Man and Young Woman in the third part. All this serves to give the play a generic or "abstract" feel rather than individual or concrete.

The pervasive lack of context, the emptiness of the stage and the absence of a linear story and individualising details reduce the characters, at moments at least, to the vulnerability, dependence and incompleteness they share with everyone else present in the theatre. The precariousness of their love and their craving for recognition signal towards the overall existential precariousness of human beings. As Judith Butler has argued in *Precarious Life*, "we all live with [...] a vulnerability to the other that is part of bodily life, a vulnerability to a sudden address from elsewhere that we cannot preempt. This vulnerability, however, becomes highly exacerbated under certain social and political conditions, especially those in which violence is a way of life and the means to secure selfdefense are limited" ([2004] 2006, 29). Of course, Butler is primarily concerned with life under conditions of political oppression and actual threats to "life and limb," but it arguably remains within the remit of her conception of precariousness to claim that love, too, is a condition that exacerbates human vulnerability. In each scene of tucker green's play, the characters are reminded of their vulnerability resulting from their lack of self-sufficiency, their dependence on the uncontrollable love of an uncontrollable other and their exposure to emotional violence. Notably, although the play makes extensive use of venomous insults, its most distressing moments are often wordless. In scene five, for instance, after B has unveiled to A that he has become bored by "it"—most probably sex—A's anxious question "Are you tired of me?" is left hanging in the air by B's inconclusive answer, "Yeh. No. *Beat.* Well ..." (22). Similarly, part two ends in painful silence. After Man and Woman's tenacious struggle for an apology, Woman eventually lays down her arms and says sorry. Having thus weakened her position, she expects Man to do the same and "*gestures for him to say something*" but there is only "[*s*]*ilence, for as long as it can be held* (72; italics in the original). It is through recognising the characters' emotional suffering in situations like these that the audience may be reminded of their own inescapable vulnerability and hence experience not only empathic but also egocentric emotions.

I do not think recognition of this latter kind will usually take the form of fully conscious, propositional knowledge. As Leys suggests, in order to think about affect without reverting to a dualistic conception of mind and body, it might be necessary to abandon the position that equates cognition and intentionality with "the human capacity for producing linguistic propositions" (2011, 470). This means a shift away from what Linda Zerilli describes as the "intellectualist doctrine," the position that "tends to treat all aspects of human thought and action in terms of cognition" and according to which "our orientation to the world is wholly conceptual, with 'conceptual' understood here in the specific sense of the mental grasping of true propositions" (2015, 261–62). Against this, Zerilli proposes to "advance an understanding of intelligent action and judgement in which affect and reason are understood to be mutually imbricated in modes of conceptuality" (2015, 262) and that "insists on the irreducible entanglement of thinking and feeling, [...] propositional and nonpropositional knowledge" (2015, 266). In the light of a "conceptualist but non-intellectualist" (Zerilli 2015, 272) mode of understanding, then, I suggest that the audience's affective response to tucker green's play does not follow from the acquisition of the articulate knowledge that they are precarious beings in the sense of Butler's or similar philosophical assumptions, but from the intuitive realisation that the characters' existential vulnerability that surfaces in (crises of) love is something they share.

No matter to what extent this realisation becomes articulate knowledge or remains a vague intuition, the affective response it engenders is irreducibly intentional. It is intentional because it cannot be prised away from that which causes it, which includes the physical situation of the theatre performance, the consciously grasped thematic content of the play and the maybe conscious, maybe subconscious recognition of human precariousness. In Zerilli's words, "intentionalism involves a mode of concept possession that does not necessarily entail intellectualism" (2015, 282), which allows affects to be intentional even if it is beyond the subject's capacity to formulate their "aboutness" in a verbal proposition. Even a play as abstract and opaque as tucker green's, therefore, elicits affects related to its thematic content.

Conclusion

Recognition of thematic content takes on different degrees of awareness or, as Wetherell puts it, "affective responses are triggered by conscious cognitions (e.g. memories and perceptions) and non-conscious subjective appraisals" (2012, 62). But even the latter still precipitate intentional, content-related affects. With regard to literary texts, Hogan argues that the "complex emotional experience" they can produce "is inseparable from the depictive content" (2011, 22). When it comes to theatre, I contend, the affective experience is likewise entangled with the depictive content of the play, while the physical presence and proximity of actors and audience members, the sense of exposure and intimacy I have described above, reinforce its bodily dimension. In the mind/body interactivity elicited by theatre, in other words, the body is arguably more active than in the reading process, but affective audience response cannot be disentangled from the activities of the mind.

The claim that a play like tucker green's *a profoundly affectionate, passionate devotion* elicits affective responses that are inseparably bodily and mental and, moreover, intentional—in the sense that they are, not exclusively but substantially, about its thematic content—is of course open to question. It might be objected that if the performance does indeed evoke a sense of precariousness, this is primarily due to the performance situation, while the content plays only a secondary role. Affective activation, in this view, would occur independently of and before the conceptual processing of the content, which then only retrospectively shapes and directs the affective response. This argument would form an analogy to Toby's view in *The Effect* that the increased levels of dopamine and all the resulting symptoms are already there—caused by the antidepressant agent—before they are interpreted by the conscious mind as love. Similarly, it could be argued that the theatre situation in itself elevates the audience's level of affective activation, which is then explained and intentionalised by the mind in relation to the thematic content. But even if this might make sense on an abstract, theoretical level, it has no impact on actual experience. There is no perception of a pure theatre situation that is not already meshed with its entire context, including its thematic content, just as there is no pure experience of raised or lowered levels of dopamine without a context in which they are understood. Tristan is sure he is in love because for him, ultimately, bodily and mental experience cannot be reasonably separated and when he feels love, it is what it is. Similarly, if the spectator of tucker green's play experiences precariousness, it is what it is and cannot be divided into the bodily and the mental components of this experience, which inextricably rests on both and consists of both.

References

Ahmed, Sara. 2004. *The Cultural Politics of Emotion.* London and New York: Routledge.

Billington, Michael. 2012. Review of *The Effect*, by Lucy Prebble. *Guardian*, November 14.

———. 2017. Review of *a profoundly affectionate, passionate devotion to someone (-noun)*, by debbie tucker green. *Guardian*, March 7. Accessed December 20, 2019.

Butler, Judith. (2004) 2006. *Precarious Life: The Powers of Mourning and Violence.* London: Verso.

Cavendish, Dominic. 2017. Review of *a profoundly affectionate, passionate devotion to someone (-noun)*, by debbie tucker green. *Telegraph*, March 7. Accessed December 20, 2019.

Clapp, Susannah. 2012. Review of *The Effect*, by Lucy Prebble. *Observer*, November 18.

Fisher, Helen. 2004. *Why We Love: The Nature and Chemistry of Romantic Love.* New York: Henry Holt.

Hemming, Sarah. 2012. Review of *The Effect*, by Lucy Prebble. *Financial Times*, November 15.

Hogan, Patrick Colm. 2011. *What Literature Teaches Us About Emotion.* Cambridge: Cambridge UP.

Letts, Quentin. 2012. Review of *The Effect*, by Lucy Prebble. *Daily Mail*, November 14.

Leys, Ruth. 2011. "The Turn to Affect: A Critique." *Critical Inquiry* 37 (3): 434–72.

Nathan, John. 2012. Review of *The Effect*, by Lucy Prebble. *Jewish Chronicle*, November 16.

Prebble, Lucy. 2009. *Enron.* London: Bloomsbury.

———. 2012. *The Effect.* London: Bloomsbury.

Purves, Libby. 2012. Review of *The Effect*, by Lucy Prebble. *Times*, November 14.

Shouse, Eric. 2005. "Feeling, Emotion, Affect." *M/C Journal* 8 (6). Accessed February 24, 2020.

Singer, Irving. (1984) 2009. *The Nature of Love. Vol. 2, Courtly and Romantic.* Cambridge, MA: MIT Press.

Szlawinska, Maxie. 2012. Review of *The Effect*, by Lucy Prebble. *Sunday Times*, November 18.

Vesey-Byrne, Joe. 2017. Review of *a profoundly affectionate, passionate devotion to someone (-noun)*, by debbie tucker green. *Independent*, March 7. Accessed December 20, 2019.

Wehrs, Donald R. 2017. "Introduction: Affect and Texts: Contemporary Inquiry in Historical Context." In Wehrs and Blake 2017, 1–93.

Wehrs, Donald, and Thomas Blake, eds. 2017. *The Palgrave Handbook of Affect Studies and Textual Criticism*. London: Palgrave Macmillan.

Wetherell, Margaret. 2012. *Affect and Emotion: A New Social Science Understanding*. London: Sage.

Zerilli, Linda. 2015. "The Turn to Affect and the Problem of Judgement." *New Literary History* 46 (2): 261–86.

CHAPTER 5

Political Dramaturgies of Affect: Anthony Neilson's *God in Ruins* and *The Wonderful World of Dissocia*

Liz Tomlin

The turn to affect, in the broadest sense, is commonly located as a movement that has occurred within the humanities and social sciences. In the context of theatre studies, it is important to note that this might more accurately be termed a *re*turn, given that, in the words of Erin Hurley, "questions of feeling have always been central to theatre" (2010, 2). This has not, however, always been the case in the European discourse and practice of political theatre with which this chapter will engage.

Bertolt Brecht's well-known scepticism of theatres that sought to trade in emotional operations (2015) is often misinterpreted as an outright rejection of the political currency of emotion. But it is nonetheless the case that his vision of a Marxist political theatre necessitated that emotional responses were sought primarily as a means to a rational end that was arrived at through the cognitive judgement of the spectator. Such is also the case, Sarah Grochala argues, in the tradition of British drama from

L. Tomlin (✉)
University of Glasgow, Glasgow, UK
e-mail: Elizabeth.Tomlin@glasgow.ac.uk

M. Aragay et al. (eds.), *Affects in 21st-Century British Theatre*,
https://doi.org/10.1007/978-3-030-58486-3_5

George Bernard Shaw to David Edgar characterised by the thesis play that "yokes together the dialectical discussion of a political issue with a realist dramaturgy" (2017, 13). This dominant historical lineage of British political theatre is distinguished through its continuing adherence to a rational, dialectical narrative structure that plays predominantly to a cognitive, analytical reception and analysis.

The turn to affect that characterises Hans-Thies Lehmann's theories of the postdramatic has offered one of the most sustained challenges to the dramatic, dialectical model, inherited from both Brechtian and Shavian traditions, that has proved particularly durable in the British context. In the wealth of scholarship that has engaged with Lehmann's seminal publication, *Postdramatic Theatre* (2006; originally published in German in 1999), the importance of affect to the political currency of Lehmann's model of the postdramatic was initially somewhat overshadowed by debates concerning the role of text and dramaturgical innovations that challenge dramatic form. However, in his more recent work, Lehmann emphasises that the postdramatic is explicitly "a theatre of affectivity" (2016, 433) that is, moreover, engaged in "an affective interrogation of dramatic theatre" (2016, 435) and contends that it is in this affective charge and interrogation of the dramatic model that its political potential is to be found.

Although Lehmann does not explicitly engage with the affect theorists or debates that underpin this volume, the affective charge he envisages is not one that enhances narrative or rational argument through the invocation of recognised and calibrated emotional states, but rather a sensation of intensity that disturbs meaning, shocks the spectator's learned cultural expectations and capacities of interpretation and so remains resistant to rational, or even emotional, cognitive processing. In this, his understanding of the politics of affect would, like that of theorists such as Brian Massumi (2002), following Baruch Spinoza and Gilles Deleuze, rest on its capacity to exist as prepersonal and asocial and so beyond ideological manipulation or critique. In the context of Lehmann's postdramatic, the politics of affect lie in the capacity of certain theatrical strategies to viscerally shock and disorientate the spectator out of her habitual mode of perception through a transgression of accepted aesthetic boundaries and cultural assumptions. Such shock, he has always argued, is only conceivable within a form that ruptures the aesthetic frame of the dramatic theatre to which the spectator is habituated. However, in his more recent work on the postdramatic tragic impulse, Lehmann begins to speculate as to whether the *political* charge of the affect of shock may lie most securely within dramaturgies that rupture the aesthetic boundaries of the theatre event—dramatic or postdramatic—through the intervention of "real actuality" (2013, 99).

This chapter will contest Lehmann's proposal that political potential is limited to dramaturgies that embrace the irruption of "real actuality" by turning to Anthony Neilson's "theatre of affect" (Reid 2017, 3), which seeks to deliver a shock of the kind that Lehmann advocates, but retains the aesthetic framework of theatre intact. My first example, *God in Ruins* (2007; unpublished), can be seen to operate a reality effect that momentarily suggests a nonaesthetic reality has ruptured the theatrical framework, but is quickly revealed to be a representational dramaturgical device.[1] Nonetheless, I will propose that the momentary affect of shock, at the point when it might have been real, is indistinguishable from visceral sensations that may occur during performances that have, in actuality, been ruptured by a nonaesthetic reality. Moreover, in my own experience as an audience member attending *God in Ruins*, the relief provided by the realisation that the ontological status of the dramaturgy remained securely within the confines of an aesthetically structured event permitted cognitive self-reflection on my visceral and momentary response of unease. This self-reflection, I argue, far from reducing the political charge of the affective shock, enhanced it through cognitive activity that might not have been arrived at in those instances in which the irruption of the real is sustained and ostensibly authentic.

In my second example, *The Wonderful World of Dissocia* (2004; published in Neilson 2007a, 1–89), there is no such apparent rupture of the aesthetic frame by "real actuality"; here it is the aesthetic, and I will argue broadly dramatic, frame itself that is sundered into two. Yet, once more, the secure ontological framework of the dramaturgy that contains the rupture within its aesthetic boundaries is precisely what enables the political charge to operate. In this instance, I will propose that the disorientation produced by the affective shock of rupture acts in tandem with expressionist dramaturgical strategies, through which the spectator is immersed into the representational world of act one, only to experience, along with the protagonist, the violent irruption of act two and the visceral shock that this engenders. Such expressionist dramaturgies may also be defined as affective in their engagement of the audience's sensory involvement and emotional response, but their political potential would be dismissed by

Lehmann given their alignment with recognised modes of feeling and cognitive engagement that run counter to the autonomy and disorientation of the affective shock he advocates. Here, Neilson's use of affect aligns more closely with theorists such as Sara Ahmed (2004) and Carolyn Pedwell (2014), who resist narrow differentiation between affect and emotion and reject the dualism of bodily sensation versus cognitive activity. The argument pursued in this chapter is less interested in pitting one understanding, or definition, of affect against another, than in exploring precisely how Neilson's theatre of affect evokes, to political effect, both visceral shock—which may at the point of experience be untethered to emotional or rational processing—and sustained emotional and sensory engagement.

Above all, it is my contention that the fictional, or aesthetic, framework of the dramatic offers the ontological security that is vital for the political processing of any visceral shock to take place, and I thus reject Lehmann's conviction that it is only the shock of an irruption of the real, and the subsequent collapse of the spectator's ontological security and suspension of analytical activity, that can result in a political charge. Such a proposition would support the Deleuzian position that the politics of affect are only secured if the autonomy of affect from emotional, social or political interpretation or analysis is maintained. To the contrary, I argue in this chapter that while visceral shock can heighten awareness, self-consciousness and trigger a more acute propensity for altered perception, the political potential of such affect is only realised through subsequent cognitive processing, be that emotional, rational or both.

I will employ the term *representational theatre* for Neilson's work, although I will propose, drawing on criteria I have laid out elsewhere (Tomlin 2013a), that *God in Ruins* is predominantly dramatic, with one significant postdramatic rupture, and *The Wonderful World of Dissocia* (henceforth *Dissocia*) is expressionist drama.[2] The important factor for this chapter is that both plays remain within the aesthetic boundaries of "art" (Lehmann 2016, 440); everything is, ultimately, designed, rehearsed and then represented on stage, without any irruption of "the real." Yet this chapter will conclude not only that representational theatre, even that which is broadly dramatic, is equally capable of achieving politically charged affect but also that it is precisely *through* its containment within aesthetic boundaries which permit subsequent self-reflection and emotional calibration that the affect of shock wields its particular political charge.

Postdramatic Politics of Affect

In his recent work on contemporary tragedy, Lehmann establishes the thesis that this chapter seeks to contest. While I will draw on Lehmann's detailed exploration of a political currency that is reliant on affective resonance through shock to the spectator's ontological certainties and cultural assumptions, I will seek to question his alignment of such a currency with a tragic impulse that holds political charge only when instigated by a rupture of the aesthetic frame via a nonaesthetic irruption of the real.

Lehmann proposes that shock to the spectator can be caused by "transgression, rupture, overstepping, immoderation and excess" (2016, 390). Viewing the tragic through the lens of the "Icarian model" (2016, 410), he argues that throughout its history, "transgression, the theme of dangerous excess, has proven central, but the connection between the tragic and the theatre always takes shape in a different way" (2016, 411). Where classical tragedy offered its audience the vicarious experience of transgression undertaken by the protagonist within the fictional cosmos of the aesthetic frame, the postdramatic tragic impulse, according to Lehmann, follows in the footsteps of avant-garde artists such as Antonin Artaud by exploring how theatre's "manifestation of transgression" (2016, 410) might collapse the fourth wall in order to viscerally, rather than vicariously, affect the spectator.

Thus, affective shock, the impact on the spectator of the postdramatic tragic, can be said to be of a different order from the cathartic emotions aroused by classical tragic structures. The emotional charge of catharsis is inarguably felt, but it is also cognitively understood and recognised and named as—in the Aristotelian configuration—fear or pity. Instead, in Lehmann's argumentation, the affect of shock is rather intended to be viscerally experienced without being emotionally calibrated, precisely to confuse any cathartic emotional or rational processing of the shock that has been received. Thus, the spectator is prevented from emotional mastery of the unfolding events and denied the security afforded by feeling part of a stable interpretative community. Instead, she is left exposed to the disorientation that enables shifts of perception to occur. This, Lehmann argues, is where the political potency of the contemporary tragic lies.

However, Lehmann reserves this potential for specific models of theatre practice and, in so doing, continues to limit the contemporary dramaturgies through which a political charge can be deemed possible. Lehmann has always dismissed the proposal that dramatic theatre, as he defines it, holds the potential for political and/or tragic currency in the contemporary moment. Although he acknowledges that "[t]here is space for tragedy even organised along the patterns of traditional conflict dramaturgy" (2013, 97), he remains sceptical of its political impact, doubting that "the necessary shock to our cultural habits can be achieved within the limits of a theatre of representation" (2013, 97). This is because he holds that the familiar dramatic conventions of the "conflict model" (2016, 390) are too securely retained within audiences' horizons of expectation to permit the kind of transgression of cultural limits that would result in any transformative visceral shock to the spectator. Rather he asserts that it is only the postdramatic form that, "though always different and modulated along idiosyncratic lines, deprives normalized [*genormt*] consciousness of its mooring: its concepts pale, the certainty of judgment wavers, the sphere of calm (or calming) reflection is shut out or deferred, and cultural intelligibility is dealt a shock" (2016, 401; translation inserted in the original).

However, because the cultural authority of the very institution of theatre is always well placed to contain the disruption threatened by attempts to transgress its aesthetic conventions, Lehmann's thesis in his more recent work begins to pull away from the political potential of a theatre that may well be widely understood as postdramatic, but in which the transgressions, now normalised in a European theatre culture increasingly influenced by such dramaturgies, risk merely entertaining or even titillating, rather than shocking, an audience that is becoming accustomed to the new conventions: "In a time when aesthetic fragmentation has become the norm, almost all interruptions can be integrated into the inherited theatrical framework with almost no consequence at all. An incalculable being, the spectator, 'succeeds,' time and again, at transforming any rupture at all into a continuum [...]. The spectator readily redramatizes the intended caesura: theatre 'theatres everything up [*theatert alles ein*],' as Brecht knew" (Lehmann 2016, 441; translation inserted in the original).[3]

Lehmann thus argues that the transgression required by the tragic impulse may need to move beyond overstepping aesthetic conventions to "*interrupt*[*ing*] art itself, insofar as the latter functions as an inert component of normative culture" (2016, 404; italics in the original): "when tragedy remains within the framework of an artistic institution that transforms everything into entertainment (against which even its radical forms have no protection), it threatens to deteriorate into the mere pretense of transgression: a matter of museums and *Kulturgut*. Such transformation simply annihilates the tragic claim, which is unthinkable if no shock to cultural intelligibility occurs" (2016, 401). Therefore, Lehmann claims, the "shock to cultural intelligibility" may now require that the commodifiable artwork of theatre itself and the cultural authority and ontological security that pertain to such an event be punctured by an interruption of reality that cannot be contained within a purely aesthetic framework. Only with such a rupture "is it possible to experience a shaking or destabilising of the basic grounds of our cultural existence, even a blurring of the boundaries of the self, of conceptual understanding as such" (2013, 98–99).

Thus, as Lehmann notes, more recent theatrical practice has moved beyond postdramatic transgressions of dramatic representation to ever more radical attempts to take "the aesthetic mode of perception [...] to its limits—so that praxis, that which is serious and real, breaks through or undermines merely artful appearance" (2016, 442). He refers to such work in various ways, all of which seem to require an extended understanding of the postdramatic as previously defined in his earlier writings. At different points, he notes "a theatre of situation" (2013, 89), the "curious twilight zone between political activism and aesthetic practice" (2013, 87) or "a theatre—whether one calls it postdramatic, performance or something else—[that] will not maintain a clear distinction between its status as art and as praxis" (2016, 440).

Lehmann's discussion of the political potential of affective transgression thus traverses a number of models of theatre that might be seen to constitute, to some degree, a spectrum. At one end lies dramatic theatre, which Lehmann doubts is able to achieve "the necessary shock to our cultural habits" (2013, 97); next is the range of forms that constitute the postdramatic, which work by "taxing" the framework of the dramatic in various ways (2016, 425). At the far end of the spectrum, and examined in Lehmann's more recent work, are events such as Laila Soliman's series of performances, *No Time for Art* (2011–2013), where the aesthetic frame of the theatre event itself is ruptured, or indeed entirely scored through, by interruptions of praxis (Lehmann 2013). One precondition of the political in theatre, Lehmann asserts, "is the momentous undermining of key certainties: about whether we are spectators or participants; whether we perceive or are confronted with perceptions that function 'as if' or for real; whether we dwell in the field of aesthetic make-belief or in real actuality" (2013, 99).

In turning now to Neilson's work, I will seek to contest Lehmann's proposal that to sustain the political charge of the affect of shock, artists need to continue chasing ever more radical transgressions of theatre's aesthetic limits through ever more radical irruptions of the real. This is a tactic that fails to recognise that each rupture will, in turn, become anticipated, just as the postdramatic conventions that preceded them, by audiences who have become immune to or are titillated by what might be termed *shock-effects*. In such instances, the "affect" that is delivered is cognitively recognised as a cultural convention within a certain trend of aesthetic practice, and the political charge of its potential to genuinely shock the spectator from their cultural moorings is neutered. On the contrary, I will argue, there is renewable political currency in affects that are built into, and unique to, the dramaturgical design of the unruptured aesthetic framework in which they are employed.

Neilson's *God in Ruins* operates an ostensible rupture in the aesthetic framework of the theatre event, but one that is quickly revealed to be a reality effect, an integral and scripted part of the play. I will argue that, despite the rupture being quickly "theatred up," as Lehmann would protest, there is nonetheless political currency in the affect of shock that momentarily disturbs and disorientates. Furthermore, I will argue that it is precisely the reincorporation of the rupture back into the aesthetic framework that permits the emotional and rational calibration that theorists such as Lehmann would wish to occlude from a discourse of affective resonance that must, to protect its political charge, remain autonomous from cognitive activity. Conversely, I believe that far from blunting the political charge of the affective shock as Lehmann might contend, Neilson's reincorporation of the shock of the seemingly real back into a representational framework permits deeper cognitive self-reflection on a visceral and momentary response of unease than may be the case when the interruption of "real actuality" is authentic, sustained and unreconciled.

Reality Effects and Affective Ruptures

The reality effect I am concerned with in this analysis occurs around three-quarters of the way through *God in Ruins*, Neilson's Christmas play which I attended at Soho Theatre, London. Up until this point, the play had engaged, through expressionist rather than realist strategies, with the narrative journey of TV producer Brian (played by Brian Doherty), a modern-day Scrooge battling his demons and attempting to make contact with his estranged daughter at Christmas despite the best efforts of his ex-wife to prevent this from happening. The lead-up to the moment of rupture sees Brian coming around from a drug-fuelled stupor to be confronted by, firstly, the ghost of his dead father, and secondly, the fictional character of Scrooge.

Although both of these appearances, to borrow from Lehmann, increasingly "taxed" the representational frame of the play, such subversions were, themselves, contained within the rationalising narrative device of a drug-induced hallucination or dream world, thus remaining supported by a coherent and broadly dramatic structural framework as I have argued elsewhere (2013, xv). It was only at the point at which the house lights came up and the characters, Scrooge (Sean Kearns) and Brian, were startled and confused by the sight of an audience watching them that the narrative coherence of the play world began to crack and we briefly glimpsed the postdramatic territory that later plays of Neilson, such as *Narrative* (2013; published in Neilson 2018, 163–251), were to more fully explore. Yet even this rupture, particularly given the comedic responses of the characters and the seasonal context of the play, felt less like a postdramatic and political irruption of the real and more like a pleasurable pantomime convention. It was only when there was a flurry of activity at the back of the theatre, where a man appeared to be arguing with the usher to get past her and into the auditorium, that the aesthetic boundaries appeared to be crumbling and an affect of unease began to ripple through the audience.

The man, who looked and sounded exactly like a rough sleeper who was potentially violent and probably drunk might be expected to, was brilliantly convincing. Kearns and Doherty dropped their characters and began asking the man to leave. He became aggressive; he was an ex-soldier who had worked in Basra, was now sleeping on the streets and needed a bit of help. Although my hard-wired scepticism remained intact, there was something about the detailed authenticity of the staged event that made me very alert to my real presence in the auditorium in which these events were now unfolding and somewhat anxious about any potential exposure to come—be that from the consequences of a real intrusion or from a staged event that might suddenly demand more of me than the contract with the play I had implicitly accepted so far.

As Trish Reid argues, throughout his work Neilson has deployed numerous strategies to make spectators alert to the present moment (2017, 125); an intensification of theatre's intrinsic liveness that, for Neilson, fulfils theatre's "experiential" promise (Neilson 2007b, n.p.). In moments like this, when the ontological register of the play is ruptured—and whether the rupture is real or not—we are thrown into an increased awareness of our own present space and time and our vulnerability to exposure or of a call to action that we might be unprepared for and unwilling to fulfil. Despite the artful dialogue that ensued between the ex-soldier, Ryan, and Kearns and Doherty about the play itself, which increasingly suggested the aesthetic and designed nature of the intervention, Ryan's supplications to the audience continued to unnerve me given the context of the play and the role I had felt safe playing up until this point. The fraction of any remaining possibility that he might be a "real" ex-soldier, wounded in battle and now sleeping on the streets and hungry, who might ask me at any moment to give him a bit of spare change in the spirit of Christmas, made my absence of response, my complete denial of his presence, complicit with the ubiquitous figure of Scrooge or the figure of Brian, who had in earlier scenes given a tip of five pence to the pizza delivery man. Yet conversely, the fear of responding, acting, and giving him money, when it was overwhelmingly likely that this was an actor playing a part, was also paralysing—how stupid would such an action make me look? My relief as it gradually became clear that this was, in fact, "only theatre," did nothing to neutralise the political currency of those moments of doubt.

This rupture, at its moment of occurrence, initiated in this spectator what Lehmann describes as "the unsettling that occurs through the *indecidability* whether one is dealing with reality or fiction" (2006, 101; italics in the original). Lehmann notes that the spectators in such a context "find themselves in a double bind, calling for an aesthetic appreciation and at the same time for a reaction of responsibility which would be to some degree 'real' [...]. Ethico-political responsibility re-enters into the aesthetic experience" (2013, 100). Where I would, however, question the trajectory of Lehmann's thinking is in his doubt that such transgressions can be sustained in contexts such as *God in Ruins*, in which the irruption is an illusion, a reality effect that is revealed to be a mere aesthetic strategy and thus, in his view, neutered of any transgressive political charge. Despite the intervention of Ryan being explicitly "theatred up," it momentarily cut through an enjoyable Christmas fable as a reminder of the liveness of the action; it cut through my security as a spectator of whom nothing was asked to expose me, in that moment of being, to risk—the risk of acting in the wrong way, of not knowing whether action was actually desired of me. I experienced, in Lehmann's terms, that "passing fever of affect that makes the subject lose composure" (2016, 429), an affect in which I could only retrospectively identify the emotions of embarrassment, anxiety, fear and shame. At the moment of ontological uncertainty, the dominant sensation was a visceral and confused self-consciousness that only subsequently took the shape of an uncomfortable awareness of my own position as a privileged attendant of entertaining artistic performances in the face of someone who was ostensibly having to live on the streets and survive on handouts.

As Lehmann's thesis proposes, I was indeed dislocated, through the affect of shock, from my habitual mode of perception to an awareness of "heightened, conscious being" (2016, 438). Lehmann further argues that the spectator's experience of such excess may not promote healing, as Aristotelian catharsis intended, but quite the reverse (2016, 438). His analysis of the affect he experienced in Soliman's *No Time for Art* reflects my own experience at this moment in Neilson's play: the feeling of "lack in the face of the absence of action. The aesthetic appreciation is broken by a concrete questioning of the self" (2013, 109). The affective value of the shock was due to the very real threat that I was to be called upon to act in ways that I might not be comfortable with, in ambiguous contexts that might be aesthetic representations of the real governed by rules for my behaviour that were manifestly unclear, or might be interruptions of an unwelcome social reality that should compel me to do something. In short, I instinctively felt both compelled and unable to act. Ryan's intrusion, in Lehmann's terms, had instigated a confusion between aesthetic play and actual praxis (2016, 440), an "overstepping of the framework of reception" I had consented to when purchasing a ticket for a Christmas show (2016, 438).

Yet, as it fairly rapidly became clear that this interruption was, in fact, scripted—exposing Ryan, in turn, as a highly skilled actor, not a drunk ex-soldier who was sleeping rough—the "theatring up" of this reality effect did nothing to blunt the political charge of the affective, if momentary, shock. Conversely, as the affect of unease subsided and the risk of exposure was no longer acute, I was able to cognitively reflect on my instinctive visceral response. Through this reflection, I was forced to acknowledge to myself that my concern about how I might look to other audience members was probably way and above more important than the plight of this intruder into the hitherto secure framework of my attendance at a Christmas show. This is how Lehmann's affective charge operated for me in this instance of rupture: a dislocation of security and community by the intrusion of "the other," a disenfranchised member of the real world offering a stark reminder to the relatively privileged actors and spectators that the "goodwill to all men" that is a part and parcel of our Christmas tradition might not any more easily translate into charitable or courageous action for those spectators than it did for Brian or Charles Dickens's Scrooge. Yet, critically, the political charge of this rupture required, counter to Lehmann's proposal, a moment of contemplation permitted by the return of the ontological safety offered by the aesthetic event, in which I could process the affect of shock and cognitively—as well as self-critically—reflect on my own visceral response. Without this restitution of ontological security—that is, had Ryan proved to be "real"—I would suggest that my response to the affective shock may not have been able to escape the momentarily overwhelming anxiety and potentially narcissistic self-consciousness at how the removal of the aesthetic frame had left me and my sense of public subjecthood exposed to risk. That Ryan was a representation, a reality effect, did not detract from the political impact of the moment when it might—just might—have been real, but conversely permitted it by resettling the unease that had sent my affective reflexes hurtling towards the necessity for self-protection, thus enabling cognitive and self-critical reflection on the politics of the experience.

If such an analysis, which is necessarily subjective and inconclusive, speculatively suggests that what might be defined as the postdramatic reality effect of *God in Ruins* may hold equivalent, or even deeper, political potential than the actual intervention of any "real actuality," in the next section I pursue my interrogation of Lehmann's thesis still further along the spectrum I sketched out above as I turn to Neilson's *Dissocia*. In this case, there is no fissure in the aesthetic framework that would constitute an interruption by a "real actuality" or the illusory effect of such a rupture. Moreover, without digressing into an extensive discussion over the categorisation of *Dissocia*, I would locate the play as broadly dramatic in form, despite the characteristics—its affective charge key amongst them—that have led others, such as Reid (2007), to focus on the many ways in which it evokes Lehmann's descriptions of postdramatic dramaturgies. Whereas *God in Ruins* does momentarily fracture the enclosed, representational framework of the fictional world, as described above, *Dissocia* maintains its fourth wall throughout and follows a narrative that is consistent and coherent, given the play's internal logic as an expressionist account of reality. Here, it is the fictional frame of the protagonist itself that is sundered into two. However, I will argue that it is precisely because both the aesthetic and fictional frameworks of *Dissocia* are sustained throughout that the affective and political charge for the spectator can be strengthened and consolidated within the carefully designed, dramatic dramaturgy of Neilson's expressionist world.

Affective Expressionism

Dissocia is a play of two distinct acts, designed around a critical interval that is integral to the affective and political potential of the piece. In the first act, we are taken on a fantastical journey to the land of Dissocia, a narrative that echoes the absurd, comical and sometimes terrifying adventures of Lewis Carroll's *Alice in Wonderland* ([1865] 2017), as well as evoking other classic fantasy tales such as C. S. Lewis's *The Lion the Witch and the Wardrobe* ([1950] 2009). The protagonist, Lisa, is visited by a watch mender, Victor, who explains that her recent experiences of ill health are due to her having lost an hour during a transatlantic flight that arrived just as the clocks went back an hour to end British Summer Time. Her missing hour, he informs her, can be retrieved from Dissocia, and once she gets her hour back, balance will be restored to her life. Among the characters Lisa encounters in Dissocia are two nervous (in)security guards, a (scape)Goat who is blamed for everything and Jane from the Council, who submits herself as a victim to as many crimes as possible—including Lisa's imminent rape by the Goat—in order to reduce the number of individuals to have suffered from crime in the council's statistics. Lisa gradually learns that Dissocia is under attack from the armies of the Black Dog King, who is attempting to capture Dissocia's Queen Sarah, who has gone into hiding. As she finally succeeds in tracking down an absurdly dysfunctional Lost Property office in search of her lost hour, she is firstly informed that to have her hour back would destroy Dissocia, and subsequently that she is, in fact, the Queen who must now save them all.

This first act is fast paced, colourful, spectacular and exuberant. The dialogue is sharp and insistently witty, even in moments when the humour is at its darkest. There are songs throughout and the action is often spectacular, including an unforgettable sequence in which Jane and Lisa take to the sky in a flying car as bombs rain down around them. Amidst the chaos of Lisa's adventures, there is also the poignantly affective moment where everything darkens and Lisa curls into a foetal position chanting, "I want to go home I want to go home" (Neilson 2007a, 45). As the sounds of violence fade and Lisa whimpers in the silence, a trapdoor opens in the stage and a polar bear emerges in a mist of dry ice singing a song that starts and ends with the line, "[w]ho'll hold your paw when you die" (45–46), before disappearing back into the ground. Like all quest journeys, there is a clear and coherent narrative strand to follow but, also in common with most quest journeys, it is the moment-by-moment experience of the highs and lows of the journey that thrills, and this is underpinned by the highly affective rewards of this first act's turbo-charged assault on the spectator's senses.

Following the interval that, for me, consisted in a glass of prosecco with a close friend I saw only rarely and a high level of buzz and excitement in the packed bar of York's Theatre Royal, I returned to the auditorium eager for more of the same. Yet we were met instead with silence, an impression of whiteness, flickering fluorescent lighting, a window of perspex separating the audience from the stage, a single hospital bed in which Lisa was lying. The subsequent fourteen short scenes, marked by lights going up and lights going down, contain minimal action, sound or dialogue. Scenes one, two and four consist of a nurse entering, waking Lisa, giving her pills, leaving. The sole sound of footsteps approaching and leaving the room accompanies the beginning or end of each of these scenes. There are brief and quickly resolved moments of conflict when Lisa wants to use the phone, have a cigarette or continue dancing and singing with her Walkman on, before it is taken away. The impact on the spectator when act two begins is one of shock and disorientation. There is a palpable sense of comedown in the auditorium. The energy is slowly sapped from the audience, through the long silences of repetitive scenes where little happens. Heart rates slow. Shoulders sink. The world of the theatre becomes a place where you no longer want to be: bleak, cold and depressing. We all, it feels to me, have been ripped from the play we were part of and are left to find our bearings somewhere much less appealing.

Neilson's attraction to manipulating the affective potential of theatre is clearly foregrounded in Reid's sustained analysis of his work. Arguing that critics should pay more attention to "the forms and textures of Neilson's work" rather than a simple focus on the content, Reid confirms Neilson's commitment to a theatre that is "experiential" and "visceral" in its effect on the audience (2007, 489). She further argues that "*Dissocia*'s effects are substantially dependent on the deliberate violation of conventional rules regarding sign density. The first half is ostentatiously replete with signs—colour, movement, sound, music, shifts in linguistic register and heightened and mixed performance style—while the second is extraordinarily static and muted. [...] the play's overall effect is substantially dependent on a collision between two extreme types of signifying practice" (2007, 490).

It is, perhaps, no great revelation that well-crafted representational theatre that sustains an unruptured aesthetic framework throughout is perfectly able to deliver affective results, as both Reid and myself, among many others, would argue. However, contrary to Lehmann's assertion that such affective work, in the absence of any breach in theatre's aesthetic boundaries, will struggle to shock the spectator's cultural habits sufficiently to invoke a political charge, I will now argue that the affective dramaturgies of *Dissocia* were designed to do precisely that—and in the case of this spectator at least, were successful in so doing.

There are clues laid out for the spectator throughout act one that suggest that the world of *Dissocia* is not a fantastical land that really exists in this fictional world, but a mindscape circumscribed entirely by Lisa's subjective experience of the world around her through the lens of her dissociative disorder. In addition to the infiltration of sounds from the "real" world, throughout her journey, Lisa is threatened in Dissocia by the Black Dog King, a clear reference to depression, and the Dissocians are desperate for the return of Queen Sarah of the House of Tonin, a reference to serotonin, the so-called happy chemical of the human body that is often in short supply for those suffering from depression or anxiety.

In act two, Lisa lies drugged up with medication in a psychiatric hospital. After the first two scenes where she has barely moved sufficiently to take the pills she is given, she gathers her belongings and tries to escape. At the end of scene five, she plays her Walkman and we can just make out the music from the flying car scene of her adventures in Dissocia. In scene six, she dances manically with her Walkman on, until she is restrained by the nurse and has it taken away. In later scenes, Lisa has visitors. Her sister Dot harangues her for her selfish behaviour and the impact this has had on her mother and family: "all because you can't manage to take a few pills twice a day" (82). In the penultimate scene she is visited by Vince:

VINCE: I thought you wanted to get better.
LISA: I *do* want to get better.
VINCE: Well, yes, you say that but then you don't take your *medication*—
LISA *sighs heavily.*
VINCE: Yeah, well, you can fucking sigh, but what can I do? All I can do is nag you to take the fucking pills and then you resent me for nagging you, I just—
Pause.
I don't know if I can do this anymore, I really don't—
[…]
LISA: […] but you don't understand—
VINCE: That's not my fault! It's not my fault that I don't understand! (87; italics in the original)

It is in these final, and brief, exchanges with Lisa that the politics of the piece begin to land. Because for those spectators who have not personally experienced Lisa's journey through depression to mania to neuroleptic sedation, our perspective on her neurological states of mind would more usually be from the outside looking in, through the eyes, perhaps, of the sister or boyfriend who want her to be well and cannot understand why she will not take the medication designed to maintain a state free from psychosis. Yet, as Anna Harpin argues, *Dissocia* explicitly rejects the limitations of realist representations of "madness" that tend to invite a "diagnostic gaze": "Realism tends to remainder the contents of 'mad' experience in some ways as outside the dramatic frame and, thereby, implicitly participates in an othering of such states of mind. Madness in such works is, frequently, reduced to identifiable surface behaviours that are framed as 'ill,' behaviours that exceed the limits of the internal logic of the playworld" (2014, 189). Realist representations of "madness" in theatre, Harpin contends, are most often constructed from the perspective of those, both onstage and off, who are deemed normal, looking at those whose behaviour is framed as aberrant and abnormal. Conversely, in *Dissocia*, the audience is invited to experience an expressionist reality through the perspective of Lisa's neurological lens.

Where Harpin's analysis focuses in detail on the political potential of Neilson's dramaturgy to signal "an acute awareness of the ambiguity that lies at the heart of current notions of mental illness" (2014, 188), I am most interested here in the specific way in which Neilson's invitation to the audience to experience the world as Lisa does is extended predominantly through eliciting particular affective responses that map onto those of the protagonist. We, too, delight in the flying car, we are shocked by the noise of the falling bombs, we feel deeply saddened as Lisa lies whimpering and we share her delight at the appearance of the polar bear. But most of all we, too, are stunned by the rupture of the adventure that lands us in act two: the silence, lack of colour, sterility and absence of any stimulation. We smile to hear the flying car music reprised on the Walkman and are relieved and energised by the scene in which Lisa sings and dances around the ward. As Harpin asserts, "by aligning an audience's journey with Lisa's and further making that experience sumptuous with pleasure he [Neilson] asks that one reassess one's own mode of engagement with the subject of madness and reality. […] Neilson harnesses the pleasure of aesthetic experience to ethical effect" (2014, 197). The ethical, and I would argue political, effect relies on the combined deployment of the two different conceptions of affect I noted in the introduction: the emotional manipulation of the audience's affective experience as they travel with Lisa on her journey and the disorientating shock to their expectations at the beginning of the second half. Having spoken at length to the political potential of the latter, I would like to turn now to the political potential of the former.

Here, I would argue that affective alignment with the protagonist's emotional states does hold political potential in a way that would be dismissed by those theorists who believe, with Lehmann, that for affect to hold political charge it must evade any mode of cognitive processing, emotional as well as rational. I would argue, on the contrary, that emotional cognitive processing is vital to the politics at play in *Dissocia*. This is because mental states unlike our own are peculiarly difficult to comprehend through discursive or rational contemplation. To think of moments of extreme sadness or grief is not to arrive at clinical depression. To think of moments of elation is not to arrive at mania. Thus, public discourse too often resorts to "common sense" responses to behaviour not born of common or rational neurological states of mind. Vince speaks on behalf of the Everyman or woman when he declares to Lisa that he simply does not understand why she would stop taking her medication when she knows that this will make her ill. But what we may be unable to understand rationally, we might just be able to access through affective, emotional experience. This is precisely Neilson's aim, as he outlines in the foreword to *Dissocia*: "Hopefully, when she is asked in the second act why she doesn't take the medication [...] the audience—having been deprived of the spectacle of the first half and any conclusion to its narrative—will understand on a visceral level why she is drawn to her condition" (2007b, n.p.). Here, as Harpin argues, "Neilson aims to dissolve the presumed unintelligibility and incommunicability of experiences of mental illness" (2014, 198).

Because, if the audience do not understand, they are at least perhaps able to feel something analogous to the impact that lands with the rupture from mania into the lethargy and comedown of neuroleptic medication. This is the political charge, as Reid argues, that arises "through felt experience as opposed to intellectual engagement and judgement" (2017, 82). Through Neilson's expressionist dramaturgy, the affective strategies in *Dissocia* operate precisely by containing and immersing the spectator not only inside the play's fictional framework, but inside the neurodivergent mind of its protagonist from which the neuronormative spectator is forced to confront an alien manifestation of their more familiar perspective: that of the family, friends and medical profession who are unable to understand. While the emotional engagement induced by Neilson's fictional framework may not transgress the "limits of [...] 'cultural intelligibility'" in an aesthetic sense, as Lehmann's affective shock would require (2013, 97), I would argue that Neilson's use of affect does disrupt the pathologising of mental health disorders by the dominant social codes and legal apparatus that seek to contain the more extreme manifestations of neurodiversity. Neilson achieves this through a dramaturgy that catapults the spectator into the protagonist's world of mania, only to deliver a shocking rupture after the interval that aesthetically replicates, for the spectator, the affective experience of medication and withdrawal undergone by the protagonist.

The combined affects of emotional alignment and disorientating shock hold strong political potential, given the affective resonance that long outlives any memories of the detailed text or narrative of the production. Revisiting this piece eleven years after seeing it, before returning to the play text, what remained with me was a heart-breaking singing polar bear and the palpable gut wrench when the curtain went up after an interval of buzz and prosecco that hit me with the aesthetic equivalent of a clinical comedown. In my own subsequent engagements and interactions with friends undergoing journeys such as Lisa's, that sense and the insight it brought with it has never left me, and my perception of those who resist medication has been irrevocably enlightened by the affective residue of the performance, which enabled me to "feel," rather than necessarily understand, states of being that I was not able to rationally comprehend.

Conclusion

While I have drawn above on my own subjective experience of *God in Ruins* and *Dissocia*, my analysis does substantiate the legitimacy of a politics of affect that reaches beyond Lehmann's insistence that transgressive shock within unruptured aesthetic frameworks will struggle to escape the "risk of cancelling itself out immediately" (2016, 401). Moreover, I have argued that the political charge of Neilson's affective dramaturgies is achieved, in these two pieces, not only through the employment of affective shock, but also through affective, expressionist dramaturgies that evoke states of emotional, and so cognitive, engagement. In *God in Ruins*, I have argued that the politics lies in the very restitution of the aesthetic boundaries that permit emotional and rational cognitive processing of the affective shock to take place. In *Dissocia*, I have claimed that the politics works through the combination of affective alignment of the spectator with the emotional states of the protagonist and the affective shock that disorientates both protagonist and spectator and rips the latter viscerally from their emotional moorings. The aesthetic frameworks that operated without real rupture in both instances offer the ontological security in which, I would argue, we are best placed to dare to open ourselves up to the vulnerability of being truly shocked or affected in ways that we had not anticipated. In the context of the return to affect in the tradition of political theatres, Neilson's work demonstrates the value in folding the revitalised interest in the affective charge back into a discourse of intended, and political, effect on the world that lies beyond the time and space of the theatre event in ways that can transcend the momentary disorientation of the individual spectator.

Notes

1. *God in Ruins* premiered at Soho Theatre, London, on November 29, 2007. The analysis in this chapter is taken from my notes on the performance.
2. In translations of Lehmann, the term *representational* is often used as synonymous with *dramatic*. In previous work, I have argued that all theatres that are designed, rehearsed and performed are representational (2013b). Thus, the term works well here to subsume the contested binaries of dramatic and postdramatic in opposition to dramaturgies where the representational apparatus is ruptured or scored through by something "real" that cannot be contained within the aesthetic boundaries of theatre.
3. The German citation comes from Brecht (1957, 30).

References

Ahmed, Sara. 2004. *The Cultural Politics of Emotion*. London and New York: Routledge.

Angelaki, Vicky, ed. 2013. *Contemporary British Theatre: Breaking New Ground*. Basingstoke and New York: Palgrave Macmillan.

Brecht, Bertolt. 1957. *Schriften zum Theater. Über eine nicht-aristotelische Dramatik*. Frankfurt am Maine: Suhrkamp.

———. 2015. *Brecht on Theatre*. 3rd ed. Edited by Marc Silberman, Steve Giles and Tom Kuhn. London: Methuen.

Carroll, Lewis. (1865) 2017. *Alice in Wonderland*. London: Legend.

Grochala, Sarah. 2017. *The Contemporary Political Play: Rethinking Dramaturgical Structure*. London: Bloomsbury.

Harpin, Anna. 2014. "Dislocated: Metaphors of Madness in British Theatre." In Harpin and Foster 2014, 187–215.

Harpin, Anna and Juliet Foster, eds. 2014. *Performance, Madness and Psychiatry: Isolated Acts.* Basingstoke and New York: Palgrave Macmillan.

Hurley, Erin. 2010. *Theatre & Feeling.* Basingstoke and New York: Palgrave Macmillan.

Jürs-Munby, Karen, Jerome Carroll and Steve Giles, eds. 2013. *Postdramatic Theatre and the Political: International Perspectives on Contemporary Performance.* London: Bloomsbury.

Lehmann, Hans-Thies. 2006. *Postdramatic Theatre.* Translated by Karen Jürs-Munby. London and New York: Routledge.

———. 2013. "A Future for Tragedy? Remarks on the Political and the Postdramatic." In Jürs-Munby, Carroll and Giles 2013, 87–110.

———. 2016. *Tragedy and Dramatic Theatre.* Translated by Erik Butler. London and New York: Routledge.

Lewis, C. S. (1950) 2009. *The Lion, the Witch and the Wardrobe.* London: Harper Collins.

Massumi, Brian. 2002. *Parables for the Virtual: Movement, Affect, Sensation.* Durham, NC and London: Duke UP.

Neilson, Anthony. 2007a. *The Wonderful World of Dissocia/Realism.* London: Bloomsbury.

———. 2007b. "Foreword." In Neilson 2007a, n.p.

———. 2018. *Plays 3.* London: Bloomsbury.

Pedwell, Carolyn 2014: *Affective Relations: The Transnational Politics of Empathy.* Basingstoke and New York: Palgrave Macmillan.

Reid, Trish. 2007. "'Deformities of the Frame': The Theatre of Anthony Neilson." *Contemporary Theatre Review* 17 (4): 487–98.

———. 2017. *The Theatre of Anthony Neilson.* London: Bloomsbury.

Tomlin, Liz. 2013a. "Foreword: Dramatic Developments." In Angelaki 2013, viii–xxvi.

———. 2013b. *Acts and Apparitions: Discourses of the Real in Performance Practice and Theory 1990–2010.* Manchester: Manchester UP.

PART II

Affects and Politics: Identities, Institutions, Ideology

CHAPTER 6

Black Lives, Black Words at the Bush Theatre: Art, Anger, Affect and Activism

Lynette Goddard

Talking About Race, Rage and Black Theatre

In *Why I'm No Longer Talking to White People about Race* (2017), Reni Eddo-Lodge acknowledges that she is following in the footsteps of her predecessor Black feminists Kimberlé Crenshaw, Angela Davis, bell hooks, Audre Lorde and Michele Wallace to discuss an intersectional approach to feminism that accounts for racialised experiences of gender. Eddo-Lodge had noticed the sometimes innocuous, and often explicit, ways in which conversations about race and the intersectionality of racial and gendered oppressions were closed down in white feminist spaces where she was in the minority as a Black woman. The title of Eddo-Lodge's book presents a provocation about the difficulties of talking about race with white people who resist fully understanding where Black people are speaking from or refuse to acknowledge our concerns about intersectionality. The difficulties that Eddo-Lodge refers to are in no small part affective: during and after such conversations, we incur an exhausting emotional labour and

L. Goddard (✉)
Royal Holloway, University of London, Egham, UK
e-mail: L.P.Goddard@rhul.ac.uk

M. Aragay et al. (eds.), *Affects in 21st-Century British Theatre*,
https://doi.org/10.1007/978-3-030-58486-3_6

expense. Talking to white people about race can produce and reproduce bodily anxieties in the moment; we can be left with residual feelings afterwards. Yet, despite its provocative title, Eddo-Lodge makes a case for why structural racism makes it imperative to talk about race and between races.

The emotions related to talking about race that Eddo-Lodge identifies were prevalent in the earlier waves of 1980s and 1990s Black feminist theorising from which she draws. There are particular echoes of hooks's work on "killing rage: ending racism" and Lorde's elucidation of the uses of anger for women responding to racism. hooks describes being "reluctant to 'talk race' because it hurts. It is painful to think long and hard about race and racism in the United States" (1995, 3). Lorde maintains that "[w]omen responding to racism means women responding to anger; the anger of exclusion, of unquestioned privilege, of racial distortions, of silence, ill-use, stereotyping, defensiveness, misnaming, betrayal, and co-optation" (1984, 124). She describes anger in affective terms as "a powerful source of energy serving progress and change" (1984, 127) and speaks of using productive anger as an activist space from which to propel action for change.

Although neither hooks nor Lorde uses the term "affect," their Black feminist work on confronting racism is affective in nature *and* subject matter; it is about dealing with difficult emotions such as rage and anger and about galvanising one's affective and emotional responses in the service of feminist political action and activism. Their use of terms such as "anger," "pain," "fear" and "rage" signals to the affective bodily responses, feelings and thoughts related to "talking about race" and racism. Lorde writes "[e]very Black woman in America lives her life somewhere along a wide curve of ancient and unexpressed angers" (1984, 145) and she reflects upon her own anger as "a molten pond at the core of me" (1984, 145). hooks states that "[c]onfronting the great resurgence of white supremacist organizations and seeing the rhetoric and beliefs of these groups surface as part of accepted discourse in every aspect of daily life in the United States startles, frightens, and is enough to throw one back into silence" (1995, 3). The centrality of affect and feeling in their contributions preempts some of the preoccupations of the more recent turn to affect in the humanities and allows us to situate more recent affect theory work within a lineage of Black feminist scholarship.

Indeed, the legacy of 1980s and 1990s Black feminist scholars is palpable in the work of recent affect theorists such as Sara Ahmed and Sianne Ngai. Ahmed explores how Lorde's work on anger propels a vision for the future and action for change by acknowledging that "[w]ithin Black feminism, the passion of anger is crucial to what gives us 'the energy' to react against the deep social and psychic investments in racism as well as sexism" (2014, 75). Ahmed identifies anger, rage and shame as three affects of injustice and argues that "feeling better for some might involve expressing feelings of anger, rage and shame," because "emotions that have often been described as negative or even destructive can also be enabling and creative" (2014, 201). A focus on anger and rage also corresponds with what Ngai terms "ugly feelings" (2005, 6) wherein a person feeling such emotions might experience associated feelings of anxiety or shame. As explained by Ngai, "the morally degraded and seemingly unjustifiable status of these feelings tends to produce an unpleasurable feeling *about* the feeling (a reflexive response taking the form of 'I feel ashamed about feeling envious' or 'I feel anxious about my enviousness')" (2005, 10; italics in the original). But whereas Ngai looks at "envy" and "irritation" as a way of favouring "minor and generally unprestigious feelings [...] over grander passions like anger and fear" (2005, 6), hooks and Lorde explored the potential for engaging the seemingly negative "grander passions" as a basis for political action. When it comes to Black women, anger could be perceived as a negative emotion, as epitomised by the supposed "angry Black woman" trope. But Ahmed, hooks and Lorde encourage the proactivist harnessing of angry energies in the pursuit of change and progress. Eddo-Lodge also embraces the idea of the angry Black woman as a symbol of defiance: "The angry black woman cannot be reasoned with. She argues back. She is not docile, sweet or agreeable" (2017, 185).

Talking openly about race is difficult and can be risky, awkward and uncomfortable, leading to heightened emotional anxieties, internal tensions, hostility and silencing on the subject. As Harvey Young suggests, there is a "widespread reluctance to talk about race" (2013, 3), which stems from a sense of anxiety that seeing and applying meaning to race is in itself a form of racism: "To enter such a *difficult dialogue* would threaten our credentials as twenty-first-century thinkers who have advanced beyond last century's logic of the 'color line' and possess the capacity to see beyond the rigidly defined racial categories of the past. To talk about race feels dangerous. There is the possibility of slippage, a verbal gaffe or, perhaps worse, a sincere and honest opinion that does not jibe with contemporary groupthink" (Young 2013, 3; italics in the original).

Direct conversations about race are also shied away from in the British theatre industry and in much theatre scholarship, which tends to subsume overt discussions of race under veneers of "equality and diversity" policies and initiatives. While historically there are a limited number of contemporary British plays that expressly address issues of race and racism, a number of recent plays have begun to examine race and racism in the UK through big-issue themes such as relations between Black communities and the police and debates about immigration and asylum.[1] A growing interest in these concerns coincides with the #BlackLivesMatter campaign, which since 2013 has increased public awareness of these issues by posting bystander footage of incidents of heavy-handed policing onto social media platforms and being a site for cultural debate and activism. Correspondingly, a number of contemporary British plays have also responded to these concerns.

This chapter analyses one such theatrical response: the *Black Lives, Black Words* UK seasons produced by the Bush Theatre in 2015, 2016 and 2017.[2] My analysis of *Black Lives, Black Words* draws primarily from Black scholarship on race, rage, anger and emotion that sits alongside the more recent intersectional explorations of affect in work by Ahmed and Ngai, amongst others. I assess the third production of *Black Lives, Black Words* (Bush Theatre 2017) through reference to the emotional registers that are related to Black people experiencing racism and to the challenges of talking about race. In particular, I examine race and emotion with a focus on portrayals of anger, activism and microaggressions as seen in the content of the plays, the world realities to which these representations relate and the affects generated by the staging decisions.

Black Lives, Black Words

Black Lives, Black Words is an international project started by Reginald Edmund in Chicago, which has since been to Canada and came to London in collaboration with Simeilia Hodge-Dallaway, who runs Artistic Directors of the Future, and Madani Younis, former Artistic Director at the Bush Theatre, London.[3] Each production consists of an evening where Black playwrights and performance practitioners are invited to contribute short ten-minute plays that respond to concerns arising from the #BlackLivesMatter movement by providing a theatrical response to the question "Do Black lives matter today?" Each production is unique as the project moves from city to city, each with a different set of invited writers, spoken-word artists, poets and cast members.[4] Runs are between one and three nights and the performances are script-in-hand rehearsed readings.

Black Lives, Black Words plays express the kind of raw, visceral emotions of anger and rage that are prevalent in the race activist work, Black cultural criticism and Black feminist theory discussed earlier and work that highlights the kinds of defensive responses and denials that often occur when issues of race and racism are raised and debated. Plays in the first two *Black Lives, Black Words* UK events explored two of the big concerns for Black people living in the US and the UK: the vulnerability of Black lives in the face of police brutality and street violence and the precarious lives of asylum seekers and refugees in Europe and Britain.[5] Several of the pieces focus on the affect of grief from the perspectives of Black family members who have lost or fear losing loved ones to police brutality. This focus resonates with Ahmed's sense of grief as having an affective force. She asks, "what happens when those who have been designated as ungrievable are grieved, and when their loss is not only felt as a loss, but becomes a symbol of the injustice of loss?" (2014, 192). In the plays grief, or fear of loss, becomes the basis from which families speak out against the injustices enacted upon Black bodies by those who are paid to "protect and serve."

Yolanda Mercy's *His Life Matters* (2016; published in Edmund 2017c, 200–205) depicts a pregnant woman and her female partner waiting at a doctor's surgery and discussing whether they should keep a son who will be "disabled" by "the two things he can't change" (207)—being Black and male—which could lead to stereotyped perceptions of his behaviour and make him vulnerable to racist attacks and police brutality. The partner of the pregnant woman's explanation of not wanting to become yet another Black mother whose son is mistreated by the police, and potentially another grieving Black mother, is visceral and affective in highlighting the traumatic bodily responses that she associates with grief: "I refuse to have my name stamped on a headline with tears rolling down my face, with my weave fucked up cause I ain't slept in days. Days and weeks and years, resting on my heavy shoulders stitching pain under my eyes reflecting to the world the story of my dead son" (207). Sharmila Chauhan's *Prodigal* (2016; unpublished) is told from the perspective of a grieving Black mother and daughter who are retracing the last steps of their son/twin brother before he was fatally shot by a police officer. Affect in their anguish is further heightened by being interspersed with the memories of a white father who stresses that his police officer son is a good man who was "just doing his duty" and "had no choice" when he pulled the fateful trigger.[6]

Trish Cooke's *Left Hangin'* (2015; published in Edmund 2017c, 142–55) tackles deaths in custody through the eyes of a mother who is seeking to understand how her vulnerable son with diagnosed autism and Attention Deficit Hyperactivity Disorder (ADHD) ended up dying in police custody. This grieving Black mother refuses to accept the police version of what happened to her son in the police cell, raising questions about how the police deal with Black men with neurodivergent traits or mental health conditions. This resonates with a number of cases in the UK of Black men experiencing a mental health episode where the police have been called to help and the vulnerable person has somehow ended up dead.[7] In Cooke's play, the mother's grief is interlaced with her palpable anger about the injustice and mistreatment of her son by the authorities and her questions about whether she will ever find out what really happened or whether there will be a true and honest report. Notoriously, the Independent Police Complaints Authority have been criticised for lacking objectivity and for finding ultimately on the side of the police. Cooke's piece is connected to the reality of these issues by interspersing snippets from 2015 BBC News bulletins about deaths in custody. Such connections to the real are imperative to the affect created by the piece on the level of the mum's experience of grief. The traces of "the real" underpinning the cumulative grief, fear and anger in these pieces give the affective charge of the plays an even higher potency.

Following a £4.3 million refurbishment project, the Bush reopened with its third *Black Lives, Black Words* production, a three-night run that I attended on March 25, 2017. Four of the six plays shown address how Black people talk about race and racism with white people and how white people can become allies for concerns arising from #BlackLivesMatter campaigns against racial injustice. Plays in the third London production of *Black Lives, Black Words* examine these issues by exploring how interactions between Black people and white people are shaped by emotional forces and they use a range of performance strategies that heighten their affective force. The plays are emotive expressions of anger and revolutionary ideas, simultaneously provocative and poignant. Their deliberately unpolished style lends them a political force as pieces that seek to raise consciousness and agitate towards activism. In the Bush production, the powerful content of the plays pleads at emotional and political sensibilities about race, injustice and rightful rage, and this subject matter combined with the dramatic and performed devices to create and underscore raw and direct affective performances. These issues are portrayed in ways that foreground the characters' heightened emotional responses by showing how their expressions of anger provoke a sense of their determination for justice.

Such portrayals are evocative of Ahmed's discussion of "the relation between emotions and (in)justice" (2014, 191), in which she situates the importance of how emotions can work "to open up the possibility of restoration, repair, healing and recovery" (2014, 191).

Understanding affect in the *Black Lives, Black Words* productions is also as much about understanding the experience of being in the audience watching the performance and the emotions evoked through the evening as it is about the content and contexts of the individual plays. The short-play, rehearsed-reading format resulted in compressed and impressionistic performances, a raw provocative style that directly articulated their main concerns and got straight to the heart of pertinent issues arising within the #BlackLivesMatter debates. Correspondingly, the short-play format necessitates a particular analytical approach. I will focus on one or two key moments from each play that capture the essence of the affective/emotional quality explored either in the play's content or in specific staging decisions.

Rage, Anger and Creative Activism in Reginald Edmund's *Speaking for the Unheard Voices*

hooks foregrounds the importance of acknowledging and expressing "constructive healing rage" as "a necessary aspect of resistance struggle. Rage can act as a catalyst inspiring courageous action" (1995, 16). Lorde also proposes using anger constructively in the quest for action and change. Lorde maintains that "[a]nger is an appropriate reaction to racist attitudes, as is fury when the actions arising from those attitudes do not change" (1984, 129) and she encourages women "to tap that anger as an important source of empowerment" (1984, 130). Ahmed develops Lorde's argument to consider how "[a]nger is creative; it works to create a language with which to respond to that which one is against" (2014, 176). Ahmed suggests that emotions such as anger are integral to collective action against injustice, noting that "challenging social norms involves having a different affective reaction to those norms, partly by 'feeling' their costs as a collective loss" (2014, 196). She maintains that "'feeling' [is] crucial to the struggle against injustice" (2014, 196): "We need to respond to injustice in a way that shows rather than erases the complexity of the relation between violence, power and emotion" (2014, 196). Black rage is manifestly an underlying propeller of movements such as

#BlackLivesMatter where activists unite in action against injustice. Yet Black anger and rage are too often frowned upon when expressed in ways that are not deemed acceptable. When Black activists take to the streets to protest against racial injustice or police brutality, for example, these are often too quickly reported in the media as riots.

Edmund's *Speaking for the Unheard Voices* (2017; published in Edmund 2017c, 122–33) explores ways of using Black rage against injustice constructively and collectively through creative means as a necessary step in propelling the call to action. Edmund explains, "I started Black Lives, Black Words because I felt there needed to be an opportunity for me as a playwright to speak out against the sins committed in this world inflicted upon black bodies [...]. This in turn caused me to wonder what other artists were out there that possess this overwhelming desire to speak out for the unheard voices" (2017b, vii). Speaking for unheard voices links to Lorde's assertions about the importance of moving from silence to voice in advocating for antiracist discourses and pursuing the causes of social injustices. In creative terms, *Black Lives, Black Words* evokes Lorde's sense that "poetry is not a luxury" but rather a necessary "way we help give name to the nameless" (1984, 37) and speak for the unheard.

In the play, Edmund and Hodge-Dallaway play themselves as characters named R (An African-American Male) and S (A Black British Female) to give voice to the notion of creating a shared Black activist solidarity across the Atlantic and explain how they became united by an ambition to use theatre to recognise and remember prematurely lost Black lives. R and S are thinking about the same issues and facing the same challenges about race relations—him in the US and her in the UK. They perform verbatim extracts from exchanges between them on live messaging and Skype video calls that resulted in them coming up with the idea to internationalise *Black Lives, Black Words* in order to move from silence to activism. Having the characters speak words written by the other as they read each other's messages aloud draws attention to transatlantic parallels as some of his experiences are recounted by her and hers by him. Their reactions to memories of everyday racism, racist graffiti and racist bullying convey a sense of injustice about the mistreatment of Black youths by the police and explore how they can respond creatively to speak for the unheard. Police officers are employed to "protect and serve" their communities, a duty that, too often, is not equitably applied to Black people. Racial stereotyping makes the Black male body vulnerable to police violence, with the police rarely being held accountable. R and S's rage and anger about the vulnerability of Black bodies being mistreated by the state are heightened in response to R's anxiety about being a Black man out on the streets in the US: "With so many lives being taken here, it's getting to me. I'm scared to leave the house. Who knows maybe I'll be next" (Edmund 2017a, 129). They unite in their quest to use theatre to raise awareness about #BlackLivesMatter issues by finding socially conscious artists who have something to say in response to the injustices that are happening in our communities and can speak for those who can no longer speak for themselves, the—permanently silenced—deceased.

Emotional and affective qualities in *Speaking for the Unheard Voices* are further underlined by R and S speaking some of the key words and phrases pertaining to police violence in unison as a chorus, which culminates in a closing roll call where the choral repetition of the mantra "speak for the unheard voices" is interspersed with the names of some of the many who have lost their lives on the streets or while being held in custody:

> Artists that want to speak for the Trayvon Martin
> Speak for the Unheard Voices
> Sandra Bland
> Speak for the Unheard Voices
> Eric Garner
> Speak for the Unheard Voices
> Tamir Rice
> Speak for the Unheard Voices
> Jermaine Carby
> Speak for the Unheard Voices.
> Rekia Boyd
> Speak for the Unheard Voices
> Mark Duggan
> Speak for the Unheard Voices
> Michael Brown
> Speak for the Unheard Voices
> Speak for the Unheard Voices
> Speak for the Unheard Voices
> Speak for the Unheard Voices
> Speak for the Unheard Voices. (134–35)

Defensiveness, Denial and White Fragility in Idris Goodwin's *#Matter*

Robin DiAngelo argues that white fragility in conversations about race stems from "a deeply internalised sense of superiority that we [white people] are either unaware of or can never admit to ourselves" (2018, 2). DiAngelo explains: "[t]hough white fragility is triggered by discomfort and anxiety, it is born of superiority and entitlement. White fragility is not weakness per se. In fact, it is a powerful means of white racial control and the protection of white advantage" (2018, 2). She suggests that a range of defensive emotional responses including anger, fear, guilt and "behaviors such as argumentation, silence, and withdrawal from the stress-inducing situation […] work to reinstate white equilibrium as they repel the challenge […] and maintain our [white people's] dominance within the racial hierarchy" (2018, 2). DiAngelo's ideas about how white fragility can work to impede discussions about race are explored in Goodwin's *#Matter* (2015; published in Edmund 2017c, 16–27), which also uses the device of two people communicating on a social media platform to explore how white fragility and defensive responses impact upon the possibility for Black and white people to talk about race and the #BlackLivesMatter debates. In contrast to Edmund's play, where R and S arrived easily at a shared manifesto for building *Black Lives, Black Words* on an international scale, Goodwin captures the struggle to communicate across race and the challenges that Black people face in trying to get even well-meaning white people to acknowledge and understand how racism works.

In Goodwin's play, the couple are former childhood neighbours that almost became high-school lovers. They end up debating whether saying #BlackLivesMatter is divisive in a country that prides itself on multiculturalism. Black character Kim writes a social media post that responds to "[a]nother body. Another name. Another image / Has circulated. The latest body. Name. The newest image to haunt" (17). White character Cole is at first empathetic to her words, writing "It's shameful" (17), adding "likes" to her posts and endorsing her calls for equality, until Kim types "a hash tag and three words"—presumably #BlackLivesMatter, although it is not stated. At this point, Cole takes offence and types his own hash tag and three words—presumably #AllLivesMatter, although again unstated. A debate ensues in terms of whether her three words are divisive. Cole dislikes the expression of race and focuses on the idea of "the human experience" (18) to the detriment of understanding the specifics of race. As the play moves from a social media debate to the reality of them sitting down together to discuss the issues, it becomes more of a treatise about brokering understanding between races, about Kim needing to be strong in the face of Cole's white fragility and about her imploring him about the need for white people to listen to Black experience without feeling the need to defend whiteness, to commandeer Black experience or to ask questions like "don't all lives matter?"

Cole's comments sum up problematic responses to Black experiences of racism, including his suggesting that Kim is making Black suffering worse than others, that rage is not strategic and ultimately that "AllLivesMatter." These are the kinds of issues that Black activists are confronted with when dealing with white fragility, which is a misplaced sense of vulnerability that demands increased affective and emotional labour from Black speakers in conversations about race. While the Internet and social media have enabled Black voices to be heard and allowed the global reach of the #BlackLivesMatter movement, the kind of denial of experience being spouted by Cole reflects age-old defences against charges of racism—the sense, for example, that there is no such thing as "white lives matter." Cole implores Kim to look at a bigger picture, to recognise the experiences of "poor white folks who live in black communities [...]. All lives KIM" (21–22), and he asks "Do white lives *not* matter?" (23; italics in the original). Goodwin's piece evokes difficulties identified in Eddo-Lodge's *Why I'm No Longer Talking to White People about Race* about getting white people to talk about race and listen through defences and denial, such as the tendency to deny that there is a racial dynamic at play in, for example, a hate attack, a police stop and search or incidents of police violence. Although Cole sees himself as an ally in the struggle against racism, he still falls foul of such defensive responses and Kim challenges him for being adamant that they are equal.

Eddo-Lodge indicates that conversations about race with white people have to be carefully negotiated, else risking reaffirming problematic presuppositions: "As the heckles rise and the defiance grows, I have to tread carefully, because if I express frustration, anger or exasperation at their refusal to understand, they will tap into their pre-subscribed racist tropes about angry black people" (2017, xi). In Goodwin's play, Cole voices such stereotypical criticisms, such as the idea that Kim has become an angry Black woman and that expressing rage is an unproductive response to racism. Kim's comment, "I really want to let Cole off the hook. Drop this whole thing. Tell him it's all good. But I have swallowed myself so many times to make white folks feel less uncomfortable" (26), is evocative of the historical baggage that underlies the racial dynamic between them. The overall effect of this scene is emphasised by Kim speaking at the same time as Cole to counteract his assertions and expose his lack of empathy and understanding. A style based on short sentences, quick-fire responses sometimes spoken simultaneously—indicated in the script by parallel printing of their words in two columns on the page—creates the impression that this is an urgent conversation that needs to be had:

COLE	KIM
No but it's sort of making your suffering worse than others	
	Uhm ... what did you just
[...]	
I'm all for Civil rights but looting?	
Property damage and just rage?	No-No-No
It doesn't work—	
I mean—it's not strategic	You don't...
All lives KIM That's all I'm saying—let's pull the act from the context of race We have to break this down to the root Human wickedness	

KIM
And sometimes humans kill humans because of their race. (21–22)

Cole's resistance to listening to Kim's point of view evokes the struggles that Black people face in getting white people to understand our experiences of race and racism. While the two characters do eventually arrive at a reluctant understanding, Cole's final words maximise the play's affective force after Kim dies in exactly the kinds of circumstances that she was protesting against. The pacing and poignant pauses indicated by the use of ellipsis capture Cole's emotions as he finally comes to understand what Kim had been talking about:

> Week or two later I sent Kim a message. I thanked her for the conversation. I told her we should be in touch more often. That I wanted to keep talking. Not just about this. But our lives in general. ... and then I got a message

> back ... it was from Kim's mom. There'd been ... an accident ... ... a fucking ... ... a story ... the same story ... again ... ... the same thing ... a misunderstanding ... they called it ... a failure to comply ... she failed at being silent ... so she was made silent...
> [...]
> On her wall
> I typed a hash tag
> And three words. (26–27)

Racial Microaggressions and Race Allies in Rachel De-lahay's *My White Best Friend*

Racial microaggressions are the small slights, insults and even sometimes intended compliments that Black people experience on an everyday basis. Some common racial microaggressions include asking a Black person, "where are you from? No, where are you really from?"; holding a bag more closely to oneself when a Black man walks by; being followed around a store by shop security guards or being asked too quickly if you "need help"; being told you do not talk, sound or behave "Black"; mispronouncing someone's name or anglicising it to a supposedly "easier" version; asking curious questions about Black hair and hairstyles; or taxi drivers notoriously not stopping for Black customers. As Ijeoma Oluo writes, "[m]icroaggressions are more than just annoyances. The cumulative effect of these constant reminders that you are [perceived to be] 'less than' does real psychological damage" (2018, 169). Microaggressions can be tricky to recognise as they are often seemingly innocuous, and sometimes one is not sure whether you had really experienced this, whether you heard right, whether that is what they really meant. However, microaggressions can be felt in a bodily way, in a sense that something is not quite right in the exchange, in a feeling deep in the pit of the stomach, in being caught off guard. Confronting microaggressions can lead to accusations of being oversensitive, of not being able to take a joke, of having a chip on one's shoulder or of being too angry. As Oluo concludes, microaggressions "normalize racism. They make racist assumptions part of everyday life" and "help hold the system of White Supremacy together" (2018, 172). Not challenging racist behaviour when we see it is a way of being complicit in its functioning and there is a recent push to call out such behaviours when we witness them. However, the onus should not be on Black people to call out racist behaviours, as the emotional labour of such an expectation can be draining. Indeed, Oluo enjoins white people in particular to speak out against racial microaggressions when witnessed, in recognition that it can sometimes be difficult for the Black people who are subjected to these subtle forms of racism to challenge such behaviour. In this way, white people can become necessary allies in the fight against racial injustices.

De-lahay's *My White Best Friend* (2017a; published in Edmund 2017c, 170–78) starts with a request from the writer to reshuffle the audience: "All the girls need to be at the front. All brown, black, queer, disable[d] girls, centre. All white, able-bodied men, fall back" (173). De-lahay's reconfigured audience seeks to draw attention to how power works and to create a safe space for those who are usually marginalised in order to challenge both racism and sexism. If an audience can be easily reconfigured with a simple request and within a matter of seconds, then the workings of power can be challenged. De-lahay's piece is a monologue in the form of a letter that Rachel has written to be performed by her white best friend, in which she calls her white best friend out for not being there when she needed help in the face of racial microaggressions. The performance is presented as though the best friend is reading the letter for the first time in a shared public space unaware of what will come up in the letter or the difficult emotions that the content could produce. *My White Best Friend* begins by humorously setting up the long-established friendship of women who know each other intimately and emotionally, women who have "lived together, got drunk together, experimented with drugs together, fallen in love with each other, seen each other fall in love with others. Helped mend heartbreak. Fought [...]. Laughed, cried, sang [...] at the top of our voices, in our bedrooms, in pyjamas" (173). As young women who have known each other a long time, there is a sense of familiarity between them and of sharing the kinds of experiences that best friends share no matter what their race is.

But the sense of safety in their friendship is challenged when they go to a party together at which one white guest questions the appropriateness of saying #BlackLivesMatter—"*Why are they allowed to say that? Black lives matter? Like, Is that not racist? Like, why do they matter more?* [...] *It's a little aggressive, kinda exclusive* ... [...] *we don't get a white history month*" (177; italics in the original). Another inappropriately comments that "Rachel wasn't even really his type. Like he'd never even dated a black girl before. Not that he had a problem with black girls, it was just a fancying thing. Like he wasn't really ever into girls with dark nipples. They just weren't his ... thing" (178). They settle in awkward silence, Rachel's white friend not knowing what to say and choosing to avoid the potential conflict. A party is a place for frivolity, for shared fun, and rationally they were too drunk to engage in a heavy political conversation. Rachel's white best friend missed the chance to stand in solidarity with her Black best friend, to act as an ally in the face of racism, and the monologue imagines the argument that ensues when Rachel challenges her friend for not speaking up to support her in the face of such racist microaggressions now or in the past. Their silence—Rachel's in not really challenging her friend, only imagining it, and her friend's in not intervening and challenging the racist guests—maintains the status quo and the kind of complicity that allows racism to go unchecked. The idea of a complicit silence and swallowed emotions links to discussions about the difficulty of having conversations about race with white people. De-lahay states, "[i]t's hard to talk about race in this country. There's something scary about it" (2017b). Eddo-Lodge cites Lorde in reflecting that "[o]ften, there will be no one fighting your corner but yourself. It was black feminist poet Audre Lorde who said: 'your silence will not protect you.' Who wins when we don't speak? Not us" (2017, 187). Similarly, the idea of speaking up resonates with Ahmed's sense of the importance of finding a way of reacting "to what one is against" (2014, 174). Anger would be an appropriate response to the pain of racist microaggressions.

Admittedly, I was not sure about De-lahay's monologue when it started. In an evening that had until then been fundamentally about how to support and remember Black lives, I did not initially see how a piece with the title *My White Best Friend* would fit. I wondered about why De-lahay was writing about white people rather than focusing on Black experience. However, the piece emerged as a strong and powerful provocation against white privilege, showing how microaggressions can cause hurt and highlighting the importance of open and honest dialogue between Black and white friends. The title *My White Best Friend* plays on the phrase "I can't be racist, one of my best friends is Black," which is sometimes used to deny racist attitudes and behaviours. In this case, it is the "white best friend" who fails to stand up against racism for their "Black best friend," which makes her complicit in sustaining the attitudes that enable structural racism to pervade. As with the other pieces outlined here, *My White Best Friend* invites white people to listen, to understand and then to play a part as allies in the cause of #BlackLivesMatter and activating social justice.

Witnessing Police Brutality in Mojisola Adebayo's *The Interrogation of Sandra Bland*

I have so far focused on performance pieces in which feelings or affects apply to the emotional responses of the characters to each other in the face of racism and racial injustice. Adebayo's *The Interrogation of Sandra Bland* (2017) is affective both in the content that is portrayed and in its manipulation of verbatim dramatic devices to produce affects in the play as watched by audiences. Sandra Bland (d. July 13, 2015) was a twenty-eight-year-old African-American woman who was found dead in a police cell three days after being arrested by Texas State Trooper Brian Encinia in what should have been a routine traffic stop on July 10, 2015. While the official cause of death has been widely reported as suicide by hanging, questions have been raised about the circumstances leading up to Bland's death. Adebayo was taken with Bland's story, as many of us were, a Black woman who was an activist social media campaigner in the #BlackLivesMatter movement becoming one of the names in the list of deaths in police custody. To create the performance, Adebayo transcribed the full police dashcam evidence of Encinia's roadside encounter with Bland and crafted it to be performed by a core group of seven Black women and a community chorus of one hundred culturally diverse women playing Bland, plus one white man playing Encinia and one white woman playing the second officer that arrives at the scene after Encinia calls for backup. An inherent intensity of feeling emerges from the heightened verbatim exchange between Bland and the officer, in which he repeatedly shouts at her to "GET OUT OF THE CAR!" (Adebayo 2017, 165) and threatens to forcibly yank her out before drawing his stun gun on her:

> Step out of the car! […] Step out or I will remove you. […] I'm going to yank you out of here. […] You are under arrest! […] I said get out of the car! […] GET OUT OF THE CAR! […] I WILL LIGHT YOU UP! GET OUT! […] Get off the phone! […] Put your phone down! […] Put your hands behind your back and turn around. […] Stop moving! […] Stay right here. Stand right there. (164–67)

The short form of the play emphasises just how quickly the situation escalated from the initial stop to the officer's threats of violence as Encinia attempts to physically remove Bland from the car and restrains her on the ground. However, Bland is empowered by the Black women who share the speaking of her words, their multiple voices popping up from around the auditorium as they stand on different podiums set around the space and some in amongst the audience. The use of a community chorus amplifies the Black women's voices to respond loudly and collectively—sometimes two or more voices in unison—to Encinia's demands. The chorus created a magnified effect of unified Black women's voices to match the boom of the shouting white male officer's voice. In this way, Bland's responses to the officer resonate with ideas of Black women collectively turning anger into a defiant refusal to acquiesce to unjust, violent, behaviour towards them. At the same time, Bland appears vulnerable in the exchange, dressed only in a maxidress, repeating phrases to the officer and in several lines distressed and crying as she speaks. As much as she is challenging him, affects of frustration and despair are created and underlined by the use of the chorus, repetition and shared, collective, voices:

Bland Seven:	*(Crying.)* This make you feel real good don't it.
All:	It make you feel real good don't it?
Bland Seven:	A female for a traffic ticket, / for a traffic ticket.
Bland One:	Don't it make you feel real good Officer Encinia?
Bland Two:	I know it make you feel real good.
Bland Three:	You're a real man now.
Bland Four:	You just slammed me, knocked my head into the ground.
Bland Five:	I got epilepsy, you motherfucker! (Adebayo 2019, 182–83)[8]

The women playing Bland demand to know "[w]hy am I being apprehended?" (Adebayo 2017, 176), challenging Encinia's assertion of authority—"[y]ou're doing all of this/for a failure to signal?" (177)—and emphasising his use of excessive force—"[y]ou're about to break my fucking wrist!" (181). Capturing the defiance of Black women answering back to Encinia's confrontational questioning style empowers them to respond to him as a gesture of resistance to the long history of institutional racism that manifests itself in the way the police treat Black people. Adebayo's transcript of the arrest of Bland is a powerful use of verbatim technique, modelled to maximise the emotional and testimonial power of the piece. As a theatrical response to the #BlackLivesMatter and #SayHerName movements, *The Interrogation of Sandra Bland* is a short play with a large affective impact, the echoes of which remain long after leaving the auditorium.

Concluding Thoughts

Issues related to the #BlackLivesMatter movement are strong, affective, sensitive, powerful and evocative. Apart from Adebayo's piece, the rehearsed-reading format of the third London production of *Black Lives, Black Words* meant limited stage action and putting the emphasis on the words, which is where I have focused my analysis. That said, each piece deployed certain elements of performance or writing style to accentuate the expressions of emotions in the plays—the one-woman third-person narrative of *My White Best Friend*, the conflicting views of the Black and the white characters in *#Matter* and the use of verbatim transcript in *The Interrogation of Sandra Bland*. The content of the plays and the performance strategies of the third London production of *Black Lives, Black Words* maximise their consciousness-raising potential by creating an emotionally charged evening that promotes an activist purpose for Black theatre in Britain. These are impassioned pieces, whose performance strategies and short-play format mean that they move quickly through a range of emotional affects, up and down, from the start to the peak of each play. They drove home the evening as one in which questions were raised about the politics of race, rage and justice and about the intersection between art, activism and affect.[9]

Notes

1. See, for example, Roy Williams's *Fallout* (2003), Oladipo Agboluaje's *The Hounding of David Oluwale* (2008) and Urbain Hayo (aka Urban Wolf) and Tom Wainwright's *Custody* (2017), which examine the relationship between young Black men and the police past and present. Bola Agbaje's *Detaining Justice* (2009), Rachel De-lahay's *Routes* (2013), Lemn Sissay's adaptation of Benjamin Zephaniah's novel *Refugee Boy* (2013) and Zodwa Nyoni's *Nine Lives* (2014) all depict characters seeking asylum and citizenship in the UK.
2. Recordings of the first two London seasons and some of the US *Black Lives, Black Words* productions are available on YouTube. The second London production of *Black Lives, Black Words* (2016) was performed in collaboration with Theatre Royal Stratford East while the Bush Theatre was undergoing refurbishment work. The third London production of *Black Lives, Black Words* (2017) coincided with the publication of an anthology that included thirty-two of the playtexts for the first time (Edmund 2017c).

3. Artistic Directors of the Future is an initiative founded and managed by Hodge-Dallaway to create new Black and Global Majority artistic directors through training and opportunities.
4. Black British playwrights and practitioners who contributed to the first three seasons include Mojisola Adebayo, Oladipo Agboluaje, Trish Cooke, Rachel De-lahay, Winsome Pinnock and Somalia Seaton.
5. The second London production of *Black Lives, Black Words* was staged in 2016 amidst the height of the so-called migrant crisis, to which several of the plays respond.
6. Citations are based on my transcription of the YouTube recording of the play, "*Black Lives, Black Words*: Part Two: *Prodigal* by Sharmila Chauhan."
7. See, for example, the cases of Roger Sylvester, who died on January 19, 1999, eight days after being detained outside his home in Tottenham under the Mental Health Act, and Sean Rigg, who died at the entrance of Brixton Police station on August 21, 2008.
8. *The Interrogation of Sandra Bland* was first published in the *Black Lives, Black Words* anthology in 2017 (Edmund 2017c, 156–68), from which most of my citations are taken. This block citation, however, is drawn from the rehearsal script published in *Plays Two* (Adebayo 2019, 163–85) because it demonstrates more clearly how Adebayo has crafted the transcript to be performed with multiple actresses sharing the speaking of Bland's words.
9. This chapter was completed before the police killing of George Floyd in Minneapolis on 25 May 2020, which has further heightened awareness about police brutality, protesting against Black deaths in custody, and how white allies can support the cause for racial justice that are discussed in this chapter. #BlackLivesMatter #BlackPlaysMatter.

References

Adebayo, Mojisola. 2017. *The Interrogation of Sandra Bland*. In Edmund 2017c, 156-68.

———. 2019. *Plays Two*. Introduced by Lynette Goddard. London: Oberon.

Agbaje, Bola. 2009. *Detaining Justice*. In Williams, Kwei-Armah and Agbaje 2009, 185–269.

Agboluaje, Oladipo. 2008. *The Hounding of David Oluwale*. London: Oberon.

Ahmed, Sara. 2014. *The Cultural Politics of Emotion*. 2nd ed. Edinburgh: Edinburgh UP.

Bush Theatre. 2017. *Black Lives, Black Words*. Accessed February 24, 2019.

Cooke, Trish. (2015) 2017. *Left Hangin'*. In Edmund 2017c, 142–55.

De-lahay, Rachel. 2013. *Routes*. London: Bloomsbury.

———. 2017a. *My White Best Friend*. In Edmund 2017c, 170–78.

———. 2017b. "Rachel De-lahay: 'Being a Brown Woman Is Political in Itself.'" Interview by Kate Kellaway. *Observer*, March 19. Accessed September 17, 2019.
DiAngelo, Robin. 2018. *White Fragility: Why It's so Hard for White People to Talk about Racism*. Boston, MA: Beacon.
Eddo-Lodge, Reni. 2017. *Why I'm No Longer Talking to White People about Race*. London: Bloomsbury.
Edmund, Reginald. 2017a. *Speaking for the Unheard Voices*. In Edmund 2017c, 122–33.
———. 2017b. "Thoughts from the Managing Curating Producer." In Edmund 2017c, vii–ix.
———, ed. 2017c. *Black Lives, Black Words*. London: Oberon.
Goodwin, Idris. (2015) 2017. *#Matter*. In Edmund 2017c, 16–27.
Hayo, Urbain and Tom Wainwright. 2017. *Custody*. London: Team Angelica.
hooks, bell. 1995. *Killing Rage: Ending Racism*. New York: Henry Holt.
Lorde, Audre. 1984. *Sister Outsider: Essays and Speeches*. Freedom, CA: Crossing Press.
Mercy, Yolanda. (2016) 2017. *His Life Matters*. In Edmund 2017c, 200–205.
Ngai, Sianne. 2005. *Ugly Feelings*. Cambridge, MA: Harvard UP.
Nyoni, Zodwa. 2014. *Nine Lives*. London: Bloomsbury.
Oluo, Ijeoma. 2018. *So You Want to Talk about Race*. New York: Seal Press.
Sissay, Lemn. 2013. *Refugee Boy*. London: Bloomsbury.
Williams, Roy. 2003. *Fallout*. London: Methuen.
Williams, Roy, Kwame Kwei-Armah and Bola Agbaje. 2009. *Not Black and White*. Introduced by Nicolas Kent. London: Methuen.
Young, Harvey. 2013. *theatre & race*. Basingstoke and New York: Palgrave Macmillan.

CHAPTER 7

"Feeling Feminism": Politics of Mischief in Contemporary Women's Theatre

Marissia Fragkou

In *Living a Feminist Life*, feminist cultural theorist Sara Ahmed describes feminism as an embodied practice that involves coming up against walls (2017, 163). This process, Ahmed continues, which may bring things to a point of shattering, enables feminists to experience fragility as the "wear and tear of living a feminist life" (2017, 163). For Ahmed, feminism then appears as "a fragile archive, a body assembled from shattering, from splattering, an archive whose fragility gives us responsibility: to take care" (2017, 17) and "as an affective inheritance" (2017, 20) that is often "understood as a problem of will: a way of going one's own way, a way of going the wrong way" (2017, 65). In considering feminism as a process and practice of "coming up against walls," Ahmed utilises the figures of the feminist killjoy and willful subject and discusses them in relation to affect and language.[1] In short, a feminist killjoy is "an affect alien," a figure "not made happy by the right things" (2017, 57) who gets in the way of popular norms of happiness. By extension, a willful subject implies

M. Fragkou (✉)
Canterbury Christ Church University, Canterbury, UK
e-mail: marissia.fragkou@canterbury.ac.uk

M. Aragay et al. (eds.), *Affects in 21st-Century British Theatre*,
https://doi.org/10.1007/978-3-030-58486-3_7

someone who persistently "speaks the language of injustice" (2017, 71; see also Ahmed 2014), but whose "will does not coincide with that of others, those whose will is reified as the general or social will" (2010b, 64). In this sense, both cause disturbance to consensual forms of happiness and are marked as figures that stir trouble.

Ahmed's critical approach emanates from her ongoing interest in "what [...] emotions do" (2004, 4) and forms part of the wider affective turn taking place in the humanities and social sciences since the beginning of the new millennium. Affect and feminism share much common ground, as they both place emphasis on the "significance of matter, materiality and the body" (Pedwell and Whitehead 2012, 117); in the context of feminist studies, the turn to affect can be then read as a *re*turn that further contributes to the recent recalibration of the feminist movement. As Anu Koivunen observes, feminism's preoccupation with affect and affectivity facilitates "investigating and conceptualizing the subject of feminism as embodied, located and relational" (2010, 8). Feminist thinkers revisit questions of embodiment, affect and affectivity and the role of emotions in shaping different regimes of knowledge. For example, Carolyn Pedwell and Anne Whitehead underscore "the impossibility of objective knowledge detached from embodied location" and argue for "the potential for affect to provide different, and potentially transformative, ways of knowing" (2012, 119). Feminist and queer theories of affect consider that affect and emotion interdependently "stick" to each other (Ahmed 2010a, 32) and use affect as "a means of theorizing the social" (Koivunen 2010, 18). It is with this line of thought that this chapter shares allegiance; for this reason, I am not drawing a distinction between affect as prelinguistic and physiological and emotion as socially positioned, but rather use affect to suggest both the physiological and the social.

Ahmed specifically proposes the term *impression* (2004, 6; 2010a, 32) to describe both the cognitive and emotive processes at work when objects come in contact or "press" against each other. Her proposition to look at affect and emotion as impressions is particularly helpful in the context of scholarship concerned with the affective imprints theatre and performance leave on the audience. In addition, Ahmed's focus on impressions chimes with Lauren Berlant's understanding of affective atmospheres. According to Berlant, bodies respond "to the atmospheres in which they find themselves" and these "affective responses [...] exemplify shared *historical* time" (2011, 15; italics in the original). Borrowing from critical frameworks of feminist affect theory, and especially the work of Ahmed and

Berlant, I am here particularly concerned with examining how the work of contemporary women playwrights and theatre makers in Britain both presses on and is impressed on by the affective atmospheres of the present.

In this sense, this essay will contribute to the growing scholarly interest in the revitalisation of feminism that has urged women to reconsider the damaging legacy of postfeminism and neoliberal capitalism (Diamond et al. 2017; Gorman et al. 2018). I am here following Elaine Aston's thinking about the position of feminism in contemporary women's playwriting to more broadly examine how contemporary theatre work by women negotiates affect. Aston was the first scholar to apply Ahmed's theorisation of the cultural politics of emotion to work by women playwrights. Tracing the affective impressions left by feminism, her article "Feeling the Loss of Feminism: Sarah Kane's *Blasted* and an Experiential Genealogy of Contemporary Women's Playwriting" examined how particular plays articulate anxieties about the "loss of feminism" and a "feminist fatigue" through the adoption of experiential dramaturgies that "are called upon to critique a contemporary lack of *caritas*" (2010, 589). In a more recent article, "Enter Stage Left: 'Recognition,' 'Redistribution,' and the A-Affect," Aston observes a socialist feminist renewal in millennial plays by women. Turning to the influence of Bertolt Brecht's legacy on socialist feminist dramaturgies, Aston proposes that this is now mobilised through what she terms the "A-affect," which "works through strategies of heightened affectivity" and whose objective "is to *move* audiences towards a reorientated perception of 'socially-conditioned phenomena'" (2018a, 302; italics in the original).[2]

Following Aston, I also argue for the importance of placing contemporary women's theatre work within the context of previous affective impressions left by feminism, which, taking my cue from Ahmed, I will refer to as *feminist archives* that form the basis of a feminist renewal. At the same time, it is crucial to examine how those archives are in dialogue with the feminist politics more broadly mobilised in the work of twenty-first-century women theatre makers. In other words, I am interested in how women theatre makers currently address feminist politics as "a tear in the social fabric" (Ahmed 2017, 171) that invites us to reinvent ways to take care (Ahmed 2017, 17). In the following pages, I will be examining the figures of the feminist killjoy and willful subject in conjunction with what I name a *politics of mischief*. This interest in mischief is inspired by Erica Whyman, Deputy Artistic Director at the Royal Shakespeare Company (RSC), whose current vision for the company's newly opened studio space

The Other Place is driven by "radical mischief." For Whyman, this focus offers "the possibility of joy and humour and naughtiness and playfulness" to be part of the exploration of current political issues (Whyman 2014). According to the *Oxford English Dictionary*, one of the meanings of *mischief* is "playful misbehaviour" or "playfulness that is intended to tease or create trouble." Mischief thus shares common ground with the feminist killjoy's capacity to "turn disturbance into a cause" (Ahmed 2010a, 32) and I will consider how it can be read as an affective feminist theatrical strategy that stirs trouble and reorientates an audience's perception towards material experiences of inequality and injustice. In order to do so, I will focus on two British theatre pieces created and produced by women during the second decade of the new millennium: Alice Birch's *Revolt. She Said. Revolt Again.* (2014) and Sh!t Theatre's *Letters to Windsor House* (2016; published in 2017).

Revolt. She Said. Revolt Again.: A "Feminist Killjoy" Manifesto

Birch emerged on the British stage in 2011 and has been hailed as "one of the most important female, and feminist, theatrical voices in the UK" (Escoda forthcoming) and "one of the most exciting playwrights in British theatre" (Simon Stephens quoted in Bowie-Sell 2011). She has collaborated with all-women theatre groups such as Clean Break and Rash Dash and female directors such as Whyman and Katie Mitchell. She has received prestigious awards, such as the 2014 George Devine Award for Most Promising Playwright for *Revolt. She Said. Revolt Again.* (henceforth *Revolt.*) and the 2018 Susan Smith Blackburn Prize for *Anatomy of a Suicide* (2017a), a play staging three generations of women and their connection to the trauma of suicide.

Affect holds a central position in Birch's work. In her analysis of the playwright's first produced play, *Many Moons* (2011), Clara Escoda suggests that the play "disrupts the obviousness and naturalness of the affective underpinnings of neo-liberal capitalism, which favours the efficient management of emotions in the public sphere" (2018, 22). This refusal to abide by "the efficient management of emotions" and, instead, stir trouble through the affects of anger and indignation becomes the key driving force of *Revolt.* The play was commissioned by the RSC and performed as part of the Midsummer Mischief Festival in 2014 at Stratford's The Other

Place. For the festival, four women playwrights were asked to respond to feminist historian Laurel Thatcher Ulrich's provocation that "well-behaved women seldom make history" (1976), first appearing in a 1970s scholarly article and taken up as a popular slogan in the 1990s. As Birch often mentions, this statement "pissed her off" and propelled her to write *Revolt.*, a play exploring revolt in both form and content (Birch 2017b).

Although the "angry feminist" label can prove limiting for the work of women in the theatre, as British playwright Ella Hickson points out (quoted in Montironi 2018, 173), it is important to highlight the role anger has played in mobilising feminist subjects (Fragkou and Goddard 2013). To put it briefly, anger has provided a language for addressing a long history of experiences of violence suffered by women, which Ahmed labels as "politics of pain" (2004, 172). As she suggests, "anger is creative, it works to create a language with which to respond to that which one is against, whereby 'the what' is renamed, and brought into a feminist world" (2004, 176). Similarly, anger enables Birch to create a dramatic form that responds to women's stories of pain and vulnerability. Birch has stated that "in order to write a 'revolutionary play,' she 'need[ed] to invent a new form'" (quoted in Escoda forthcoming). Her desire to reinvent form resonates with French feminism's critique of phallogocentrism, particularly Julia Kristeva's (1985) ideas on revolutionary language, which seeks to articulate an alternative voice to linear patriarchal narratives.[3] The play's feminist lineage can also be traced back to other theatre work by women—from Hélène Cixous's *Portrait of Dora* (1976), to Eve Ensler's *The Vagina Monologues* (1998) and Sarah Kane's *4.48 Psychosis* (2000)—that challenges phallogocentric structures and rejects realism as a "prison-house of art for women" (Case 1988, 124), whilst also alluding to vocabularies borrowed from task-based and feminist performance art that place emphasis on the materiality of the female body.

Revolt. is written in the form of an instruction manual organised into four acts that are further divided into shorter scenes, each beginning with an invitation to "Revolutionize…." As per the opening stage directions, the piece is written for a cast of six; it should be staged without set and props and every scene should have at least one female in it (Birch 2014, 45). Similar to Ahmed's "killjoy survival kit," a kind of "what to do list" that stresses the role of survival as "a feminist project" (2017, 236), Birch's voices navigate modes of survival within contemporary patriarchal structures through a particular focus on language, work and the body as sites of revolt—for this reason, the play can be described as a "killjoy manifesto" (Ahmed 2017, 251). As I will demonstrate below, the play's stylistic experimentation is further enhanced by the different dramaturgies adopted in each scene and the inclusion of an explosion at the end of the third act, "literally destroying the play's form itself" (Escoda forthcoming).

In unravelling its "politics of mischief," *Revolt.* tries to undo hegemonic and naturalised representations of the female body and voice whilst also exploring female desire and pleasure. In doing so, it applies pressure on habitual interactions as fundamentally problematic and rooted in patriarchal values by revealing some uncomfortable truths about the implications of language in framing identity. Such strategies, I argue, further promote a feminist politics of perception in the theatre that articulates the urgent need to remobilise feminist politics in the public sphere as a "caring" project. I am here borrowing Hans-Thies Lehmann's term *politics of perception*, which, he argues, is rehearsed by "an *aesthetic of responsibility*" (2006, 185; italics in the original). In his seminal book *Postdramatic Theatre*, Lehmann makes a case for a politics of perception that reanimates "the bond between perception and action" (2006, 184) mitigated by our daily exposure to images of precarious lives. Following Lehmann's argument in conjunction with Ahmed's understanding of feminism as a "fragile archive" (2017, 17), this responsibility would translate into caring for the feminist project.

In developing her own "killjoy manifesto," Ahmed suggests that "[a] manifesto not only causes a disturbance, it *aims* to cause this disturbance. [...] A killjoy manifesto must be grounded in an account of what exists. [...] [It] thus begins by recognizing inequalities as existing" (2017, 251–52; italics added). In the first scene of act one, titled "Revolutionize the Language (Invert It)," the explicit reference to an intimate sexual act becomes a battleground of power and desire between two voices who negotiate linguistic choices. This is where Birch playfully explores what language *does* to draw attention to existing power inequalities: the female voice objects to the male's phrases, such as "I want to make love to you," "I want to peel your dress" or "spread your legs," whilst at the end she reclaims language and power through her vagina: "I am Blanketing and Locking you and Draining the Life of you with my Massive Structured Beautifully built Almighty Vagina" (55). Reverting to the old feminist trope of reclaiming power through the female sex organ elicits laughter but also anger, as it (sadly) articulates its ongoing relevance and necessity for the twenty-first century.

Mischief is the driving force in a subsequent scene, "Revolutionize the Work (Engage with It)," where a female worker reclaims her body and free time by asking her—presumably male—employer to give her Mondays off to get some sleep. By refusing to abide by aspirational narratives of the "top girl" and neoliberal models of productivity that have eroded divisions between work and free time, the female voice willfully insists on making the same demand:

- I want Mondays off.
- Do you feel you'll be more productive?
- That's not my motivation.
- Is it about protest?
- It's about sleep. (68)

Trying to understand the reasons for her persistence, her employer rehearses a series of patriarchal clichés such as asking if she is pregnant or whether she suffers a mental breakdown or advising her to eat some chocolate because "it makes women happy" (69). To prove her demands unreasonable, he reminds her about the new vending machines and the fully operational bar at work. The female voice, however, insists on "speak[ing] out about [her] unhappiness with the very obligation to be made happy by such things" (Ahmed 2010b, 60) and unapologetically ends the discussion with the deadpan expression, "I'll see you on Tuesday" (69).

In "Revolutionize the Body (Make it Sexually Available. Constantly)," Birch's politics of anger and mischief draws attention to contemporary debates on rape and sexual harassment, which have resurfaced as ongoing urgent issues for women in the new millennium. Whilst the play rehearses well-known feminist arguments about the sexualisation and consumption of women's bodies, Birch also homes in on how female objectification and physical exposure interlace with wider practices of neoliberal capitalism. In the scene, a woman who decides to lie in one of the aisles of a supermarket exposing her body, which is also covered in watermelon, is confronted by the store's management, who rehearse the marketing vocabularies of commitment, health and safety and choice:

- [...] we're Happy you chose our store as the place in which you wish to Buy those melons

- We fly those melons in from all sorts of countries so you can just Have them
- Without having to think where they came from. [...]
- That's a choice we're really happy you can freely make
- We made the label "these watermelons come from Florida via Guatemala and back" really very small indeed, just so you don't have to feel guilty
- Guilt-free shopping is really important to us. (73)

The dialogue's playfulness and irony render vocabularies of commitment to customer satisfaction absurd, thus revealing the odious implications of the neoliberal market, such as the exacerbation of climate change and unequal conditions of labour. The neoliberal rhetoric of choice and freedom are both exposed as "gaping divides" (Gorman et al. 2018, 278) and thus empty of significance. Similarly, the female voice alludes to the failure of postfeminist vocabularies of choice, individual success and female empowerment. Through evoking histories of injury and pain, she narrates her various (failed) attempts to undo her objectification: "I have rubbed iodine, bleach and the gut of a rabbit into my skin until it began to burn. I have nearly emptied my body of its organs" (75). The failure to unmark her body as sexually available urges her to reverse her tactic: "Choose. My body is no battleground, there is no longer a line of defense—I Am Open. [...] This body this land is unattackable, unprotected, unconquerable, unclaimable, no different from air around it or bodies coming in because there Is no one to come into, you cannot overpower it because I have given it you cannot rape it because I give it and because I choose it" (76). This passage evokes the naturalisation of images of violence against women that continue to populate various media; its focus on an indignant female voice who still has to fight the same battles to achieve equality and ownership of her body reverses postfeminist narratives of sexual empowerment. In this context, the play's affective dramaturgical strategies shift the focus from pain and anxiety to rage against the loss of care for feminism; in this respect, it resonates with other women playwrights whose work is underpinned by "an experiential drive to feeling the loss of feminism," such as Kane and debbie tucker green (Aston 2010, 577).

Birch's text explores "feminism as self-breakage" (Ahmed 2017, 171) and "re-assemblage" (Ahmed 2017, 17); in addition to indignation, it presents exhaustion as a recurrent affective trope. Following Ahmed, part of the feminist project is to "come up against walls," to be "exhausted by what we come up against" and to find modes of survival to carry on feminism's work (2017, 163), taking care of feminism as a "fragile archive" (2017, 17). "Taking care" of feminism also means caring for women: the second act is replete with disillusionment and anxiety due to a notable lack of care between women. Staging three generations—a mother, a daughter and a grandmother—it ponders the impressions of second-wave feminism and its failure to provide a meaningful intergenerational dialogue as well as guidance as to how to take care of young women. In trying to navigate her relationship with her daughter Agnes, Dinah confronts her mother for the lack of affection in their own relationship: "I came from nowhere kind [...] and I haven't been able to give anything good to my girl" (83). Throughout the scene, Dinah refers to how tired both she and her daughter are: "I am so very tired I don't know what to do" (85). Towards the end of act three, a single voice speaking a lengthy monologue in one go contemplates where "we fucked it up" (99). For her, women's optimism about feminist progress is compromised by the competitive politics of individual choice, which has led to "new forms of female confinement" (McRobbie 2009, 122): "because [...] your choice and my choice have turned out to be not the fertile soil we thought we were standing two feet apart upon but dry and arid and empty and alone" (99).

Birch further complicates the notion of choice by showing how women have learned to self-inflict violence on their bodies "as a choice." Act two ends with Grandma and Agnes cutting out their tongues (85), whilst in the third act, one of the female characters chops her head off (90). The intertextual references at those points to other plays by women, such as Timberlake Wertenbaker's *The Love of the Nightingale* (1988; published in Wertenbaker 1996, 282–354) and Liz Lochhead's *Mary Queen of Scots Had her Head Chopped Off* ([1987] 2009), further inscribe the play within a legacy of women's playwriting that has explored the experience of violence against women performed by agents of power—with the self-infliction of such acts in Birch's play exposing the inherent violence and the internalisation of patriarchal discourse as perennial issues.[4] The mischievous treatment of "choice" is further pronounced in act three, when one of the voices repeats "my choice" while frantically "running around" working her body towards exhaustion (95). This repetition evokes the word's undoing: at the end, the voice exclaims that the only way women would be safe is if they actually refrained from going outside, as "it would be Nicest for everyone" (96)

In her performance review of the play's 2016 Soho Rep production in New York, Elizabeth M. Phillips observes how the piece, in addition to exhaustion and indignation, further staged the affective atmosphere of "disgust and terror" (2016, 671). Indeed, moments of heightened affectivity throughout the performance underscore impressions of disgust and terror through the suffering of the female body: in act two, anorexic granddaughter Agnes vomits when the family is sitting at the table to eat. According to Phillips, that particular scene left her with an intense impression where "sight and smell were ineluctable" (2016, 671).

Act three further explores mischief alongside dissonance as affective strategies that make feminist "rage legible and felt" (Aston 2010, 591). As I have argued elsewhere, dissonance as dramaturgical strategy may serve a feminist politics of perception in the theatre (2019, 132). Dissonance is affective; as an "inharmonious or harsh sound" (*Oxford English Dictionary*), it can bring physical discomfort and relates to the feminist experience of "being out of tune with others" (Ahmed 2017, 40). Opening with the instruction "Galvanize," the third act slowly unravels through a series of parallel vignettes where speech overlaps and stage actions and content offer the impression of a chaotic landscape. Escoda draws attention to Birch's use of uppercase letters as an example of "an affective type of playwriting" (forthcoming). In her opening stage directions for *Revolt.*, Birch herself notes that the use of capital letters together with punctuation "help the actor in terms of the pacing and the weight of their words" (45). Act three contains several lines that are wholly rendered in capital letters; this highlights the dynamic of the spoken word and the juxtaposition of different voices, thus making manifest what "we come up against" (Ahmed 2017, 256): "WOMAN FOR SALE! WHOLE HUMAN FOR SALE! IN THE NAME OF AHM SOMETHING REALLY BIG—WOMAN FOR SALE, ENTIRE WOMAN FOR SALE" (96). By thus articulating dissonance, the voices in *Revolt.* willfully take up a position against patriarchal structures whilst also challenging feel-good postfeminist attitudes that celebrate individual success and promote "the illusion of positivity and progress" for women (McRobbie 2009, 10).

This scene of dissonance culminates with a blast that, as noted earlier, destroys the play's form (Escoda forthcoming). This is presaged when one of the characters in act three suggests that "Actually it's a Massive Fuck Off Explosion we're after. Because really. Really there's nowhere else to go" (94). Echoing Ahmed, the blast foregrounds feminism as a "fragile archive" subject to processes of shattering and reassembling (2017, 17).

Following the blast, act four presents reassemblage as an affective strategy that marshals "killjoy" politics. Four female voices advocate a feminist renewal to fight against patriarchy and neoliberal capitalism; more specifically, they debate how sadness might serve as a driving force for this renewal:

- I am sad.
- It won't work if you are sad.
- It won't work if you aren't. It failed. The whole world failed at it. It could have been so brilliant. How strange of you not to feel sad. Who knew that life could be so awful. (101)

At the play's ending, the hope for the revitalisation of feminism thus merges with anxiety about its possibility. "Hope," Ahmed continues, "animates a struggle; hope gives us a sense that there is a point to working things out, working things through" (2017, 2). As a future-oriented affect, it also encompasses anxiety, "as some of the things we wish for will fail to happen, or be fundamentally undermined" (2010b, 182–83). By articulating an "anxious hope" (Ahmed 2010b, 182) about the futures of feminism, the complex constellation of affective atmospheres impressed in Birch's voices makes an urgent call for its revitalisation.

Whilst mourning the failures of feminism and the falsity of postfeminist narratives of progress and individual choice through reference to the "unhappy" archives of women's experience, Birch's angry feminist killjoys insist on reminding the world of the injustices women continue to suffer in the twenty-first century. *Revolt.*'s feminist politics of perception draws attention to mischief and willfulness as strategies that resist and disrupt practices of marketisation and victimisation of the female body and voice and revitalise feminism as an embodied practice.

The Feminist Precariat: *Letters to Windsor House*

Sh!t Theatre is an all-female theatre company who, like Birch, made their debut in the second decade of the new millennium. Louise Mothersole and Rebecca Biscuit, the company's performers and artistic directors, write, perform and produce theatre work that merges vocabularies of performance art, autobiography, cabaret and DIY aesthetic. Influenced by Lois Weaver and the legendary US feminist theatre company Split Britches (Mothersole and Biscuit 2017), the company's work can be further placed alongside postdramatic performance vocabularies and also shares allegiance with contemporary feminist performance art such as the work of UK-based Ursula Martinez, Bryony Kimmings and Rash Dash. Sh!t Theatre has been described by critics as "funny feminist agit-prop" (Gardner 2015) and "riotous, punky, properly angry feminist theatre" (Tripney 2015). Deeply invested in the intersections of gender and contemporary conditions of precarity, the company has created pieces such as *Job Seekers Anonymous* (2013; unpublished), which investigates the topic of unemployment for young women, *Women's Hour* (2014; unpublished), commissioned by Camden People's Theatre for their feminist festival "Calm Down Dear," and *Guinea Pigs on Trial* (2014; unpublished), which revolves around the politics of pharmaceutical companies. The company is the recipient of several awards and nominations, including a Total Theatre Award for Best Emerging Company in 2013 and a Fringe First for *Letters to Windsor House* (henceforth *Letters*) in 2016.

As a contemporary state-of-the-nation piece (Tripney 2017), *Letters* navigates the affective landscape of precarity in twenty-first-century Britain. It tackles issues such as the housing crisis, the prioritisation of private over public ownership and the lack of access to narratives of happiness and the good life for the young so-called Generation Rent. Similar to work by contemporary women playwrights such as Hickson, Lucy Kirkwood or Laura Wade, among others, and underpinned by an acute concern with "neoliberal capitalism and its capacity to structure feelings of economic and social precarity" (Aston 2018b, 131), *Letters* navigates the affective atmospheres of neoliberal Britain and the "cruelty" of aspirations of upward mobility and home ownership. Berlant suggests that cruel optimism can be traced when "the object/scene that ignites a sense of possibility actually makes it impossible to attain the expansive transformation for which a person or a people risks striving" (2011, 2). In this sense, Berlant argues, the present is experienced as an "impasse," a time where "the traditional infrastructures for reproducing life—at work, in intimacy, politically—are crumbling at a threatening pace" (2011, 5). Against this backdrop, *Letters* taps into survival tactics for navigating the precarious present.

The piece revolves around the two performers' experience of sharing a small council flat in Hackney, East London, a part of the city that has been undergoing significant regeneration activity. Across the street, the new luxury housing complex of Woodberry Park irretrievably changes the landscape of the neighbourhood and exacerbates class inequalities. Toying with the oxymoronic names of the blocks of flats in the area, such as Windsor House and Buckingham House, the performers introduce us to their shabby flat and neighbourhood before revealing the inspiration for their piece. during their time at Windsor House, they have been receiving a series of letters and brochures addressed to previous tenants. Assuming that they contained important information, they decide to open them and track down the people addressed on the envelopes.

Despite the serious nature of the topic, Sh!t Theatre approaches it through a cabaret comedy style. Comedy is a significant driving force across the company's oeuvre: as Mothersole and Biscuit admit, they aim to create "a joyful experience for the audience and also for ourselves on stage" (2017). Berlant also acknowledges the potentiality of comedy and "the politics of a cartoonish simplicity [...] for diminishing affectively what it is much harder to diminish effectively" (2011, 244). In disconnecting politics from negative attachments such as pain, fear, shame and disillusionment, comedy, she argues, "reopen[s] the space for the political as it is lived to become a space of genuine flourishing" and might "motivate the body politic to perform modes of intimate, physical, live reciprocity in the ordinary spaces of life itself?" (2011, 244). As they navigate the ordinary spaces of their life in Hackney, then, Mothersole and Biscuit use laughter and mischief as reflexive political strategies, combined with a tongue-in-cheek naivety and, sometimes, "cartoonish simplicity" (Berlant 2011, 244). Through such means, *Letters* reveals the uncomfortable truths of huge financial inequalities in contemporary Britain and causes disturbance in happiness narratives attached to home ownership and, more broadly, in neoliberal narratives of progress. This is achieved by drawing attention to the odious implications of urban gentrification, such as the displacement of low-income communities and the deepening of class divisions and how these are further fuelled by biopolitical mechanisms of debt. As Maurizio Lazzarato highlights, "property remains one of the major political stakes of neoliberalism" (2012, 8); neoliberalism's promise that "'everyone [is] an owner,'" he continues, has "plunged us into an existential condition of the indebted man, at once responsible and guilty for his particular fate" (2012, 9). Following Lazzarato's line of thinking, the perception of home ownership as an indicator of personal fulfilment and progress for the neoliberal subject cultivates feelings of anxiety and loss and exacerbates class inequalities.

The company's playful naivety and mischief seek to reverse the negative affects associated with debt and are inextricably connected to their intentional rejection of "virtuosity" (Mothersole and Biscuit 2017). This is particularly evident in their DIY stage aesthetic and set design, composed of perishable items such as cardboard boxes and an old sofa, as well as in their playful "nonexpert" approach to their material. In their role as amateur detectives, they marginally breach the law: they admit that they know that it may not be legal to open the letters, but refer to the Postal Services Act's use of the pronoun "he" to indicate any unlawful tampering with someone else's letters as an excuse for doing so (Sh!t Theatre 2017, 29). During the performance, they detail their attempts to excavate whatever information they have found about the flat's previous tenants and share this by only slightly changing their names. Thus, in order to locate Rob Jecock, "not his name but almost his real name" (36), a recipient of adverts for baby products and magazines on breast cancer, they leave him a series of Facebook messages and stalk him at work, because they "care" (55). Their amateur detective activity continues when they visit one of the luxury apartments at Woodberry estate as "an eccentric lesbian couple from Cambridge" and potential buyers (60) and secretly film their conversation with the estate agent, which they show during the live performance.

The piece's dramaturgy revolves around the various ephemera that connect to the history of their home and their neighbourhood. These include photographs from their flat, such as Reggie the cat, their "awards' shelf" (25–26) or the various local shops such as "Simply Organique—an old Costcutter which this year changed its name, but none of its stock" (31). In *An Archive of Feelings*, Ann Cvetkovich argues that "[i]n the absence of institutionalized documentation or in opposition to official histories, memory becomes a valuable historical resource, and ephemeral and personal collections of objects stand alongside the documents of the dominant culture in order to offer alternative modes of knowledge" (2003, 8). While Cvetkovich largely discusses the archive in relation to queer trauma, Mothersole and Biscuit's personal archive seeks to capture an affective impression that also evokes happy feelings about place brought by specific objects and memories. In *The Promise of Happiness*, Ahmed reminds us that "objects acquire value through contact with bodies" (2010b, 23). In *Letters*, this is particularly pronounced when Louise narrates how she was made "ridiculously happy" when they turned their narrow balcony "where the pigeons shit" into a small garden by bringing a roll of artificial grass (32). Such affective attachments to noninstrumental, "silly" objects inscribe the performers as affect aliens and directly challenge neoliberal understandings of happiness and ownership.

As an antidote to "institutionalized documentation" (Cvetkovich 2003, 8), the affective archive the performers share with the audience is amateurish and intimate: the photographs are grainy and unfocused, without any attempt at stylisation or embellishment; the performance's published script, which includes the details of all the photographs shown, repeatedly uses words like "awful" or "shit" to express disgust about visual evidence depicting the inside of their flat or themselves in the neighbourhood. Such strategies clearly contrast with the glossy images accompanying the stylish magazines they receive in the post. Wobbly video footage of fleeting impressions of the neighbourhood, such as "a pile of mattresses" or "a bulldozed council estate filmed through a hole in a fence" (40), is mixed with an audio of soft jazz music from a Woodbury Park advert and a male voiceover detailing the benefits of the housing development, whose "whole idea is about people coming together as a community" (41).

In gathering material for their archive, Mothersole and Biscuit attempt to capture a feeling of community in order to undermine neoliberal marketing language's appropriation of such concepts. This community has a particular class identity attached to precarity and debt. As the performers discover through letters sent by banks and Her Majesty's Revenue and Customs (HMRC), some of the previous tenants have fled the country, leaving their debts behind. In a consciously naïve and facetious way, they playfully reverse debt's negative affective attachments, such as "guilt, fear and bad conscience" (Lazzarato 2012, 130), and laugh at the thought of trying to save money: "How do you end up saving money these days? Who even has any savings? It is so '90s!" (48).

Another thread interwoven into the piece concerns precarity and its affinity with dispossession: in a comic reprise of the theme song taken from the popular 1980s TV series *Full House*, Mothersole and Biscuit sing, "whatever happened to predictability? [...] How did I get to living here?" (30). Precarity is foregrounded through the illustration of the poor conditions of living in their flat and explicit references to Charles Dickens's (2005) *Oliver Twist*. In doing so, they draw connections between Dickensian and neoliberal London; while they remake and sing songs from the British musical *Oliver!* (Bart and Coe 1960), a quote from Stephanie Polsky's *Ignoble Displacement: Dispossessed Capital in Neo-Dickensian London* (2015) shown in a projection spells out this connection: "The logic of contemporary Conservatism is truly Dickensian: their main concern is to prevent the poor from making demands on society" (46). The reference to "the poor" connects to the number of homeless people who set up their tents in their neighbourhood, to whom the performers refer as their "new neighbours" (45): "Next to Windsor is an unused patch of concrete three meters wide. People who don't have flats build homes out of cardboard and canvas before they are moved on, only to return days later" (80). In an attempt to illustrate the precarious conditions of living without a home, the performers use cardboard boxes to build a shelter on stage, which progressively resembles a small house. At the end of the show, following their announcement that their favourite local pub, the "Happy Man," will be demolished soon as part of the area's regeneration, the performers begin to furiously destroy their cardboard house leaving a pile of debris on stage. This is a moment of heightened affectivity that evokes Guy Standing's *precariat*, a neologism deriving from the words *precarious* and *proletariat*. According to Standing, the emergence of the precariat coincides with the "increase of labour market flexibility" (2011, 1). Not unlike Lazzarato's *homo debitor*, the precariat identity is marked by emotions of fear, anger, anomie and anxiety incurred by insecure labour conditions connecting to debt structures (Standing 2011, 22; Lazzarato 2012, 23–24).

In *Letters*, the performers' personal affective geographies vis-à-vis the implications of the rapidly changing landscape of neoliberal cities and their tactics of "accumulation by dispossession" (Harvey 2010, 249) work as reminders of the need to find solidarity and care. Against the "crisis of care" identified by Nancy Fraser, among others—the result of how the "financialized form of capitalism is systematically consuming our capacities to sustain social bonds" (Fraser 2016a; see also Fraser 2016b)—as well as against a postfeminist moment that privileges a competitive, individualistic, white middle-class femininity, the piece proposes an ethics of care as a feminist project. As "[c]are ethics points to the centrality of social relations and emotions for understanding our world" (Lawson 2007, 4), Mothersole and Biscuit's exploration of care begins with their friendship and love for each other. "Love," Ahmed argues, "makes the subject vulnerable, exposed to, and dependent upon another" (2004, 125). This vulnerability is made palpable through the confessional monologues the performers share with each other, which affectively shift the tone of the piece from a light-hearted treatment of memory to a reminiscence that evokes feelings of guilt, pain and fear. Hidden inside cardboard boxes designed to look like postboxes, they speak their intimate thoughts and feelings in the form of letters. The audience becomes privy to some uncomfortable truths, such as the time when Mothersole threw herself off the balcony because her girlfriend split up with her. Biscuit shares her affective response to the event, a mixture of feelings of pain interlaced with love: "[t]hen you jumped off the balcony and I thought you'd died and my reaction [...] was to immediately have a heavy nosebleed and start my period at the same time. That was my reaction to thinking I'd lost you. To bleed everywhere" (52). The interdependency of Mothersole and Biscuit's relationship as both friends and company partners also entails feelings of anxiety and entrapment not dissimilar to Berlant's understanding of the impasse: "[e]verything you do," Biscuit says, "affects me because you are my friend and my working partner and my entire career is tied up with you and with us, so when it doesn't work it's terrifying and I feel trapped" (53).

In sum, the confessions shared between the performers draw attention to love as dependency and to the role of cohabitation in shaping identity and relations of care. Cohabitation is presented as precarious, fostering a constellation of feelings ranging from pain, guilt and entrapment to joy and love, and it teaches them how to take care of each other. This care and love defines their identity as relational and dependent. As Biscuit confesses, "You and me is now my identity, rather than just me" (81). Through an embodied and relational exploration of the precarious nature of their identity, the performers thus assemble an "intimate public" (Berlant 2011, 226) as a strategy of survival within neoliberalism's impasse. For Berlant, an intimate public is a space that can provide ways away from the current impasse: "any person can contribute to the intimate public a personal story about not being defeated by what is overwhelming" (2011, 226–27). By exposing the failings of their relationship or the fact that they no longer share the same flat—which is revealed at the show's final scene—their friendship and story of cohabitation appears as a "fragile archive" subject to breakage and reassemblage (Ahmed 2017, 17). At the same time, Mothersole and Biscuit also evoke affects of joy and happiness living together as affect aliens made happy by the wrong things. Their embodied approach towards their performance material and their politics of mischief allow them to navigate the impasse and to explore the lack of *caritas* or crisis of care as a feminist challenge to *take care*. In doing so, they apply pressure to and affectively challenge the workings of neoliberal capitalism while also inviting audiences to rehearse their own small acts of mischief after they leave the theatre.

Conclusion

As shown, Birch's *Revolt.* and Sh!t Theatre's *Letters* cruise the contemporary affective atmospheres of patriarchy and neoliberal capitalism that create conditions of precarity. Following an explicitly feminist and queer strand of affect studies, this essay has approached affect as "embodied, located and relational" (Koivunen 2010, 8), not distinguished from emotion; in other words, affect has been understood here as a socially produced and circulated rather than exclusively presubjective experience that rehearses a political imperative: to take care. Such an imperative reinscribes feminism as an embodied and relational practice subject to breakage and reassemblage.

In this light, both examples discussed here stage affect aliens who adopt mischief as a political strategy that impresses a critique on neoliberal vocabularies of progress and claims that feminism is a dead project. Fuelled by a complex constellation of affects including indignation, exhaustion, joy, laughter, hope and anxiety, *Revolt.* and *Letters* mischievously trouble consensual perceptions of happiness that obscure conditions of inequality and injustice and amplify "the scripts available for what counts as good life" (Ahmed 2017, 264). Such a focus coincides with the resurgence of feminism in the theatre as an embodied politics of perception driven by willful feminist subjects who expose fantasies of progress and share hopes for social change. By reanimating feminist struggle, work by contemporary women theatre makers might mobilise sentient subjects who feel the revitalisation rather than the loss of feminism.

Notes

1. For a more extensive discussion, see also Ahmed (2010b, 2014).
2. The quote "socially-conditioned phenomena" is a direct citation from Brecht ([1957] 1964, 192).
3. Birch admits she was not aware of Kristeva's work when writing the play (Birch 2017b).
4. In *The Love of the Nightingale*, central female character Philomele has her tongue cut after being raped by her sister's husband. In Lochhead's play, which explores female power, Queen Mary of Scotland is beheaded by her cousin Queen Elizabeth I.

References

Ahmed, Sara. 2004. *The Cultural Politics of Emotion*. London and New York: Routledge.

———. 2010a. "Creating Disturbance: Feminism, Happiness and Affective Differences." In Liljeström and Paasonen 31–44.

———. 2010b. *The Promise of Happiness*. Durham, NC and London: Duke UP.

———. 2014. *Willful Subjects*. Durham, NC and London: Duke UP.

———. 2017. *Living a Feminist Life*. Durham, NC and London: Duke UP.

Angelaki, Vicky, ed. 2013. *Contemporary British Theatre: Breaking New Ground*. Basingstoke and New York: Palgrave Macmillan.

Angelaki, Vicky and Dan Rebellato, eds. Forthcoming. *The Cambridge Companion to British Playwriting since 1945*. Cambridge: Cambridge UP.

Aston, Elaine. 2010. "Feeling the Loss of Feminism: Sarah Kane's *Blasted* and an Experiential Genealogy of Contemporary Women's Playwriting." *Theatre Journal* 62 (4): 575–91.

———. 2018a. "Enter Stage Left: 'Recognition,' 'Redistribution,' and the A-Affect." *Contemporary Theatre Review* 28 (3): 299–309.

———. 2018b. "Structure of Class Feeling/Feeling of Class Structure." *Modern Drama* 61 (2): 127–48.

Bart, Lionel, composer and Peter Coe, dir 1960. *Oliver!*, CD. London and Los Angeles, CA: Decca.

Berlant, Lauren. 2011. *Cruel Optimism*. Durham, NC and London: Duke UP.

Birch, Alice. 2011. *Many Moons*. London: Oberon.

———. 2014. *Revolt. She Said. Revolt Again*. In RSC 2014, 43–101.

———. 2017a. *Anatomy of a Suicide*. London: Oberon.

———. 2017b. "Alice Birch, Dramaturge." Theatre, Drama and Youth: La Jeunesse au Théâtre, Université de Lille, 2 February. Accessed October 12, 2019.

Bowie-Sell, Daisy. 2011. Review of *Many Moons*, by Alice Birch. *Telegraph*, June 1. Accessed September 12, 2019.

Brecht, Bertolt. (1957) 1964. *Brecht on Theatre: The Development of an Aesthetic*. Translated and edited by John Willett. London: Methuen.

Case, Sue-Ellen. 1988. *Feminism and Theatre*. London and New York: Routledge.

Cixous, Hélène. 1976. *Portrait of Dora*. Translated by Ann Liddle. In Prenowitz 2004, 35–60.

Cvetkovich, Ann. 2003. *An Archive of Feelings*. Durham, NC and London: Duke UP.

Diamond, Elin, Denise Varney and Candice Amich, eds. 2017. *Performance, Feminism and Affect in Neoliberal Times*. London: Palgrave Macmillan.

Dickens, Charles. 2005. *Oliver Twist*. London: Macmillan.

Ensler, Eve. 1998. *The Vagina Monologues*. London: Virago.

Escoda, Clara. 2018. "'Her heart knows my heart for a brief moment': Mediated Affect and Utopian Impulse in *Many Moons* (2011) by Alice Birch." *Performing Ethos* 8 (1): 19–34.

———. forthcoming. "Gender and the Body in Alice Birch's *Revolt. She Said. Revolt Again.*: A 21st-Century Feminist Manifesto." In Angelaki and Rebellato forthcoming.

Fragkou, Marissia. 2019. *Ecologies of Precarity in Twenty-First Century Theatre: Politics, Affect, Responsibility*. London: Bloomsbury.

Fragkou, Marissia and Lynette Goddard. 2013. "Acting In/Action: Staging Human Rights in debbie tucker green's Royal Court Plays." In Angelaki 2013, 145–66.

Fraser, Nancy. 2016a. "Capitalism's Crisis of Care." Interview by Sarah Leonard. *Dissent*, Fall. Accessed February 10, 2019.

———. 2016b. "Contradictions of Capital and Care." *New Left Review* 100 (July–Aug.): 99–117. Accessed September 12, 2019.

Gardner, Lyn. 2015. "*Women's Hour* at Edinburgh Festival: Feminist Agit Prop." *Guardian*, August 14. Accessed February 15, 2019.

Gorman, Sarah, Geraldine Harris and Jen Harvie. 2018. "Feminisms Now." *Contemporary Theatre Review* 28 (3): 278–84.

Harvey, David. 2010. *The Enigma of Capital and the Crises of Capitalism*. Oxford: Oxford UP.

Kane, Sarah. 2000. *4.48 Psychosis*. London: Methuen.

Koivunen, Anu. 2010. "An Affective Turn? Reimagining the Subject of Feminist Theory." In Liljeström and Paasonen 2010, 8–28.

Kristeva, Julia. 1985. *Revolution in Poetic Language*. Translated by Margaret Waller. New York: Columbia UP.

Lawson, Victoria. 2007. "Presidential Address: Geographies of Care and Responsibility." *Annals of the Association of American Geographers* 97 (1): 1–11.

Lazzarato, Maurizio. 2012. *The Making of the Indebted Man: An Essay on the Neoliberal Condition*. Translated by Joshua David Jordan. Amsterdam: Semiotexte.

Lehmann, Hans-Thies. 2006. *Postdramatic Theatre*. Translated by Karen Jürs-Munby. London and New York: Routledge.

Liljeström, Marianne and Susanna Paasonen, eds. 2010. *Working with Affect in Feminist Readings*. London and New York: Routledge.

Lochhead, Liz. (1987) 2009. *Mary Queen of Scots Had Her Head Chopped Off*. London: Nick Hern Books.

McRobbie, Angela. 2009. *The Aftermath of Feminism: Gender, Culture and Social Change*. London: Sage.

Montironi, Maria Elisa. 2018. *Women upon Women in Contemporary British Drama (2000–2017)*. Würzburg: Königshausen & Neumann Verlag.

Mothersole, Louise and Rebecca Biscuit. 2017. "Sh!t Theatre: 'You Don't Have to Be a Virtuoso to Have Something to Say'" Interview by Catherine Love. *The Stage*, August 7. Accessed February 10, 2019.

Pedwell, Carolyn and Anne Whitehead. 2012. "Affecting Feminism: Questions of Feeling in Feminist Theory." *Feminist Theory* 13 (2): 115–29.

Phillips, Elizabeth M. 2016. Review of *Revolt. She Said. Revolt Again.*, by Alice Birch. *Theatre Journal* 68 (4): 670–72.

Polsky, Stephanie. 2015. *Ignoble Displacement: Dispossessed Capital in Neo-Dickensian London*. Alresford: Zero Books.

Prenowitz, Eric, ed. 2004. *Selected Plays by Hélène Cixous*. London and New York: Routledge.

RSC. 2014. *Midsummer Mischief: Four Radical New Plays*. London: Oberon.

Sh!t Theatre. 2017. *Letters to Windsor House*. London: Oberon.

Standing, Guy. 2011. *The Precariat: The New Dangerous Class*. London: Bloomsbury.

Tripney, Natasha. 2015. Review of *Women's Hour*, by Sh!t Theatre. *The Stage*, August 25. Accessed September 12, 2019.

———. 2017. "Is Europe 'Infecting' British Theatre Culture?" *The Stage*, February 16. Accessed February 16, 2019.

Ulrich, Laurel Thatcher. 1976. "Vertuous Women Found: New England Ministerial Literature, 1668–1735." *American Quarterly*, 28 (1): 20–40.

Whyman, Erica. 2014. "RSC's Erica Whyman: 'We Could Be Much More Rebellious.'" Interview by Catherine Love. *WhatsOnStage*, June 30. Accessed February 12, 2019.

Wertenbaker, Timberlake. 1996. *Plays 1*. London: Faber.

CHAPTER 8

Contemporary British Theatre, Democracy and Affect: States of Feeling

Cristina Delgado-García

Theatre and Democracy in the UK, 2010–2019

The UK has undergone considerable democratic stress in the 2010s and, unsurprisingly, British playwrights have turned their attention to democratic developments in the same period.[1] Examples abound: Tim Crouch's short play *John, Antonio and Nancy* (2010; published in 2015) reflected the discursive repetitiveness, vacuity and interchangeability of political discourse using child performers whose lines repurposed words spoken by the main party candidates during the UK's 2010 general election campaign. James Graham's output in this decade saw him shifting his focus to various procedural aspects of democracy—from the scheming behind parliamentary pairing, whipping and coalition formation in *This House* (2012) to polling-station drama in *The Vote* (2015; published in 2016, 22–30), a play set and broadcast live on television on the 2015 general election night.[2] Topically, Jack Thorne's *Hope* (2014) focused on the ethical

C. Delgado-García (✉)
University of Glasgow, Glasgow, UK
e-mail: Cristina.DelgadoGarcia@glasgow.ac.uk

M. Aragay et al. (eds.), *Affects in 21st-Century British Theatre*,
https://doi.org/10.1007/978-3-030-58486-3_8

dilemmas for the Labour council of a working-class town, considering the possibility of local resistance to centrally imposed austerity budgets. David Greig's version of Aeschylus's *The Suppliant Women* (2016; published in 2017), to which I return later, narratively pivots on the citizens' vote on offering protection to asylum-seeking women. Rob Drummond's *The Majority* (2017) premiered after the 2014 Scottish independence referendum and the 2016 referendum on the UK's EU membership and used spectators' votes as a dramaturgical device to punctuate a story about political participation.

This volume is concerned primarily with playwright's theatre, but the decade's work from across the performing arts engaging with democratic institutions, processes and effects is too significant to dismiss. *#TORYCORE* (2011–2017), a series of gigs by theatre makers Lucy Ellinson and Chris Thorpe with guitarist Steve Lawson, set verbatim extracts from Conservative Party documents to sludge and doom metal music—a form deemed fit to express the material and affective consequences of conservative governments. London-based queer feminist collective Femme Feral's *THERESAMAYSMACKDOWN* (2016–2019) similarly sought to articulate the angry desire to fight back against governmental/structural violence through the medium of organised group wrestling. In a participatory vein, Kaleider's piece *The Money* (2013) was dramaturgically structured around consensus building and budget administration, while Ellie Harrison's event *This Is What Democracy Looks Like!* (2015), held in London's Queen Elizabeth Olympic Park, fostered roving conversations between citizens and their newly elected representatives in a cycling vehicle equipped with one steering wheel and seven inward-facing saddles. Commissioned for the anniversary of the 1918 Representation of People Act, Selina Thompson's *Sortition* (2018) considered arrangements alternative to electoral representation.

Institutionally, the engagement with democracy has ranged from the corrective to the oblique. National Theatre Wales put forward "The Big Democracy Project" (2014–2016), a programme of activities aiming to "explore how art and creativity can play a part in helping communities across Wales re-engage with the democratic process" (Gwalchmai 2014). The project used online voting systems and assemblies across the country as a starting point towards "a truer democracy" (Gwalchmai 2014). In London, the National Theatre sought to represent verbatim the views of those who had allegedly been neglected in the public sphere before the

EU membership referendum in *My Country: A Work in Progress* (Duffy and Norris 2017). The National Theatre of Scotland's one-night event *Dear Europe*, scheduled to coincide with the then-assumed date of departure from the EU (March 29, 2019), featured six new performances that mostly favoured an indirect treatment of the EU referendum—from Alan McKendrick's *Cadaver Police in Quest of Aquatraz Exit*, a dystopian gig-theatre piece about life in an island prison, to Leonie Rae Gasson's *Death Becomes Us*, a performance that began with headphone- and blindfold-wearing audiences listening to a recording that blended the aesthetic of ASMR-stimulating sounds,[3] control-related eroticism and Vote Leave's invocations to take back control, before being invited to witness a rallying musical performance by Kenyan-Scottish singer Beldina Odenyo Onassis and a chorus of migrant nonbinary people and women.

This rich body of work representing, responding to and seeking to supplement democratic politics attests to democracy's prominence as a concern across theatre and performance in the 2010s and merits close examination. As a first step towards such an enquiry, this chapter advocates for attention to the operations of feelings both in democracy and in democracy-invested theatre and performance and offers a rationale and model for such a focus.[4] In so doing, I seek to make room for feelings alongside other, more familiar concerns that have preoccupied the discipline in relation to democracy—namely, representation, assembly, debate, consensus, disruption and, increasingly, agonism (on the latter, see Fletcher 2003; Fisher and Katsouraki 2017; Harrop 2018; Malzacher and Sellar 2017; Tomlin 2019). In this regard, I take heed of Chantal Mouffe, whose work situates affect as instrumental to the functioning, deterioration and potential enhancement of democracy, particularly in the present moment. With a renewed appreciation of affects in and for democracy, and in and through the arts, the chapter proposes an affective turn in the discipline's examination of texts and performances dealing with democratic matters—a turn that probes what democracy feels like, the function and effects of such feelings and the ways theatre may compose, diffuse or suppress affects. By way of illustration, I offer an affective study of Greig's *The Suppliant Women*, a piece representative of a broader stance in British theatre, whereby a strong attachment to democracy is performed despite the negative affective and material states democracy is shown to produce and legitimate.

Democracy and Affect in Our "Populist Moment": A Theoretical Framework

In line with broader cultural biases (Ahmed 2004), feelings are often portrayed as inimical to democracy for their alleged pernicious effect on discussion, voting and the irruption or ill management of conflict. George E. Marcus summarises this long-standing criticism: "democracy is [often found] wanting because of the apparent inability of the electorate to deliberate" (2002, 30); for democracy to thrive, so the argument goes, we must "minimize the evocation of passion and enhance the function of rationality"—in short, activate a "dispassionate citizen" (2002, 31). Despite research on the role that emotion plays in voting (Coleman 2013), attention or deliberation (Hall 2007) and criticisms of deliberative models of democracy (Mouffe 2000, 83–96), the charges against feelings in relation to democracy are pervasive and popular. Marcus writes in a North American context in the early 2000s, but British readings of recent political events in the UK and abroad testify to this. Days before the 2016 EU referendum, the *Guardian* newspaper cautioned: "The best starting point for Britain to reach a sound decision on Thursday is to cool the passions of the heart, and listen to the head" (Editorial 2016). Later that year and reflecting on both the results of that referendum and the election of Donald Trump as president of the US, political essayist Pankaj Mishra wrote: "we cannot understand this crisis because our dominant intellectual concepts and categories seem unable to process an explosion of uncontrolled forces [...]. [W]e find ourselves in an age of anger, with authoritarian leaders manipulating the cynicism and discontent of furious majorities" (2016).

Mouffe's scholarship on democracy offers an important corrective to the entrenched prejudice towards feelings in politics, particularly in her recent work on populism. Reclaiming the much-maligned term "populism," Mouffe uses it to refer to processes where a collective, heterologous, dissensual, anti-establishment and passionate popular will is galvanised (2018, 82–83).[5] Understood in this sense, populism does not necessarily equate to stoking right-wing sentiments or the withering of democracy. Populism may indeed, for Mouffe, be oriented leftwards, towards a "radical democracy": the "radicalization of the existing democratic institutions, with the result that the principles of liberty and equality become effective in an increasing number of social relations" (2018, 40; see also Laclau and Mouffe 2001). Indeed, this is the reorientation that

Mouffe proposes in a historical conjuncture she describes as our "populist moment," in which, after the financial crisis that began in 2008, "the neoliberal hegemonic formation is being called into question by a variety of anti-establishment movements, both from the right and from the left" (2018, 5).

Affect, Mouffe argues, can be instrumental in this populist shift towards the left. Programmatically, she proposes: "A left populist strategy aims at the crystallization of a collective will sustained by common affects aspiring for a more democratic order. This requires the creation of a different regime of desires and affects through inscription in discursive/affective practices that will bring about new forms of identification" (2018, 76–77), "practices that beget identification with a democratic egalitarian vision" (2018, 73). In other words, to "create the conditions for a recovery and deepening of democracy" (2018, 80) in Western liberal democracies, the loosely understood left needs to harness the political potential of affects. These, Mouffe believes, can contribute to the questioning and transformation of what is understood and/or felt as *common sense* in the Gramscian use of the term and induce new forms of political subjectivity around a desire for deeper liberty and equality within democratic frameworks.[6]

The argument for the democratic importance of affects is not new in Mouffe's work, though she had previously prioritised the term "passions."[7] Closer examination of Mouffe's ongoing engagement with passions/affects reveals that she envisions two uses of feelings in paving the way towards radical democracy. In *The Democratic Paradox* (2000), she suggests that the transition towards the agonistic, plural, radical democracy she espouses "requires providing channels through which *collective passions will be given ways to express themselves* over issues which, while allowing enough possibility for identification, will not construct the opponent as an enemy but as an adversary" (2000, 96; italics added). Yet her later work, written in our "populist moment," additionally emphasises the need to *mobilise* and *foster new affective regimes* attuned to the process of radicalising democracy (2018, 76–78). Mouffe therefore situates the expression, enlistment and creation of passions/affects as key to this process of radicalising democracy.

In this regard, and crucially in relation to this chapter, Mouffe continues the work she had undertaken previously in arguing that art and culture are an important part of those heterogeneous practices capable of producing new common desires and affects around liberty and equality and of bringing about new subjectivities galvanised around these axioms, thus *contributing* to the unsettling of neoliberal hegemony and the radicalisation of democracy (2013, 85–106; 2018, 77). The notion of contribution is central here as, for Mouffe, "critical artistic practices represent an important dimension of democratic politics. This does not mean, though, […] that they could alone realize the transformations needed for the establishment of a new hegemony" (2007, 5). To illustrate how art can disrupt hegemony, provoke new desires and identifications and contribute to the radicalisation of democracy, Mouffe offers examples drawn from socially engaged practices, artivism and institution-led initiatives: from Alfredo Jaar's interventions in public space to the anticar street parties of the direct action movement Reclaim the Streets to the Museu d'Art Contemporani de Barcelona's workshops "Of Direct Action Considered as One of the Fine Arts," held in October 2000 (Mouffe 2013, 94–103).

Mouffe's theorisation of left-wing populism, affects and radical democracy is certainly not immune to criticism.[8] Her work disregards the unpredictability and uncontrollability of affect as an autonomous intensity, as theorised in affect studies and described in the introduction to this collection. Indeed, artists' ability to orchestrate or reorient audiences' feelings in a particular direction may be less straightforward than Mouffe's presuppositions would seem to suggest. Mouffe's confidence in the political potential of affects themselves could also be tempered. As Jodi Dean notes, art may indeed "circulate political affects" but, in so doing, may also quench political energy, "displacing political struggles from the streets to the galleries" (2012, 13). Liz Tomlin warns that "enabl[ing] artists and audience to feel, and indeed to reflect, that they are contributing to the project of radical democracy […] can too easily become, in Sara Ahmed's terms, a non-performative" (2019, 110)—that is, a practice that does not have the effects it names despite appearing to do so (Ahmed 2012, 116–17). Mouffe is indeed invested in the productive correlation between the rousing of "affects aspiring for a more democratic order" (2018, 76), the formation of a popular, transversal will and the radical transformation of democracy, but it is also possible to envision—as Dean and Tomlin do—less successful scenarios between these steps: short circuits, dissonances or formations of collective will that are only brief. In addition to this, Mouffe's strategic examples of antihegemonic artistic practices share a clear orientation towards public spaces and politically inflected public actions, leaving ample room for questioning the affective-political traction of work that seeks to do nothing suchlike. More broadly, her vision of the arts as a potential contributor to a left-wing populist agenda is arguably instrumentalising. While cognisant of these criticisms, I want to retain Mouffe's scholarship on democracy and affect tactically, as it can be productive for theatre studies on at least two counts, which I will now examine.

Theatre and Democracy: New Questions to Ask

Theatre is often posited by academics and practitioners as a scaled-down parliamentary or deliberative democratic space. It has been described as a place where "assembled citizens *view and consider* representations of their world enacted for them in the immediacy of live performance" (Kritzer 2008, 1; italics added) and as a "fundamentally a democratic place—[…] where *debate and dispute, thought and memory* are transformed into what John McGrath himself called 'a good night out'" (Greig 2016; italics added): a place for viewing and reviewing, thinking and debating. Theatre can make a contribution "in all areas central to the working of a democracy," McGrath noted, "to scrutinize our values, to contest the borders of our democracy, to give a voice to the excluded, to the minorities, to guard against the tyranny of the majority, to criticize without fear, to seek true and multifaceted information, to combat the distorting power of the mass media, to define and re-define freedom for our age, to demand the equality of all citizens" (2002, 137, 139). In these views of theatre as a model for and motor of democracy, the implied understanding of democracy is predicated on assembly, representation, debate and thought. Recent and excellent edited collections, such as Shirin Rai and Janelle Reinelt's *The Grammar of Politics and Performance* (2015), Tony Fisher and Eve Katsouraki's *Performing Antagonism: Theatre, Performance & Radical Democracy* (2017) and Peter Eckersall and Helena Grehan's *The Routledge Companion to Theatre and Politics* (2019), also devote little attention to the role of passions/affects *in* or *towards* democracy. For example, the introduction to *Performing Antagonism* notes that politics cannot be reduced to "reasoned deliberation," as it "involves complex emotional and affective forms of identification, of passions and desires," but it explicitly casts aside "the problem of affect" (Fisher 2017, 9). Edited by Stephen Bottoms, *Contemporary Theatre Review*'s special issue on "Electoral Theatres" does acknowledge the importance of feelings but mostly in relation to the act of voting (Bottoms 2015). My first invitation is thus to take to heart Mouffe's attention to the affective dimension of democracy: to truly consider passions to be on an equal footing with the conceptual, symbolic, material and processual facets of democracy.

Second, Mouffe's scheme draws a distinction between (a) existing hegemonic regimes of desires and affects, (b) the generation of an antihegemonic, potentially collective affective experience, (c) the popular will or collective subjectivity that these affective configurations have the potential to induce and (d) the contribution that a passionate, collective and popular will can make to questioning the dominant hegemony and pushing for the reconfiguration of democracy in radical ways. This model can productively structure our attention by sharpening our focus on (a) the desires and passions that underpin our sociopolitical context and the ways they are maintained and (b) the affects that are expressed or activated in the theatre in relation to hegemony. Understanding these may help better situate theatre's potential contributions to (c) collective will formation and (d) democratic radicalisation.

In light of Mouffe's populist-affective turn towards radical democracy, then, my suggestion is that theatre studies take a step back to recognise that, in its various incarnations, democracy is a political structure, a set of practices and an ideal traversed by complex, multidirectional affective flows that affect and are affected by attitudes, beliefs, attention, reasoning, behaviour and decision making at individual, collective and institutional levels. Thus, before asking whether the affects generated textually and/or performatively in the theatre are efficacious for the desire to transform democracy, as per Mouffe's design, I suggest we should feel our way through the present condition. What does liberal democracy feel like in the UK in the politically turbulent decade of the 2010s? For whom does it feel like this, and for whom may it feel otherwise? What models of democracy are presented in contemporary British theatre, and what are the affects that buttress them? How are those affects composed in the text and on the stage? And importantly, what is the function of such feelings in a historical conjuncture in which democracy is under stress? Perhaps then, in the knowledge of what affects and what democratic formulations we would like to overcome, we can begin to consider how to orient passions towards radical democracy, how a populist-affective movement such as the one espoused by Mouffe might be materialised in the theatre—and, indeed, *pace* Mouffe, whether such passionate feelings towards democracy play a useful role in the present moment. I begin to pursue these questions through an examination of affect and democracy in Greig's version of Aeschylus's *The Suppliant Women*.

"Lest One Day the Citizens Fill My Hall": Democracy, Fear and Awe in David Greig's *The Suppliant Women*

Directed by Ramin Gray, *The Suppliant Women* was a coproduction between Actors Touring Company (ATC) and the Royal Lyceum Theatre Edinburgh, where it premiered in October 2016. Much promotional attention was focused on the striking topicality of the play's original preoccupations: asylum seeking, misogyny and democracy under stress (Gray 2017, n.p.). Truly, Greig's version makes no significant changes to the story of the Danaids as presented in Isabel Ruffell's literal translation, which was the basis for Greig's work on this piece (2016).[9] The Danaids, the 50 daughters of Danaos, arrive in Argos fleeing forced marriage to their Egyptian cousins and beg Pelasgos, king of Argos, to protect them. Initially resistant to giving asylum to the women, the king decides to propose to his citizens that they vote on the matter. The city votes in favour of taking the women in but threat looms at the end of the play, as an Egyptian herald arrives in Argos attempting to force the women to return to their cousins. While the Danaids do stay—thanks to the king's intervention—they are also forewarned by the citizens of Argos: "Refugees bring cold winds. / Evil pains follow, and bloody wars" (Aeschylus and Greig 2017, 46), so they should not "push things too far" (47). I will tend to the production later; for the moment I want to tease out the affectively complex, even troubling, model of democracy that is presented textually.

Greig's narrative fidelity to Aeschylus's text is also an exercise in affective fidelity, an affective archaeology of sorts: it often digs deep to unearth and expose the characters' feelings—the Danaids', Pelasgos's—in ways that cannot be easily extricated from democracy.[10] In Greig's version, as in Aeschylus's, the women's fear is not only expressed in relation to the prospect of forced marriage to their Egyptian cousins, but also regarding a city whose representative and democratic vote could easily turn against them. As it is widely known, the boundaries of the *demos* in ancient Greece are demarcated according to geographical location, gender and social position, but attention to feelings in the text suggests that these boundaries operate *within* and *because of* an affective economy of fear. As Ahmed notes, "[f]ear creates the very effect of 'that which I am not'" (2004, 67) and, in so doing, it delineates borders: borders between the fearing self and the feared object/subject, between one's integrity and that which is perceived to threaten it, between self and that which must be fled or fought. When the king receives the Danaids, trepidation also takes over him: "Fear grips me hard now" (23). In a self-focused move, the fearful women become fearsome for Pelasgos. Overcome by this intense bodily experience, the king expresses a desire for greater agency and control, presumed to be possible through emotion's alleged contrary—reason:

> I just need to think. Thought limits danger.
> I need to go deep into this like a diver
> Staying clear-headed,
> Keeping my grip. (24)[11]

The king's desire for "grip" expresses a need for self-possession at a point of affective disturbance:

> I shudder to look at your flags of asylum,
> I shudder to think of the blood they bring with them.
> No. No. No. (22)[12]

It also conveys his wish to maintain control over the city, to avoid its pollution. When the Danaids threaten suicide, the king expresses fear—not for their lives, but for the city's future shame: "If you die here like that, the name of this city / Will be spoken in whispers of shame forever" (26). His "No. No. No" voices an impassioned rejection of the women, their plight and the feelings these arouse in him. Thus, although fear ripples through *The Suppliant Women*, the feeling is neither shared nor brings subjects together in the first instance. Rather, fear in the play firms up the boundaries between those whom the representative of the democratic city *feels* he has a duty to protect and those whom he *feels* could be left out.

Greig's portrait of democracy, also in keeping with Aeschylus's, similarly provides an intriguing connection between leadership, feelings and direct votes. The king has a change of heart and decides to intervene in the Danaids' request for asylum. Yet the solution, the direct vote on the matter, is presented in ambivalent terms. First, the king implies that a collective vote is the only legitimate course of action on the grounds that the consequences will be shared, collectively, by the city (22). But later, however, it is fear *for the self* and fear *of passionate citizens* that support the leader's decision for a vote:

> […] [T]he city must vote,
> Lest one day the citizens fill my hall.
> Chanting in fury
> Righteous with anger
> "Letting in migrants caused Argos to fall." (23)

It is not, or not only, the potential fall of the city that motivates his decision but, rather, the possibility that he may be held accountable for it: "What price will I pay? Blood. Blood. Blood. / Blood on the meadow for the sake of some women?" (26). There is also an implicit hierarchy of feelings in the king's position, as pity for the existing suffering of women/migrants/outsiders in the present can and must be suppressed and superseded by compassion for *the potential* suffering of the (male) citizens/insiders and their leader *in the future*:

> […] I see you women
> Making a claim on the gods of my city.
> I know it means trouble.
> I know I don't want it.
> I know I won't take them to war out of pity. (22)

Even as the king affirms not wanting "to give these girls up," the admission is immediately followed by a clarification of motive: "Those doves on a rock / Could bring vengeance upon us" (24). Greig also maintains from Aeschylus the sense that the feelings of the voters can be swayed through rhetoric:

> I'll teach Danaos what to say in his speech.
> I'll prepare ground so the town's sympathetic
> And use all my skill to win you the vote. (28)

And indeed, Danaos describes the king's speech as "dripp[ing] with the art of persuasion" (32) in Greig's version, which only just hints at Ruffell's caution of a "somewhat pejorative" undertone in Aeschylus's original phrasing (2016, 28n). Thus, direct vote is not portrayed in Greig's version as a political practice where matters of significance are offered for the citizens' consideration without vested interests or mediation from leaders, nor is democracy celebrated as a system for governing that is inherently more compassionate towards strangers, newcomers or those at risk. Rather, direct vote is presented as subject to leaders' tactical rousing of emotions and as a means to allow the *demos*—and particularly the self—to save face, retain control during uncertainty and disseminate responsibility in times of crisis. That the result of the vote in *The Suppliant Women* is favourable to the asylum seekers is, under these circumstances, not particularly redemptive of democracy and its workings. This, as I elucidate later, jars with the celebratory stance on democracy and its representatives articulated in the performance.

The most important affective-stylistic divergences from the literal translation with regard to democracy are those that contribute to its presentation as an unknown form of government for the Middle Eastern female migrants. In Ruffell's literal translation, the women know of direct democracy and its functioning from their very first intervention and present themselves as "not flee[ing] / in an exile that had resulted from a blood-crime / convicted by a vote of the city" (2016, 3). Yet Greig's version significantly omits this early reference, which later allows him to portray the Danaids' ignorance and curiosity in asking "How did the city make its decision? / How does it work, this thing called 'democracy'?" (31). Ruffell's literal translation is suggestive of their inquisitiveness, rather than ignorance about democracy and its voting system: "Tell me how the conclusion has been ratified / how the people's ruling hand reached a majority" (2016, 27). So is Philip Vellacott's: "Tell us this one thing—what does their decision say? / What action is laid down by the prevailing vote?" (Aeschylus 1961, 72). Greig's version therefore introduces and emphasises geocultural distance between the "women of Egypt, / Neighbours of Syria" (11) and Argos, making the latter's democracy an unknown object of curiosity and awe for the former, an unknown entity holding the promise of protection of individual rights and the end of heteronormative violence.

A similar cultural distance is emphasised in Greig's version with the arrival of the Egyptian men and their herald. In Ruffell's literal translation, the female chorus appeals to "leaders, nobles of the city" to intervene and prevent their return to Egypt, to which the herald retorts, "You'll see many lords, the sons of Aigyptos, soon" (2016, 40); Vellacott's translation uses very similar terms and phrasings (Aeschylus 1961, 80–81). Greig, however, omits the chorus's appeal and adjusts the herald's intervention, highlighting that the distinction between Greek male figures of protection and Egyptian male figures of oppression also depends on democracy as a form of authority and decision making: "Forget about Argos. *Forget about voters.* / The sons of Aegyptos are your masters now" (41; italics added). A little earlier, the Egyptian men illustrate their ways thus:

This is how we solve a problem,
Force! Force! Force! Force!
What you want no longer matters.
You are lovely, hair and dresses
Come to meet our fists, your masters. (39)

Greig's version does not only oppose the Argive citizens to the Egyptian men, but in contraposing the former's voting to the latter's use of force it makes fear democracy's allure: the fear that the alternative to democracy can only be brutality. In so doing, Greig's *The Suppliant Women* recreates at this point a persistent, damaging binary steeped in hegemonic affective associations: on the one hand, Western democracy paternally offering the promise of safety, even if the fear that this might be withheld or withdrawn underscores this hope; on the other, the terrifying, undemocratic, violently misogynist East. This binary supports deeply entrenched stereotypes that position the West as culturally, socially and politically superior to the East.

While the production's promotional material signalled the actuality of Ancient Greece's social-ethical challenges and, implicitly, the power of the people's vote to overcome these, reading the playtext for affects offers a much less celebratory vision of this lineage. Greig's palimpsestic writing on democracy is underscored by divisive, self-protective, ethnocentric fear and patriarchal power. This instils in the script a subtle trace of what Astra Taylor calls "democracy's dark history" but would be better described as democracy's violent past and present: its history "of oppression, exploitation, demagoguery, dispossession, domination, horror, and abuse," existing in paradoxical tension with its "history of cooperation, solidarity, deliberation, emancipation, justice, and empathy" (Taylor 2019, 13).

ATC's Production of *The Suppliant Women*: Mixed Feelings

In the remainder of this chapter, I want to focus on the *representational-democratic feel* of the performance—that is, the orchestration of an atmosphere reminiscent of representative democracy for its presentation of (s)elected members to stand in for community—and its interplay with visions of democracy in the text and our historical moment. Described as "thoroughly democratic" (Fisher 2016), ATC's production of *The Suppliant Women* was keen on performance tropes on representation. In every city where it was performed, the *demos* was represented through a large community cast of amateur performers that had been recruited locally and thoroughly trained to perform as the protagonist chorus of Danaids, the Egyptian cousins and the citizens of Argos, with only three professional actors as the chorus leader, Pelasgos and Danaos/the Egyptian herald. A second layer of local representation was offered by ATC's adaptation of the libation ritual to precede performance, whereby a "local dignitary, politician or prominent member in the community," new each night, was in charge of offering context for the play, detailing how it had been financed, explaining the amateur make-up of the chorus (Gray 2017, n.p.) and reenacting the ritual pouring of wine along the thrust stage as an offering to Dionysus. The democratic quality that casts and libation performers impressed upon the show was therefore predicated on the onstage presence of "the people" of the community: their irrefutable standing in for the broader community evokes the representational ideal of democratic institutions.

Yet, amidst reviews that praised ATC's production for its fulfilment of Greig's vision of the theatre as a democratic space (Fisher 2016; Sierz 2017), Maddy Costa's unfavourable appraisal stands out:

> On Wednesday 15 November, that person [offering the libation] was Eleanor Kelly, chief executive of Southwark Council. That's Southwark Council who, according to a blog post published on 14 November 2017, [...] "hold top place for the local authority with the most number of homeless households in Bed & Breakfast/hostel accommodation over the 6 week limit." The same Southwark Council that, according to figures published in July 2016 by another activist group, [...] has "1,270 empty council homes, yet ... turns away 47% of homeless survivors of domestic violence." Whatever democracies should do to help the vulnerable, the minority, it doesn't look like this. Viewed through that lens, the libation—Kelly pours red wine over the front of the stage—begins to lose its romantic aspect, its spiritual dimension, and comes across instead as an act of waste. (2017)[13]

Costa rightly identifies a jarring between the production's gesture of respect for the city's dignitaries, their assumed espousal of democratic and egalitarian values and the indignity caused/permitted by the democratic institutions they represent. It is worth noting that the libation was not always poured by a local politician—in the performance I saw at the Royal Exchange Theatre in Manchester on March 17, 2017, this was performed by the then director of the Whitworth and Manchester City Galleries, Maria Balshaw. The friction between form, content and its real-life referents nonetheless stands. *The Suppliant Women*, a story about the rupture of the status quo, is framed by the libation in terms of fidelity to ancient traditions and deference towards a community's authorities, distinguished figures, taxpayers and patrons; a story about the plight and demands of outsiders is embodied by local residents—outsiders, perhaps, only to the theatre as an area of economic activity and whose cultural-ethnic heterogeneity is ambiguously subsumed under the production's emphasis on locality.

My final observation is on the *radically democratic* feeling of the performance: its strong arousal of left-wing populist-democratic affects à la Mouffe. Indeed, the chorus *felt like* the Mouffian heterologous, dissensual, passionate collective subject determined to demand safety and equality and, in so doing, radicalise democracy—the chorus evokes the "tireless agitators" (Taylor 2019, 5) that make an increasingly egalitarian democracy possible. Zachary Dunbar and Stephe Harrop describe well the oppositional energy of the female chorus and the overriding power of their onstage presence: "They are individually distinctive, displaying different levels of energy and physical skill. They lack the disciplined, drilled uniformity often associated with idealizing visions of the tragic chorus. But, at the show's best moments, *this doesn't matter at all.* Confronting the singular figure of the Argive king (Oscar Batterham), these massed suppliants [...] could easily be the Amazons he initially conjectures them to be" (2018, 150–51; italics added). And later: "The women's vocal text [...] is sometimes audible and sometimes not, getting lost in the rush of bodies, and the heavy scuffle of feet. *It doesn't really matter*. The heart of the tragedy, today, lies in the spectacle of a group of young women, each individually distinct and distinctly of her own contemporary city, taking a stand on the tragic stage" (2018, 151–52; italics added). And yet, as Duška Radosavljević's review notes, what the performance *felt like*—a female-led, vigorous spectacle, underscored by feminist demands—is not necessarily what the performance *was*—a show authored, adapted and directed by men that reproduced patriarchal structures in its production methods: "Aeschylus's world itself, then and now, has always adhered to the deeply entrenched power mechanism of patriarchy, and this production authored by men remains within it even if its rallying cry brought about by the women working on the show has us feeling otherwise" (2017).[14]

Similarly, the chorus may have aroused a regime of desires and affects attuned to the project of a deeper democracy: a more capacious, compassionate and egalitarian form of self-government and social organisation. But the circulation of these alluring progressive passions must not obfuscate how much related questions *do* matter. How are these radical-democratic affects produced? Who gets to feel thus? Who does not? What is the function of these affects, generated and circulated thus, in this moment? One of the strengths of ATC's production of *The Suppliant Women* was its physical and vocal training of the local female chorus, whose energetic choreography, singing and chanting conjured the sustained fear, anxiety and audacious resolve of the asylum-seeking Danaids (Hemming 2017). Arguably, however, the extreme distress and resolution of the migrants they embody is leveraged to generate positive affects towards the inclusive potential of our democracy: the suffering and defiant endurance of others reassuringly confirms to us that our age-old democracy is good, that voting can bring a safer world into existence. In addition, the material and affective work of "agitating" falls upon the stranger in the narrative but, in performance, "these women look like us; they come from among us; they could be us" (Hemming 2017): the local casts facilitate what at best might be described as an anticipatory modelling of "the people" within a community fighting for a radical democracy; at worst, the use of the amateur chorus in ATC's performance may be said to allocate the suffering, courage and tenacity of foreigners to the local *demos.*

In short, Aeschylus's tragedy and Greig's version textually displayed mixed feelings on democracy and its workings, holding at once the promise of compassionate government and a foundational association with fear, exclusion, ethnocentrism, dubious leadership and easily manipulated voters. Despite this, the affective commitment of ATC's production lies firmly within tradition keeping, deference towards authorities and performative tribute to the democratic representation of "the people" through casting and libation ritual. Although the performance does have an undeniably hopeful radical-democratic feel, this hinges upon the local casts' metabolisation of newcomers' suffering and disruptive, militant work.

Conclusion

I began this piece with an incomplete survey of theatre's salient interest in democracy in the period between 2010 and 2019, to which I wish to return now. These works insist on the need for reflection on democratic matters in a decade when UK democracy has undergone considerable stress and scrutiny, but they also call for a nuanced understanding of the role and function of affects in and for democracy in the present moment. Democracy not only regulates the material conditions of life within a state, it also produces states of feeling and is partly subjected to them. As such, any examination of democracy and its representation/evocation in the theatre is thus incomplete without a consideration of affects: how democracy feels across constituencies and agents, how such feelings have socio-political functions and important symbolic-material effects and how theatre contributes to the perpetuation or, as Mouffe would have it, the disruption of such affective economies. My overall sense is that reading theatre and performance for affect suggests that these works generate, reproduce and circulate a series of feelings that "stick" to democracy—melancholy, rage, fear, perplexity, hope—and that these feelings also make democracy "stick" with particular permanence in our political imaginary.[15] *The Suppliant Women* is a case in point: it reproduces a model of democracy that is traversed by "ugly feelings" (Ngai 2005) and yet, mobilising democratic tropes of representation and participation, it succeeds in appearing triumphantly and "thoroughly democratic." In so doing, it contributes to maintaining an attachment to democracy despite its shortcomings to deliver on representation, the equal flourishing of all members of society, the configuration of rigorous public debate and the ethical consideration of the nonhuman world in political decision making in our contemporary moment. This arguably retains hope for a radical democracy while perhaps fossilising the horizon of imaginable forms of governing that may be materially, affectively and environmentally nurturing for all, across borders.

Notes

1. In this period, there have been four general elections, two country-wide referendums, two prime ministers have stepped down and two unelected others have succeeded them. The UK has also displayed signs of the increasing difficulty in disentangling liberal democracies from corporate interests. The austerity measures implemented by UK Conservative-led governments since 2010 exemplify how "state power [is] unapologetically harnessed to the project of capital accumulation via tax, environmental, energy, labor, social, fiscal, and monetary policy as well as an endless stream of direct supports and bailouts for all sectors of capital" (Brown 2012, 46–47). The 2016 referendum on the UK's withdrawal from the EU has further illuminated unresolved problems at the core of democratic pro-

cesses: among others, the extent of parliamentary sovereignty (Eleftheriadis 2017), the make-up of the electoral *demos* (Wren-Lewis 2019), the complications resulting from different referendum results across the four constituent nations of the UK and known irregularities in campaign financing and data use (see Hern 2019; Wren-Lewis 2019). While it is established that there is neither a single definition nor uniform practice of democracy (Brown 2012, 44; Fishman 2017), these events demonstrate that the received understanding of democracy as the "rule by the people" (Fishman 2017) is incomplete and being put to the test.

2. A dramatised reading of an updated version of this play, retitled *The Vote 2019*, was held at Bush House, London, on general election night on December 12, 2019. Graham has also explored democratic issues in his writing for television drama: *Coalition* (2015) and *Brexit: An Uncivil War* (2019).
3. ASMR stands for Autonomous Sensory Meridian Response and is defined as the "feeling of well-being combined with a tingling sensation in the scalp and down the back of the neck, as experienced by some people in response to a specific gentle stimulus, often a particular sound" (*Oxford English Dictionary*).
4. As discussed in the introduction to this volume, the terms *affect*, *emotion* and *feeling* are not always defined and used consistently in the literature. This chapter respects terminology in sources and uses *affect* and *emotion* as conceptually distinct but coterminous, with boundaries that are not always easy or necessarily useful to delineate. Following Erin Hurley (2010, 10–23), my use of *feelings* encompasses both.
5. For Mouffe, a left-wing populist strategy is pertinent to the present moment for three reasons: populism provides a disruption of the equation of democracy with consensus, which she sees as indicative of postpolitics; populism foregrounds "the *demos* as an essential dimension of democracy," allowing for the "construction of 'a people' in a transversal way" (2018, 82, 83), opposing oligarchy across constituencies; and finally, populism acknowledges "the role of the affective dimension in the political forms of identification and the importance of the mobilization of common affects" (2018, 83; see also Errejón and Mouffe 2016, 55).
6. Antonio Gramsci's notion of "common sense" (*senso commune*) refers to the sets of hegemonic beliefs about the world and society that have come to be perceived as natural and self-evident despite their constructed and politically entrenched nature (Gramsci 1971, 323–49).
7. For Mouffe, "passions" are "a certain type of common affects, those that are mobilized in the political domain in the formation of the we/they forms of identification" (2014, 155) and evoke both the collective and conflictual she places at the centre of democracy (2014, 149).

8. For criticisms of Mouffe's *For a Left Populism* within political theory, see Matthew Longo (2018) on the practicalities of this left turn to populism and the dispersed nature of the public sphere in the present.
9. My thanks to Professor Ruffell for kindly sharing her translation and granting permission for me to cite it in this chapter.
10. Greig introduces small changes to the affective landscape presented in the literal translation, which I highlight in the notes unless of direct relevance to democratic matters.
11. Greig's version produces here a sharp opposition between feeling and thinking and one that is distributed along gender and moral binaries. In his text, the king's stated "need to think" is challenged by the female chorus thus: "Feel!— / Feel! Feeling finds Justice—Justice finds Mercy" (24). In Ruffell's literal translation, however, the king asks for "deep consideration," which the chorus neither opposes nor suspects: "Consider, then, and become entirely justly / a respectful local representative" (2016, 19). Philip Vellacott's translation similarly sees the chorus respecting the king's request for reflection: "Think! And befriend us / Justly, religiously" (Aeschylus 1961, 66).
12. Greig intensifies Pelasgos's affective reaction and stages more emphatically a struggle between his body's uncontrollable sensations and the self-command seemingly offered by thought, with the king stating twice that his body trembles with the uncertainty the women bring and underscoring this with a triple assertion of what he does know: "I know it means trouble. / I know I don't want it. / I know I won't take them to war out of pity" (22). Ruffell's translation captures a less violent tension between sensation, feelings and understanding—the king does shudder, though only once, and the conviction delivered by knowledge in Greig's version is but the expression of an uncertain wish: "I wish this affair of strangers to the city does not become harmful, / and may no strife come to the city from unexpected / and unlooked-for events. The city has no need of them" (2016, 16). Vellacott's earlier translation (Aeschylus 1961, 64–65) is in line with Ruffell's.
13. Costa hyperlinks her sources. See Housing Action Southwark and Lambeth (2017) and Sisters Uncut (2016).
14. Costa (2017) also highlights a contradiction between the rousing effect in performance, giving credence to female empowerment, and the cultural, symbolic and material injustices masked by these affects. For alternative views, see Elaine Aston (2016), Sarah Hemming (2017) and Aleks Sierz (2017). I also wish to acknowledge Aston's recent monograph *Restaging Feminisms*, which deepens her feminist reading of *The Suppliant Women* in arguing that "the community chorus in combination with Greig's demotic-poetic rendition of the tragedy" render "ideas-affections" that critique and

weaken patriarchalism (2020, 68). Aston's book was published while this edited collection was in production, and therefore too late for this chapter to engage meaningfully with its arguments.

15. On the "stickiness" of affect, see Ahmed (2004, 11–16).

References

Aeschylus. 1961. *Prometheus Bound; The Suppliants; Seven Against Thebes; The Persians.* Translated by Philip Vellacott. London: Penguin.

Aeschylus and David Greig. 2017. *The Suppliant Women.* London: Faber.

Agamben, Giorgio et al. 2012. *Democracy in What State?* New York: Columbia UP.

Ahmed, Sara. 2004. *The Cultural Politics of Emotion.* London and New York: Routledge.

———. 2012. *On Being Included: Racism and Diversity in Institutional Life.* Durham, NC and London: Duke UP.

Aston, Elaine. 2016. "Feminism, Theatre and Democracy." Review of *The Suppliant Women*, by Aeschylus and David Greig. *Drama Queens Review* (blog), October 16. Accessed October 6, 2019.

———. 2020. *Staging Feminisms.* London: Palgrave Macmillan.

Bottoms, Stephen, ed. 2015. "Electoral Theatres." Special issue, *Contemporary Theatre Review* 25 (2).

Brown, Wendy. 2012. "We Are All Democrats Now…" In Agamben et al. 2012, 44–57.

Coleman, Stephen. 2013. *How Voters Feel.* Cambridge: Cambridge UP.

Costa, Maddie. 2017. Review of *The Suppliant Women*, by Aeschylus and David Greig. *Exeunt*, November 20. Accessed October 6, 2019.

Crouch, Tim. 2015. *John, Antonio and Nancy. Contemporary Theatre Review* 25 (2): 251–54.

Dean, Jodi. 2012. *The Communist Horizon.* London: Verso.

Drummond, Rob. 2017. *The Majority.* London: Bloomsbury.

Duffy, Carol Ann and Rufus Norris. 2017. *My Country: A Work in Progress.* London: Faber.

Dunbar, Zachary and Stephe Harrop. 2018. *Greek Tragedy and the Contemporary Actor.* London: Palgrave Macmillan.

Eckersall, Peter and Helena Grehan, eds. 2019. *The Routledge Companion to Theatre and Politics.* London and New York: Routledge.

Editorial. 2016. "The Guardian View on the EU Referendum: Keep Connected and Inclusive, Not Angry and Isolated." *Guardian*, June 20. Accessed August 9, 2019.

Eleftheriadis, Pavlos. 2017. "Constitutional Illegitimacy over Brexit." *The Political Quarterly* 88 (2): 182–88.

Errejón, Íñigo and Chantal Mouffe. 2016. *Podemos: In the Name of the People*. London: Lawrence & Wishart.

Fisher, Mark. 2016. "An Epic, Feminist Protest Song." Review of *The Suppliant Women*, by Aeschylus and David Greig. *Guardian*, October 6. Accessed September 26, 2018.

Fisher, Tony. 2017. "Performance and the Tragic Politics of the Agōn." In Fisher and Katsouraki 2017, 1–23.

Fisher, Tony, and Eve Katsouraki, eds. 2017. *Performing Antagonism: Theatre, Performance & Radical Democracy*. London: Palgrave Macmillan.

Fishman, Robert M. 2017. "Democracy." *Oxford Bibliographies: Sociology*. Accessed August 13, 2019.

Fletcher, John. 2003. "Identity and Agonism: Tim Miller, Cornerstone, and the Politics of Community-Based Theatre." *Theatre Topics* 13 (2): 189–203.

Graham, James. 2012. *This House*. London: Bloomsbury.

———. 2016. *Plays: 2*. London: Bloomsbury.

Gramsci, Antonio. 1971. *Selections from the Prison Notebooks*. Translated and edited by Quintin Hoare and Geoffrey Nowell Smith. London: Lawrence & Wishart.

Gray, Ramin. 2017. "Director's Note." In Aeschylus and David Greig 2017, n.p.

Greig, David. 2016. "Season 2016/17 Announcement from Artistic Director David Greig." *Royal Lyceum Theatre Edinburgh*, May 3. Accessed September 24, 2019.

Gwalchmai, Ben. 2014. "Experimenting with Democracy: The Big Democracy Project." *Huffpost*, September 30. Accessed August 8, 2019.

Hall, Cheryl. 2007. "Recognizing the Passion in Deliberation: Toward a More Democratic Theory of Deliberative Democracy." *Hypatia: A Journal of Feminist Philosophy* 22 (4): 81–95.

Harrop, Stephe. 2018. "Greek Tragedy, Agonistic Space, and Contemporary Performance." *New Theatre Quarterly* 34 (2): 99–114.

Hemming, Sarah. 2017. "A Fierce, Beautiful Staging of Aeschylus's Drama." Review of *The Suppliant Women*, by Aeschylus and David Greig. *Financial Times*, November 17. Accessed October 6, 2019.

Hern, Alex. 2019. "Cambridge Analytica Did Work for Leave.EU, Emails Confirm." *Guardian*, July 30. Accessed August 14, 2019.

Housing Action Southwark and Lambeth. 2017. "Southwark Families Stuck in Unsuitable Temporary Accommodation—Some of Our Stories." *Housing Action Southwark and Lambeth* (blog), November 14. Accessed November 29, 2019.

Hurley, Erin. 2010. *theatre & feeling*. Basingstoke and New York: Palgrave Macmillan.

Kritzer, Amelia Howe. 2008. *Political Theatre in Post-Thatcher Britain: New Writing, 1995–2005*. Basingstoke and New York: Palgrave Macmillan.

Laclau, Ernesto and Chantal Mouffe. 2001. *Hegemony and Socialist Strategy: Towards a Radical Democratic Politics.* 2nd ed. London: Verso.

Longo, Matthew. 2018. Review of *For a Left Populism*, by Chantal Mouffe. *LSE Review of Books* (blog), August 29. Accessed August 19, 2019.

Malzacher, Florian and Tom Sellar. 2017. "Agonism and the Next Word." Theater 47 (1): 17–37.

Marcus, George E. 2002. *The Sentimental Citizen: Emotion in Democratic Politics.* University Park: Pennsylvania State UP.

McGrath, John. 2002. "Theatre and Democracy." *New Theatre Quarterly* 18 (2): 133–39.

Mishra, Pankaj. 2016. "Welcome to the Age of Anger." *Guardian*, December 8. Accessed August 9, 2019.

Mouffe, Chantal. 2000. *The Democratic Paradox.* London: Verso.

———. 2007. "Artistic Activism and Agonistic Spaces." *Art & Research: A Journal of Ideas, Contexts and Methods* 1 (2): 1–5.

———. 2013. *Agonistics: Thinking the World Politically.* London: Verso.

———. 2014. "By Way of a Postscript." *Parallax* 20 (2): 149–57.

———. 2018. *For a Left Populism.* London: Verso.

Ngai, Sianne. 2005. *Ugly Feelings.* Cambridge, MA: Harvard UP.

Radosavljević, Duška. 2017. "*The Suppliant Women:* A New Version for Modern Times." Review of *The Suppliant Women*, by Aeschylus and David Greig. *Theatre Times*, November 24. Accessed October 6, 2019.

Rai, Shirin M. and Janelle Reinelt, eds. 2015. *The Grammar of Politics and Performance.* London and New York: Routledge.

Ruffell, Isabel, trans. 2016. *The Suppliant Women*, by Aeschylus (Unpublished text, January 7), PDF file.

Sierz, Aleks. 2017. Review of *The Suppliant Women*, by Aeschylus and David Greig. *Aleks Sierz: New Writing for the British Stage*, November 17. Accessed October 6, 2019.

Sisters Uncut. 2016. "Shameful Southwark Council Response to Sisters Uncut Occupation." *Sisters Uncut*, July 1. Accessed November 29, 2019.

Taylor, Astra. 2019. *Democracy May Not Exist, but We'll Miss It When It's Gone.* London: Verso.

Thorne, Jack. 2014. *Hope.* London: Nick Hern Books.

Tomlin, Liz. 2019. *Political Dramaturgies and Theatre Spectatorship: Provocations for Change.* London: Bloomsbury.

Wren-Lewis, Simon. 2019. "The Brexit Referendum Was Badly Designed and Unfairly Won." *New Statesman*, January 9. Accessed August 21, 2019.

CHAPTER 9

Affect and the Politics of Abstraction in British New Writing

Philip Watkinson

It starts with a line. Not the kind of line spoken by a performer, but a horizontal line, a line drawn in chalk along the pale green of the wooden wall. This white line continues, slowly but surely, along its horizontal course. The performer clutches the chalk in their left hand, walking at a steady pace, producing this linear manifestation of continuity. The line remains at the performer's head height and passes by a zigzag, an arch and other geometric shapes but it pays them no mind. The line continues. And then it doesn't.

There is an interruption.

A puncture.

A gap in continuity.

The performer has removed the chalk from the surface of the wall for a moment.

P. Watkinson (✉)
Independent scholar, Sheffield, UK
e-mail: philip.watkinson@outlook.com

M. Aragay et al. (eds.), *Affects in 21st-Century British Theatre*,
https://doi.org/10.1007/978-3-030-58486-3_9

And then it returns, the line continues its linear journey. Until it suddenly stops.

Pauses.

And then onwards it goes again.

This is how debbie tucker green's *a profoundly affectionate, passionate devotion to someone (-noun)* (2017) begins (henceforth *a profoundly affectionate, passionate devotion*). Before any dialogue has been spoken, spectators are presented with graphic abstractions that invite but also resist interpretation. There are no discernible patterns or symbolic references, just the line and the act that brings it into being. Eugenie Brinkema has shown how, in terms of form and visual structure, anxiety can be a matter of an interrupted horizontal line (2014, 224). Like the unforeseen traumatic event that ruptures a balanced psychic disposition, the break in a line disrupts a continuous, predictable flow. This chalky prelude formalises the temporal intermittency of anxiety and sets a structural precedent for the remainder of the play, where interruptions, overlaps and misunderstandings define the social reality of the characters.

After a few minutes, part one, scene one is underway and tucker green's trademark elliptical dialogue takes centre stage:

A So is it—
B no.
A Is it that/you're—
B No it is/not.
A so it's
B there is no "it's" it's nothing there's nothing
A you're not—
B no. Nothing. There isn't.
Beat.
A My bad.
B Yeh.
A
B (2017, 3)

This dialogue is striking for its form rather than its content. In this opening scene, spectators are presented with a couple, A and B, who argue passionately but never state directly what the topic of their argument is; it is only denoted by the abstract placeholder "it's." Yet this lack of concrete detail does not lessen the power of the scene. Despite the fractured, terse language, there is something moving and familiar about the interactions between these characters. In this opening scene, tucker green lays bare the recognisable structures of romantic relationships, both real and fictional: the gaps in communication that foster anger, the contradictory recollections and incompatible interpretations that lead to mistrust and the banal everyday phrases that gain importance for how they are spoken rather than what is spoken.

In its adjectival form, the *Oxford English Dictionary* defines *abstract* as "relating to ideas or qualities rather than physical things" or in the more specifically artistic sense of "using colour and shapes to create an effect rather than attempting to represent real life accurately." Both definitions apply broadly to the aesthetics of tucker green's play, where dialogue takes precedence over physical processes—after the opening scene there is minimal engagement with objects or the set—and social reality is not seamlessly represented but its effect is achieved through formal means—rhythm, gaps and contradictions. When taken as a verb, *to abstract* means to "take out or remove something." This usage foregrounds the *act* of abstracting and underlines it as a process and a practice. But what exactly is this "something" being removed, and why? Louis Althusser provides an answer by giving his definition of abstraction a materialist twist and emphasising the agency involved when something is abstracted. According to his formulation,

> *every specific practice* (labor, scientific research, medicine, political struggle) *abstracts from the rest of reality in order to concentrate on transforming a part of reality.* To abstract is "to detach" a part of reality from the rest of it. Abstraction is, to begin with, this operation, and its result. The abstract is opposed to the concrete as *the part detached* from the whole is opposed to the whole. (2017, 50; italics in the original)

In this passage, Althusser makes clear that the act of abstraction does not simply entail the consideration of an entity independently of its context—as in, considering it abstractly—but involves dialectically opposing the relations between the entity and its context. This immediately counters the common-sense notion that an abstraction bears little relation to concrete, material contexts. Additionally, Althusser emphasises the capacity of abstraction to transform reality and as such rightly regards it as a powerful political process. As he notes in a wonderfully concise formulation, the "social appropriation of the concrete proceeds by way of the domination of abstract relations" (2017, 57). Neoliberal capitalism is a prominent example of this formulation in practice, where ideological hegemony serves to control material circumstances. At its core, neoliberalism is "a set of policies and beliefs about the economy," making it inextricable from the processes of capital accumulation (McDonnell 2018a, vii). As institutional structures that incessantly promote the primacy of the market above all else, neoliberalism and capitalism are so closely related today that to refer to them separately amounts to tautology. The abstractions of neoliberal capitalism, such as commodities, exploitation and surplus value, subsist, while the social reality of those who live these abstractions is subject to continuous flux and uncertainty. In order to critically account for the turmoil of this social reality, it is essential to consider the affects that may be produced by abstractions.

In this chapter, I read abstraction as an affective process that functions formally within twenty-first-century British drama. More specifically, I examine the ways in which British new writing is exploring how abstraction unsettles the grounds on which social and affective relations can be formed. My analysis focuses on two indicative examples of British new writing: tucker green's *a profoundly affectionate, passionate devotion* and Anders Lustgarten's *The Sugar-Coated Bullets of the Bourgeoisie* (2016). In these plays, abstraction is embedded into all aspects of the theatrical milieu, including the text—nomenclature, use of language—the staging and material conditions of performance and the political and ideological situations being explored. By mobilising abstraction as a theatrical tool, these plays express the negative affects—anxiety, fear—that proliferate in neoliberal capitalist societies, as well as gesture towards how spectators are well placed to proactively respond to the conditions that produce these affects.

In reading for affect and abstraction as form I take my methodological cue from Lauren Berlant, who does not equate the lives of the characters in cultural products—novels, plays, films—to the lives of real people, but notes how studying "the affective scenarios" of these works may allow scholars to identify the contours of contemporary life (2011, 9). By connecting affect to neoliberal capitalist processes in British new writing, I follow Berlant's claim that paying close attention to these affective scenarios is a "profoundly political" critical gesture (2011, 4). My argument is that, when examining the forms of affect in twenty-first-century British plays, the critical process of abstraction should be accounted for in the theatrical modes of (re)presentation.

Despite being both a hegemonic mode of sociopolitical experience in the context of neoliberal capitalism and a recurring aesthetic feature of contemporary performance, abstraction has received surprisingly little critical attention in theatre and performance studies. A primary reason for this bias is the assumption, among scholars and critics alike, that privileging the abstract in the text, the theatre event or the sociohistorical context being explored diminishes the ability of theatre to meaningfully and affectively engage spectators. For example, Michael Patterson claims that the more abstract a piece of theatre is, the further removed it becomes "from what is central to the theatrical experience: the living presence of the actor" (2016, 184). In his review of tucker green's *a profoundly affectionate, passionate devotion*, Aleks Sierz claims that the play "is too static—it fatally lacks a really satisfying story. It is the victory of the abstract over the dramatic" (2017). In short, abstraction is read by Patterson and Sierz as working against the efficacy of theatrical processes.

Alongside a mistrust of the abstract, there has been a strong disciplinary focus on materialism in recent years. An indicative example is Jen Harvie's frequently cited statement that cultural products are "always enmeshed in social, material and historical conditions" (2013, 16). While Harvie herself attends to the ways in which these conditions produce abstractions in the form of ideologies, this influential observation undoubtedly privileges the importance of the concrete and the material in the analysis of the sociopolitical effects of theatre and performance. When abstraction is considered, it is often in passing and indirectly, as a term that yields insights in particular contexts but is never subject to extended analysis itself. For example, figurations of abstraction feature in Emilie Morin's study of indeterminacy in contemporary British drama and Cristina Delgado-García's analysis of theatrical characters that eschew identity and individuality (Morin 2011; Delgado-García 2015). However, neither scholar attends to what exactly is meant by abstraction, and when the term is used its meaning is assumed rather than investigated. On the rare occasions that theatre and performance scholars have theoretically attended to abstraction as a formal aesthetic feature (Lehmann 2006) or an aspect of theatrical labour (Boyle 2017), the affective dimension inherent in the act of abstracting—abstraction as a producer of affect—has been left out of the analysis. This disciplinary bias has led to a limited conceptual understanding of abstraction and a lack of analysis concerning the ways in which abstractions are affectively woven into the material and ideological conditions that shape the making and reception of contemporary performance.

My analysis combines the analytical modes of Althusser and Brinkema, who read abstraction and affect respectively as formally embedded in cultural products and modern life. Brinkema argues that the study of affect has been too preoccupied with the "legible interiority of a character, a narrative or thematic expression" and "a mimetic instruction to a viewer" (2014, 36). Instead, she analyses how affects manifest in "duration, rhythm, absences, elisions, ruptures, gaps, and points of contradiction (ideological, aesthetic, structural, and formal)" (2014, 37). Such a reading of affect resonates with recent theorisations of abstraction, which is read by Alberto Toscano and Jamila M. H. Mascat as a process that permeates the structural and formal conditions which define our present historical moment (Toscano 2015; Mascat 2018). I argue that, instead of merely replicating the ethically problematic processes of abstraction that abound in neoliberal capitalist societies, British new writing is actively exploring how such abstraction unsettles the basis on which social and affective relations can be formed. By examining abstraction through theatrical means, tucker green and Lustgarten make tangible what Mascat calls the "social ontology of abstraction" (2018, 42), whereby abstraction is constitutive of social bonds and the body politic whilst at the same time perpetuating problematic sociocultural divisions.

Abstraction and Affect in Neoliberal Times

Before turning to the plays, I will briefly focus on the neoliberal part of the "neoliberal capitalist" pairing in order to unpack the social and affective impacts that this mode of governance entails. According to sociologist David Beer, what makes neoliberalism so powerful is its "ability to provoke uncertainty, to play with emotional and physical experience and to demarcate visions of what is worthwhile" (2016). Neoliberalism thus creates its own ideal subjects, who look to it for comfort amidst the widespread uncertainty of its social reality. Psychologists Glenn Adams et al. assert that the "primary feature of neoliberal selfways" is "a radical abstraction of self" from social and material contexts (2019, 191). In other words, freedom from constraint and the pursuit of individual interests are central among the cultural ideas, practices and values that neoliberalism privileges, regardless of the concomitant socioeconomic costs. It is important to note that this particular "abstraction of self" should not be understood as being "radical" in the sense of advocating for progressive sociopolitical change, but "radical" in the broader sense of having significant, far-reaching sociopolitical consequences. For example, this form of radical abstraction entails globalisation, which leads to the homogenisation and erasure of local characteristics and their transformation into cultural practices that are more conducive to capitalist modes of being—that is, an emphasis on fluidity, growth and movement—as well as the displacement of costs to preserve the present neoliberal sense of freedom (Adams et al. 2019, 193). Such displacement takes place spatially, where affluent communities outsource violent production practices to impoverished communities around the world, or temporally, where financial debt and ecological consequences are passed on for future generations to deal with (Adams et al. 2019, 193–94). In each case, the experience of freedom that the neoliberal system allows comes at a cost that is displaced, thus removing potential obstacles that could restrict that freedom in the here and now.

These acts of abstraction are intimately bound to our affective capacities and well-being, and in particular to the affect of anxiety. Beer goes as far as to claim that neoliberalism is "founded on the production of uncertainty and anxiety" (2016). From displacing ecological catastrophes to encouraging the ubiquity of financial debt, neoliberalism excels at creating situations that foster anxious responses. Furthermore, being engaged in precarious forms of labour—that is, labour that entails short-term, fixed-term or zero-hour contracts and nonguaranteed working hours—is often framed by neoliberalism as a form of freedom that allows individuals to creatively shape their lives. However, there is also the anxiety-ridden lived reality of such precarity, where working life is characterised by unstable and unpredictable processes. As Alex Foti notes, such precarity describes "the condition of being unable to predict one's fate or having some degree of predictability on which to build social relations and feelings of affection" (2004). The precarious forms of labour that neoliberalism privileges not only lead to anxiety due to a lack of stability and predictability, but also unsettle the grounds on which social and affective relations may be made. It is with this latter point in mind that I now turn my attention to *a profoundly affectionate, passionate devotion* to examine how anxiety and abstraction can manifest formally in contemporary theatrical contexts.

Anxiety, Abstraction and tucker green

tucker green's *a profoundly affectionate, passionate devotion* follows three couples and their unsuccessful attempts to communicate with each other. As Nicola Abram observes, failed communication has always been a recurring feature of tucker green's theatre (2014, 123). However, while the politics of tucker green's plays is often woven into the subject matter—for example, knife crime in *random*; the AIDS crisis in *stoning mary—a profoundly affectionate, passionate devotion* takes place in a contextual vacuum, and so to unpack its politics we must turn to the interpersonal relationships between the couples and their hopeless attempts to express the extent of and reasons for their communication breakdowns. The play debuted at the Royal Court's Theatre Upstairs in February 2017 and was directed by tucker green. In this production, the spectators are seated on rows of evenly spaced rotating stools, with the action taking place around them on a raised walkway which runs along the walls of the space. The set, designed by Merle Hensel, appears as a blank canvas, abstract in the purely aesthetic sense, with no identifiable objects, text, references or symbols being visible, other than the performers themselves and their chalk-drawn shapes.

The social and affective relations of tucker green's characters are drenched in abstraction. They are assigned abstract monikers, they speak in language that follows familiar everyday speech patterns but rarely conveys any specific details and their interpersonal relationships play out in a socially isolated environment. Following its debut, the play received mixed reviews, with critics commenting negatively on its abstract style and form. For example, Michael Billington states that the world of *a profoundly affectionate, passionate devotion* is devoid of any identifiable context and that the play is characterised by a "lack of specificity" (2017). It is worth quoting a passage from Billington's review in full to appreciate the extent to which he presents abstraction as an anathema to drama: "[t]he dialogues here take place in a social vacuum in which there is no reference to jobs, money, friends, neighbours or even basic geography: all the circumstantial details that determine not just who we are but that help to shape our relationships. This is life stripped of any context" (2017). Billington's argument here is unequivocal: the "social vacuum" and the lack of "circumstantial details" work against the play's ability to explore its chosen subject matter and minimise the points of meaningful connection with spectators.

Sierz is even more direct in his review, claiming that despite featuring many moving and insightful moments, tucker green's play "is too static—it fatally lacks a really satisfying story. It is the victory of the abstract over the dramatic" (2017). A broader bias against abstraction is evident in these reviews. As the Argentinian writer Jorge Luis Borges observed, "people tend to prefer the personal to the general, the concrete to the abstract" (2010, 111). Such thinking implies that the concrete gives people something they can readily grasp and relate to their own contexts and experiences, whereas the abstract appears to refer to something intangible and often irrelevant. In contrast to Billington and Sierz, I suggest it is through abstraction that the play derives its affective force. In the social vacuum of tucker green's play, the characters live through an iteration of a fundamental neoliberal capitalist process—that is, the radical abstraction of self from social and material contexts. Through this staging, the play asks two crucial questions: what is the relationship between neoliberal capitalism and abstraction at the level of personal identity? In a historical moment when the abstraction of an individual from their context is socially framed as preferable, how are interpersonal relationships supposed to proceed?

The first instance of abstraction that one comes across is the title of the play. The sentence presumably defines love—an act and a feeling that is intimately bound to a plethora of affects—but the word *love* is not actually present. As such, tucker green presents the associations of the thing without the thing itself; the thing has been abstracted from the context in question and all we—the characters and spectators—are left with is its material implications and intimations. The abstract position of love in the title extends throughout the romantic lives of the characters. For example, in part one, scene two, B says to A: "I want you beyond what I can say/ beyond what I got words for" (tucker green 2017, 10). It is tempting to read this statement as B attempting to describe the indescribable, to articulate with words an affective sensation that exceeds the bounds of the expressible. A deeper reading might draw on Abram's analysis of silence and the unsayable in tucker green's work, where the political weight of tucker green's plays is "borne by her discomforting insistence on failed communication" (2014, 123). According to Abram, dialogue that presents failed communication in tucker green's plays may be read as formally exploring the subjective experience of different traumas and injustices. In *a profoundly affectionate, passionate devotion*, the subjective experience of the characters aligns remarkably with the subjective experience inherent to neoliberal capitalist societies. A and B are abstracted from their social and material context whenever they interact and their continual failure to communicate effectively unsettles their ability to build social relations and feelings of affection. When B's statement is experienced and contextualised within the ubiquity of abstraction in neoliberal capitalism, their inability to linguistically convey love takes on a special significance. When watching the performance, I was emotionally engaged by the associations of the affect being expressed by B without the affect itself ever being named, meaning that what became moving was the removal or abstraction of an affect from its context. In other words, what tucker green stages as affective is the saturation of social relations with abstraction, where spectators watch as characters repeatedly attempt to express themselves concretely only to fall into elliptical statements that have a familiar pattern but do not convey any specifics.

Before continuing to analyse the layers of abstraction in tucker green's play, it is important to account for the complex relationship between the abstract and the concrete in the performance event, and how the impact of the latter facilitates the affective capacity of the former. While the staging and text of *a profoundly affectionate, passionate devotion* were strongly characterised by abstraction, the entire spatial construction seemed excruciatingly concrete in the physicality it implied. Everything that happened on the narrow semicircular stage was almost tangible; I felt engulfed by the action as it took place around me and by the speech that was delivered with rhythmical intensity and razor-sharp precision. This sense of concrete physicality was compounded by the uncomfortable nature of the seating. I felt palpably precarious as I perched on the small circular stool and rotated interminably to face towards the ever-shifting action. My spectatorial position reflected the precarious and indeterminate nature of meaning in the dialogue, where the act of effective communication remained possible but was never fully realised.

What are we to make of this tension between abstraction in the text and staging and the concrete experience of spectating? Through this tension, tucker green stages abstraction as an affective process that is immanent to concrete reality. To be clear, my reading of the play does not seek to impose any harmony over the dialectical opposition that Althusser notes is inherent to abstraction, but rather takes note of the fact that such an opposition between the abstract and the concrete is a constitutive aspect of social life. As Slavoj Žižek argues, "*a process of 'abstraction' is inherent to reality itself*: the tension between empirical reality and its 'abstract' notional determinations is immanent to reality, it is a feature of 'things themselves'" (2019, 351; italics in the original). In tucker green's play, it is precisely such a tension—between abstract dialogue that neither includes specifics nor develops the plot and the hyperrealistic everyday language—that defines the affective and social lives of the characters. Thus, both the spectatorial situation and the lives of the characters are characterised by this concrete-abstract tension, allowing tucker green to explore the extent that processes of abstraction are affectively woven into the concrete fabric of lived reality.

In order to examine the play's formal engagement with affect, I now turn to Brinkema's account of Sigmund Freud's psychoanalytical theory of anxiety. Brinkema traces an interesting shift in the way that Freud conceptualised anxiety in his early and later works. In his early writings, Freud thought of anxiety as being constituted by "an interruption that disturbs continuity and the completion of activity" (Brinkema 2014, 196). As such, "the negative affect [of anxiety] results from a blockage in the forward progress of energies, from movement's energy now gummed up" (Brinkema 2014, 193). According to this view, it is the interruption or the prospect of interruption that sets anxiety in motion for the subject.

In *a profoundly affectionate, passionate devotion*, examples of such interruptions are frequent, and as in Freud's theory, they are intimately bound with processes of desire, sex and love. A and B endlessly attempt to address and resolve their relationship issues but to no avail, and the "gummed up" sense of anxiety builds throughout the play. This continued failure manifests textually, as statements remain unfinished and vague. For example, in part one, scene three:

A ...When you do that thing...
B
A ...When you do that—did that (thing), that you do—did. With your thing. To me—
B with you.
A That you did a lot, to me—.
B With you.
A Thinking I liked/it.
B You liked it you did like me doin/it.
A When you did that—kept doin/that.
B That thing that you liked
A I didn't.
B
A Like it. (2017, 13)

In this passage the apprehensive interruptions take multiple forms and come one after another—the "/" indicating one character speaking over the other, the bracketed "(thing)" denoting intention rather than something spoken and the two gaps or "active silences" in the dialogue signalling where B says nothing at all (2017, 2). The anxiety unfolds as the characters are unable to effectively address the cause of their problems due to linguistic gaps, verbal repetitions and the incessant rhythm of dialogue that is characterised by interruption.

In Freud's later works, he reverses his previous formulation. Instead of anxiety resulting from an interruption, he believes it "derives from the *failure* or inability to interrupt a system" (Brinkema 2014, 196; italics in the original). In this revised formulation, movement and progress continue regardless of the subject's attempts to prevent them, and this impotence generates an anxious response. As the above scene progresses, A and B continue their syncopated interaction and anxiety begins to manifest as the incessant rhythmical speech that repeatedly interrupts itself. The characters are locked in an unresolved debate for the duration of the scene, which ends with a brief exclamation from B at the issues left unresolved: "Fuck" (2017, 15). This scene formalises the rhythm of anxiety; the verbal interruptions are sudden, intermittent, pressing, violent, and it is the inability of this movement to stop that provokes trepidation. Here it is important to recall the moment on which the play opened: a performer drawing a horizontal line with chalk that is then interrupted. Part one, scene three mimics the structure of the preceding chalk line, where the incessant intermittency of anxiety is staged and formalised.

To grasp the connection between this formal engagement with anxiety and processes of abstraction, it is useful to consider the subject's potential responses to anxiety. Freud outlines two acts of repression that occur in response to a traumatic event: "*undoing what has been done* and *isolating*" (1960, 33; italics in the original). The former involves a repetition of the event, which normalises it and attempts to remove the trauma from the event. In tucker green's play, this repetition takes a self-referential form, as what is repeated again and again by the characters—the attempt to communicate with a loved one—entails both the potential resolution and cause of the anxiety. In relation to abstraction, however, it is the act of isolating that holds more relevance. In response to an unpleasant or traumatic event, Freud claims that the traumatised subject "interpolates an interval during which nothing further must happen—during which he [*sic*] must perceive nothing and do nothing" (1960, 47). Thus, the traumatic event "is deprived of its affect, and its associative connections are suppressed or interrupted so that it remains isolated and is not reproduced in the ordinary processes of thought" (1960, 47). This act of isolating a traumatic occurrence, of briefly removing it from its context, is an act of abstraction. Such an act occurs in tucker green's play on both a macro level, with the abstract environment in which the temporal rhythms of anxiety play out, and a micro level, with the intervals that tucker green regularly inserts into the dialogue via the active silences of A and B.

It is in these acts of isolation that spectators formally encounter the cause of anxiety—neoliberal capitalism. If the primary feature of the neoliberal capitalist subjective experience is a radical abstraction of the self from its social and material context (Adams et al. 2019, 191), then the characters in tucker green's play are formal embodiments of these radically abstracted selves. While *a profoundly affectionate, passionate devotion* does not represent affect as causally related to neoliberal capitalism, the play formally enacts the structure of affect as it manifests within these specific sociopolitical conditions—within which, at present, spectators in the UK experience the play. This formal engagement makes tangible what Mascat terms the "social ontology of abstraction" where, in contemporary neoliberal capitalist societies, abstraction "constructs social bonds, builds up society and sustains the very structure of the body politic" (2018, 42). As tucker green's play makes clear, abstraction is a process that is woven into the affective scenarios that we live through on a daily basis.

Fear, Abstraction and Anders Lustgarten

Alongside anxiety, fear is an affect that is also closely bound to the lived experience of neoliberal capitalism. From the fear caused by social oppression to the fear of exploitation via precarious labour, neoliberal capitalism thrives on the production of fear via "hyper-individualised" selves abstracted from their social context (Wrenn 2014, 337). Despite often being deeply embroiled with past events and experiences, the primary temporal mode of fear is prospective. Fear can be characterised as a feeling or sensation that something unpleasant or harmful might happen or might have happened. Sociologist David Altheide offers a description that encompasses the formal operation of fear as an affective force: "Fear rests on the borders between expectations and realizations, between hope and reality" (2002, 26). Altheide's two-part definition highlights two different tensions inherent to fear. The first is temporal, where negative futures—"expectations"—and the lived present—"realizations"—threaten to coalesce. The second is ontological and concerns the relationship between the abstract—"hope"—and the concrete—"reality." In this section, I focus on two scenes where fear is staged in Lustgarten's *The Sugar-Coated*

Bullets of the Bourgeoise, and I explore how these scenes are dependent on a novel use of abstraction. Continuing my focus on the formal manifestations of affect, I do not pay attention to moments where something scary or frightening is portrayed on stage but instead analyse moments when the structure of fear is staged.

Written by Lustgarten and directed by Steven Atkinson, *The Sugar-Coated Bullets of the Bourgeoise* debuted at London's Arcola Theatre in 2016. The play vividly depicts the journey of a fictional Chinese village from feudalism to collectivism via the establishment of the People's Republic of China in 1949 and then transitions abruptly to 2016 and explores the integration of neoliberal capitalism into the village's contemporary communist society. Throughout the play, political ideologies clash tragically with material conditions and processes of abstraction are shown to be intimately connected with affective outcomes. In the final scene of part one, there is a section that overtly echoes Bertolt Brecht's epic theatre in both its impulse and its realisation. The scene opens with an atmosphere of starvation and desolation in the village of Rotten Peach. Almost all the trees that populated previous scenes are gone and scrap metal can be seen strewn across the stage. A character called Horseface is busy slaughtering the few remaining emaciated sheep in an attempt to source some food. Then the decaying stillness is suddenly disrupted by the sound of approaching trucks and two communist party officers, Xu and Stocky Jiao, run on carrying sacks of grain. These sacks are piled up and up until there is a huge mound on stage, while the confused villagers look on. Shortly afterwards Chairman Mao arrives on a surprise tour of the provinces to discover how their grain production is progressing. Mao observes the impoverished situation alongside the abundance of grain and becomes suspicious. After questioning the villagers and local officials as to whether they did indeed produce the huge pile of grain, only Tang, a local official, speaks: "It's not their grain. They've been starving here for months. The province requisitioned too much and they planted what was left too close and the harvest failed. And the people feel like they've failed, like it's all their fault, like—" (Lustgarten 2016, 59). Mao then asks the villagers if there is any truth to what Tang says, as "only the people can sort it out" (59). After a silence, Horseface and Lotus Blossom claim "*with guilt and reluctance*" that they did indeed produce the grain and that Tang is lying (60). Tang is arrested and Mao believes what he is told: "You've restored my faith in what we're trying to achieve" (61). As soon as Mao is driven off, Stocky Jiao and Xu reveal what is now to happen to the grain:

STOCKY JIAO: Where's he going next?
XU: Big Pickle.
STOCKY JIAO: Gives us half an hour.
XU: If we take the valley short cut, we can get it there in time. (*To peasants*) Oi, lazy fuckers, grab a bag and take them to the trucks! (61)

The same bags of grain are removed and taken to the next village on Mao's tour, so that he never becomes cognisant of the fact that the revolution is failing and the people are starving.

In this scene, Lustgarten stages a startling contradiction between the abstract and the concrete, as political ideologies jar disastrously with material conditions. The scene is rife with fear, from Mao's fear that the revolution is failing, to Xu and Stocky Jiao's fear that Mao will discover the revolution is failing, to the fear that causes the villagers to remain silent when questioned by Mao. Frank Furedi suggests that "public fears are rarely expressed in response to any specific event. Rather, the politics of fear captures a sensibility towards life in general" (2004). Such an abstract politics of fear is evident in this scene, where fear permeates the fabric of all the characters' outlooks and actions. The fear of a political ideology being revealed as flawed and failing dominates the choices made by both the party officials and the villagers. The characters are willing to do whatever it takes in concrete, material terms to uphold the truth of the abstraction; the reality is altered to fit with the unrealisable hopes and expectations. In this scene, Lustgarten vividly stages the abstract appropriation of social-material conditions via the domination of abstract relations.

The use of grain in this scene formalises the close-knit relationship between fear and abstraction. The fear results from a discrepancy between abstract expectations—the unrealistic grain production target—and concrete realisations—the lack of grain produced by the village. It is sustained by a process of abstraction, where a part of reality—the same grain moving from village to village—has been abstracted from the rest of reality—those who have produced the grain. In this scene, abstraction and fear are formally inextricable from one another. As in tucker green's play, the "social ontology of abstraction" is revealed, where abstraction is constitutive of social bonds while also generating problematic contradictions (Mascat 2018, 42). Lustgarten understands that the insidious beauty of abstract processes is that they do not have to be understood as such to have a concrete effect, and to render these processes visible is to contextualise their effects. Thus, Lustgarten embeds abstraction into the material conditions of his play, revealing the violent operation of ideology as a form of abstraction in the historical context of the Chinese communist revolution.

In the chronology of the play, a bold and critical move immediately follows the grain scene. Part two fast forwards in time to 2016 via "*a blitz of images of contemporary China*," including neon signs, high-speed trains and glimpses of "*Pudong, the space-age 'capitalist realist' suburb of Shanghai*" (62). The formal entanglement of affect and abstraction in the previous scene is immediately transposed to the context of neoliberal capitalism, and we see how the sociopolitical system that was feared in the communist era has now been integrated into contemporary Chinese society. Part two comments on the neoliberal capitalist-communist hybrid of China today, featuring an abundance of political satire and references to China's complex relations with Europe and the US. In the new context of 2016, the village of Rotten Peach is under threat from lawyers who are intent on rezoning the land "into a cutting edge business facility" (73). In order to prevent this from happening, Lotus Blossom comes up with an idea to bring publicity and tourists to the village: "a Chairman Mao impersonation competition" (84).

In the world of Lustgarten's play, as soon as neoliberal capitalism rears its ideological head, anxiety returns to the formal fold. In the appearance of multiple Mao impersonators, there are indications of Freud's two responses to anxiety, the acts of repetition and isolation. The singular Chairman Mao of the first part, a key figure in the imposition of fear, has now multiplied into four different Maos in part two—three Mao impersonators taking part in the competition, one Mao impersonator being interrogated by the police. As a means of addressing the cause of their anxiety—the village being sold to developers—Lotus Blossom uses an act of repetition to address the cause of the problem. This act of repetition is also an act of isolation, of abstracting Mao from the grand dominance of his historical position and inserting an interval into an ever-moving system that resists interruptions—the ever-expanding growth of capital, as represented by the lawyers. In this interval, proceedings are far removed from fear and anxiety, as can be seen in the amusing exchanges between the impersonators as they prepare for the competition:

MAO 1: This is a Xiangtan accent. That was Mao's accent.

MAO 2: I know that was Mao's accent. But that's not a Xiangtan accent. This is a Xiangtan accent.

MAO 1: No it's not. This is a Xiangtan accent, I looked it up on YouTube. (2016, 90; italics in the original)

The apparent lack of anxiety in this scene reveals it as an interval that attempts to deal with the rhythms of anxiety, which in turn result from the conditions of neoliberal capitalism that permeate contemporary China. A key distinction to note in this scene is that, with Lotus Blossom's initiating the Mao impersonation competition, an act of abstraction has been initiated by a character. By multiplying Mao and isolating him from his context, Lotus Blossom is fighting fire with fire, the abstract—social appropriation of social-material conditions via the domination of abstract relations—with the abstract. Thus, the abstract, like affect, is shown to be both a structural phenomenon as well as something that can be grasped and utilised by an individual. This adds another facet to our understanding of the social ontology of abstraction; the mode through which problematic sociocultural divisions are sustained may also be the mode through which those living through the divisions may respond to them.

ABSTRACTION AS AN AFFECTIVE PROCESS

The Sugar-Coated Bullets of the Bourgeoise and *a profoundly affectionate, passionate devotion* render palpable the fear and anxiety that proliferate in neoliberal capitalist societies. Through experiencing an intermingling of abstraction and affect, the spectator is placed in a position where affective states and emotional understanding are directly linked to sociopolitical processes via structural and formal means. As soon as the relationship between the personal and the political has been formalised in this way, a certain capacity for action has been engaged. This is not to say that spectators will inevitably be provoked to radical political action after going to see these plays, but rather that the plays gesture towards how well-placed spectators are to proactively respond to the sociopolitical conditions that surround them. Both plays stage abstraction not as an aesthetic state but as a process, or an "operation" as Althusser terms it. Furthermore, the radical abstraction of self that neoliberal capitalism fervently promotes is shown by tucker green and Lustgarten to be a process that shapes and dictates our everyday social relations—where there is abstraction, there is affect. The emphasis on abstraction as an affective process highlights how the process of abstracting can be initiated, modified and experimented upon by participating subjects. The stakes of this emphasis are substantial because as Delgado-García has shown, theatre is well equipped to "redefine subjectivity and intersubjective relations towards positive social change" (2015, 13). With regard to abstraction and its hegemonic ubiquity in neoliberal capitalism, a crucial step towards positive social change is to grasp how abstraction is intimately bound to agency and social processes.

As these two plays demonstrate, British new writing is actively exploring how abstraction unsettles the grounds on which social and affective relations can be formed. Both Lustgarten and tucker green's characters find themselves immersed in dramatic worlds where affects are abstract; anxiety and fear permeate the formal structures that these characters live through. As my analysis has made clear, the study of abstraction should not be limited to cultural products that appear superficially abstract. In a historical moment where abstraction is thoroughly engrained into the sociopolitical climate, scholars would do well to question and probe the limits and potentials of abstraction. By presenting abstraction as an affective process that functions formally, twenty-first-century British playwrights are asking, in terms of both affect and activity, how does abstraction move us?

References

Abram, Nicola. 2014. "Staging the Unsayable: debbie tucker green's Political Theatre." *Journal of Contemporary Drama in English* 2 (1): 113–30.

Adams, Glenn et al. 2019. "The Psychology of Neoliberalism and the Neoliberalism of Psychology." *Journal of Social Issues* 75 (1): 189–216.

Altheide, David L. 2002. *Creating Fear: News and the Construction of Crisis.* Hawthorne, NY: Aldine de Gruyter.

Althusser, Louis. 2017. *Philosophy for Non-Philosophers.* Translated by G.M. Goshgarian. London: Bloomsbury.

Beer, David. 2016. "Is Neoliberalism Making You Anxious? Metrics and the Production of Uncertainty." *London School of Economics and Political Science: British Politics and Policy* (blog), May 24. Accessed October 28, 2019.

Berlant, Lauren. 2011. *Cruel Optimism.* Durham, NC and London: Duke UP.

Billington, Michael. 2017. "*a profoundly affectionate*... Review—Couples' Rows are Painful to Watch." *Guardian*, March 7. Accessed November 27, 2019.

Borges, Jorge Luis. 2010. *The Perpetual Race of Achilles and the Tortoise.* Translated by Esther Allen, Suzanne Jill Levine and Eliot Weinberger. London: Penguin.

Boyle, Michael Shane. 2017. "Performance and Value: The Work of Theatre in Karl Marx's Critique of Political Economy." *Theatre Survey* 58 (1): 3–23.

Brinkema, Eugenie. 2014. *The Forms of the Affects*. Durham, NC and London: Duke UP.

Delgado-García, Cristina. 2015. *Rethinking Character in Contemporary British Theatre: Aesthetics, Politics, Subjectivity*. Berlin and Boston: De Gruyter.

Foti, Alex. 2004. "Precarity and N/European Identity: (An Interview with Alex Foti (Chainworkers))." By Merijn Oudenampsen and Gavin Sullivan. *Mute* 1 (28). Accessed October 20, 2019.

Freud, Sigmund. 1960. *Inhibitions, Symptoms, and Anxiety*. Translated by Alix Strachey and edited by James Strachey. New York: W. W. Norton.

Furedi, Frank. 2004. "The Politics of Fear." *frankfuredi.com*, October 28. Accessed November 12, 2019.

Harvie, Jen. 2013. *Fair Play: Art, Performance and Neoliberalism*. Basingstoke and New York: Palgrave Macmillan.

Lehmann, Hans-Thies. 2006. *Postdramatic Theatre*. Translated by Karen Jürs-Munby. London and New York: Routledge.

Lustgarten, Anders. 2016. *The Sugar-Coated Bullets of the Bourgeoisie*. London: Bloomsbury.

Mascat, Jamila M.H. 2018. "Hegel and the Advent of Modernity: A Social Ontology of Abstraction." *Radical Philosophy* 2 (1): 29–46.

McDonnell, John. 2018a. "Introduction." In McDonnell 2018b, vii–xviii.

———, ed. 2018b. *Economics for the Many*. London: Verso.

Morin, Emilie. 2011. "'Look Again': Indeterminacy and Contemporary British Drama." *New Theatre Quarterly* 27 (1): 71–85.

Patterson, Michael. 2016. *The Revolution in German Theatre 1900–1933*. London and New York: Routledge.

Sierz, Aleks. 2017. "*a profoundly affectionate, passionate devotion to someone (-noun)*, Royal Court Theatre." *Arts Desk*, March 7. Accessed September 9, 2019.

Toscano, Alberto. 2015. "The Detour of Abstraction." *Diacritics* 43 (2): 68–90.

tucker green, debbie. 2017. *a profoundly affectionate, passionate devotion to someone (-noun)*. London: Nick Hern Books.

Wrenn, Mary V. 2014. "The Social Ontology of Fear and Neoliberalism." *Review of Social Economy* 72 (3): 337–53.

Žižek, Slavoj. 2019. *Sex and the Failed Absolute*. London: Bloomsbury.

PART III

Affects and Hope: From Crisis to Utopian Feelings

CHAPTER 10

Vibrant Materials: Affective Arrangements, the Allure of Glamour and Architexture(s) in Penelope Skinner's *Eigengrau* and Mike Bartlett's *Game*

Martin Middeke

Introduction: Affective Arrangements, Intensity, Vibrancy and Intra-action

In what follows, affect will be understood as relational. That is, I am not primarily interested in individual mental or emotional states, their meaning or function, but in the transpersonal dynamics from which affects emanate. Analysing such transpersonal affective relationality implies examining environments, situations, arrays or social, historical, cultural as well as aesthetic setups that involve both human and nonhuman actants and their mutual potential of affecting and being affected. Drawing on Bruno Latour, actants—no matter whether human or nonhuman—can actively affect and

M. Middeke (✉)
University of Augsburg, Augsburg, Germany

University of Johannesburg, Johannesburg, South Africa
e-mail: martin.middeke@uni-a.de

M. Aragay et al. (eds.), *Affects in 21st-Century British Theatre*,
https://doi.org/10.1007/978-3-030-58486-3_10

change the course of things.[1] In this context, the German philosopher Jan Slaby and his team have introduced the term *affective arrangement* and thereby highlighted "an angle to focus on the ways in which putatively 'transpersonal' affect unfolds in the sites and settings of social life" (2019, 3–4). According to Slaby et al., affective arrangements have a heterogeneous character involving a wide range of physical materials in their affective dynamics. In this, and importantly for the study of theatre, human beings encounter and collide with things, objects, spaces, places, behaviours, language and discourses. What has to be investigated, therefore, in the study of affective arrangements is the physical tonality, atmosphere and suspense that emanate from such encounters, collisions and, especially, disruptions.

Building on Baruch Spinoza, Brian Massumi denominates *affect* as two different capacities of the human body that always go together: a capacity for affecting and for being affected (2015, 4). Affect, for Massumi, always entails movement, change and transition. He equates affect with "intensity," as he, like Slaby et al., goes beyond an understanding of affect as "personal feeling" or "'emotion' in the everyday sense" (2015, 3). Intensity is created by the transition—Massumi speaks of the crossing of a "threshold" (2015, 4)—from one affective state to another by the changing capacity of being affected. In his epoch-making essay "What Are Affects?," Silvan Tomkins, one of the founding voices of affect studies, juxtaposes ranges of positive (interest/excitement; enjoyment/joy), negative (distress/anguish; fear/terror; shame/humiliation; contempt/disgust; anger/rage) and resetting affects (surprise/startle) (1995, 74). Following Massumi, I suggest these ranges may best be analysed in terms of their relational and contextual incurrences rather than trying to identify them in solely personal, subjective instances. Methodologically, in this line of thought—which builds on the philosophical tradition of Spinoza, Friedrich Nietzsche, Henri Bergson and Gilles Deleuze/Félix Guattari—affect and emotion are not looked upon as mutually exclusive. Neither are affect and cognition, because the capacity of affecting and being affected also refers to the potential aggrandisement or diminishing of a body's capacity for calculated action, conscious engagement or rational connection emerging from an atmosphere of intensity, aliveness and vitality (Clough 2007, 1–2). Massumi makes clear that the contrast between emotion and affect is a solely pragmatic one: focusing on emotion entails applying oneself to personal or collective perspectives of articulated self-understanding with regard to bodily states such as, for instance, fear or shame, while the focus on affect illuminates the relational and dynamic situatedness of such emotions (see also Slaby et al. 2019, 59). For Robert Seyfert, "affects do not 'belong' to anybody" (2012, 27); rather, they are attributable to human as well as nonhuman bodies as they appear as interactions between bodies. Whether or not, in this context, affect and conscious experience are mutually dependent insofar as there is also a backflow from cognition to (new) affect is of less importance than the phenomenological rationale that affective intensity is always changing, changeable, mobile and thus ever potentially interacting with conscious thought. The affect/cognition threshold is, therefore, "contingent upon the state one happens to be in—[...] comparable to Spinoza's concept of affect (*affectus*)" as the "felt idea" (Houen 2020a, 6) of the transition from one affective state to another. Massumi, in this context, speaks of "thinking-feeling" when he describes the vitality effect inherent in every vision, "a thinking of perception in perception, the immediacy of its occurrence as it is felt" (2008). "Affect as a whole, then," he maintains elsewhere, "is the virtual co-presence of potentials" (2015, 5). In other words, a single, particular emotion can never entirely capture the dynamic impact of events, experiences, expressions, impressions and feelings:

> [W]hen we feel a particular emotion or think a particular thought, where have all the other memories, habits, tendencies gone that might have come at the point? And where have the bodily capacities for affecting and being affected that they're inseparable from gone? There's no way they can all be actually expressed at any given point. But they're not totally absent either, because a different selection of them is sure to come up at the next step. They're still there, but virtually—in potential. (Massumi 2015, 5)

I suggest that Massumi's concept of affect-as-intensity-as-potential comes very close to what Jane Bennett conceives of as the *vibrancy* of matter. Affects, for Bennett, constitute a vital materiality, that is, a tangible corporeality that "runs alongside and inside humans" (2010, viii) as a physical force of things in the process of their being encountered. If affective arrangements testify to the relational character of affect, then the study of such arrangements—in reality as much as in the theatre—entails the study of the alliance of human as well as nonhuman actants (Bennett 2010, ix). From this perspective, nonhuman objects and artefacts are not just seen as dead objects, but as vibrant matter. Bennett points out that the ignorance of the full affective range of nonhuman powers only hints at human hubris and destructive tendencies. In tune with Bennett's view,

Karen Barad replaced the term *interaction* by *intra-action* in order to emphasise that agency is not an inherent individual or human property, but rather a dynamism of forces (2007, 141). Affect, again, is configured here as a decisively dynamic, relational and, especially, transpersonal category *unfolding between intra-acting bodies* whose potentials are repeatedly being modified in their affective arrays (Massumi 2002; Rouse 2002; Hurley 2010; Gregg and Seigworth 2010; Slaby et al. 2019, 5).

In what follows, I examine the characterisation of affective arrangements in the two plays I turn to—Penelope Skinner's *Eigengrau* (2010) and Mike Bartlett's *Game* (2015)—and, thus, the way both plays and their intra-actions (re)configure the dynamic relatedness of affect in terms of intensity and vibrancy. As will become apparent, I argue that from the point of view of theatre aesthetics, affect is created by the interrelatedness of physical material that includes both the arrangement of theatrical and performative space as well as the linguistic and spatial/material arrangement of text. With regard to one-sided tendencies in theatre/performance studies whose emergence often tended to be supported by an often wilful repudiation of textual aspects, I would very much like to emphasise and indeed (re)claim that the study of affective arrangements in playwright's theatre—that is, the analysis of dynamic, modulating bodily encounters of human and nonhuman objects/materials/matter on the stage and on the page—must address the affective (read: bodily) constituents of both stage/performance and page/text and their immediate impact. Text and performance are indeed mutually dependent, interlinked aspects of the physicality of both plays at issue. If, as has been stated so far, affect can be equated with intensity and vibrancy and, furthermore, if emotion is viewed as "qualified intensity" (Massumi 2002, 27), an analysis of affective arrangements has to address what it is that "qualifies" intensity: semantic questions, narrative and plotlines, functions and meanings of actions as well as images. More important, however, with regard to affect are those aspects that *resist* such qualifications. Affect, I shall argue, becomes tangible in what resists/disturbs/disrupts narrativisation, recognition, semantics and semiotic attributions of function and meaning. Affect becomes vibrant matter in that it is more than an emotional state and, particularly, in that it creates something that is not static, but dynamic and disruptive. Studying affect in performance and text thus implies identifying *suspense*, *disruption* and *narrative noise* rather than cohesion.

In what follows, I will trace the intra-actions of characters and material objects in *Eigengrau* and *Game* and contextualise them within the framework of genre questions. The affective allure of matter, the vibrancy of objects, will be elaborated on by using the example of glamour. Both the allure inherent in glamour and genre frames rely on affective arrangements. This explains why affective arrangements are also based on a dynamics of expectation/satisfaction/frustration that unpredictably entails the entire spectrum of affective response ranging from fascination to nausea. Suspense, therefore, is always interlinked with expectation, so that the language of an event and the language of an image of this event coalesce: that is to say, no matter whether an image satisfies or frustrates an expectation, it has an affective potential beyond its semiotic or semantic function or meaning.

My affective reading of both plays counters the observation that an interpretative attempt to read meaning into actions, events or images blots out or at least obscures affective expression by turning to the physical materiality of both performative and textual setups in both plays. The intensity and vibrancy of both plays will be detected by looking at the physical/material sides of both performance and text, what I would call their architecture(s) as well as their *architexture(s)*, which I understand as the planning, constructing and designing of both structure and texture. *Textures* obviously refer to the sheer physicality of the spatial arrangements of theatre space or the bodily aspects of performance and performativity involved in the affective array of a play. But textures also pertain to the material relief of texts, that is, the bodily protrusions of material from the flat background of the page, the differences elevated from the surface of the linear progression of printed words on paper and the material embossings or topographies of written language. Obviously, there is a physical side to text and textuality—the array of words on a page, their order, positioning, regulation, character or type-face, punctuation, vocabulary, and so on. An analysis of affect understood as relational bodily impact and intensity will have to pay attention to such material manifestations of staging, writing and text in order to identify the plays' architextures.

Object Intra-action, the Allure of Glamour and the Transversality of Affect

Skinner's *Eigengrau* and Bartlett's *Game* are plays of the affective turn. The true protagonists of both plays are not their individual characters or human actants, but their affective arrangements and intra-actions. I shall argue that the intensities and vibrancy of the human/nonhuman/object intra-actions in both plays make it the spectator's and reader's task to process the physical impact of these intensities and, ultimately, to make these experiential processes evolve into ever-further thinking-feeling of new and changing/modulating affects and reflections on sensitivities and situations (Birke 2019, 91). Neither play foregrounds the mental attitudes of its "characters." As a matter of fact, neither play features a single "round character" with an elaborate psychology, a complex psychological development or motivation or a potential for change. The characters are so (stereo)type-like and so static, that none of them seems to stand a chance of being considered an avenue "to foster good ethical capacities" (Houen 2020a, 5) or elicit even a touch of empathy on the part of the spectator.[2] Neither play, in sum, places emotional content over literary form, genre or style (Van Alphen 2008, 22).

Directed by Polly Findlay, Skinner's *Eigengrau* was premiered at the Bush Theatre on March 10, 2010. Paul Taylor called the play "a black comedy about the penalties of living in an apparently post-feminist, Facebook and Gumtree-centred society" (2010, 285). Henry Hitchings wrote in the *Evening Standard* that the play constituted a "sideways look at the dislocation, untruths and feverish excitements of modern dating and mating" (2010, 285). Lyn Gardner's impression that the play enacts "an urban fairytale about a generation with nothing left to believe in while adrift in the big city" (2010, 286) is a perceptive hint at the glamourous genre *Eigengrau* is drawing from: romantic comedy and its Hollywood-like conceptions of love.[3] True to the affective arrangement of romcoms, the character configuration of the play is simple and typified: Mark is the smart, yet clichédly manipulative, callous "marketing guy" (Skinner 2010, 5), while his flatmate Tim is little more than an unambitious "fat bloke" (5) who is unsuccessfully coping with the death of his grandmother, looking to love and be loved. Cassie is a "feminist activist" (5), while her flatmate Rose, whom she found via a classified ads website, is a naïve "believer" (5) fascinated by mystical horoscopes and other "New Age nonsense" (Marlowe 2010, 287). The shallow love plotline on the surface of the play meanders around Rose and Mark's "meet cute" and the various complications and obstacles ensuing from this. In order to support the affective arrangement of the romcom course of love that she is convinced her own life should be taking, Rose vividly recalls that first meeting:

> Me and Mark have the most amazing *how we met* story ever. I was having a falafel and he was on the nearby table and I started telling him about numerology and he was really interested. And then we made friends on Facebook and he sent me this message saying how he'd Googled it and actually it's totally amazing like
>
> Just stuff he'd never thought about before and didn't realise was out there? (72; italics in the original)

This, however, turns out to be nothing but an illusion, as Mark does not only show no further interest in Rose after having coaxed her into casual sex, but also makes a move on Cassie, who at first sharply rebuffs him, but then falls for his charms and subsequently feels guilty about the ambivalence she senses is inherent in being a feminist and at the same time longing, as it happens, for rough sex. Mark talks her around by faking his feminist interest whilst ostentatiously carrying a copy of Germaine Greer's *The Female Eunuch* ([1970] 2006). Their relationship is abruptly brought to an end when she finds out that his sympathy is nothing but a scam. The affective arrangement of the romcom idea of true love includes the "happily ever after" at the end, which in *Eigengrau* is hinted at in the budding relationship between Rose and Tim as well as in Cassie's pregnancy. Rose's concluding statement, "[i]sn't this a happy ending though? I mean me and Tim. In love. Moving in together. You having a baby. It's all so perfect" (114), however, is still a sign of utter naivety and delusion about love and, hence, carries thoroughly satirical undertones.

In contrast to the elements of light comedy in *Eigengrau*, the genre setting for Bartlett's *Game*, which was premiered at the Almeida Theatre on February 23, 2015, and directed by Sacha Wares, is dystopia, which implies a tinge of the hyperbolic in its satirical reckoning with a cataclysmic decline in society fostered by mass consumption. The play centres around a young couple, Carly and Ashley, who are living at her mother's home as they are unable to buy or rent a place of their own. The play opens when they are about to look over a luxury apartment, a veritable "dream-home" (Shuttleworth 2015, 286), which they are offered for signing a business contract. This contract equals a Mephistophelean pact as their dream home is a Big Brother place not only spied into by strangers, but for which rich, bored customers pay an entrance fee, watch the couple and eventually shoot them with tranquilliser darts, turning Carly and Ashley literally into (a) game—in the sense of both pastime and hunting—for the punters. The deal incited Christopher Hart to link the play intermedially to such films as *Predator* (McTiernan 1987) or *The Hunger Games* (Ross 2012) (2015, 206). In the opening scene of the play, Ashley and Carly are marvelling at the apartment, while John, the owner of the business, is showing David, a former (traumatised) army veteran, the hides for the punters before hiring him as the suitable supervisor of the game.

However different *Eigengrau* and *Game* may be as regards genre, both plays share their affective arrangement of allure. Both plays also give evidence of the utter intensity and vibrancy of matter and, thus, of the physical nature of all affects, as they create worlds that make subject/object intra-action coalesce and indeed blur the threshold between the immaterial and the material, between alive and not alive. Both plays reveal the transversality of affect (Massumi 2015, x) as they show how an object world can come alive and how, at the same time, individuals can become thoroughly thing-like (Thrift 2010, 296). The affective arrangements of both plays address such category crossing in various ways, exemplifying not only that affect is about intensity of feeling, but also that the quality of glamour is "a key imaginary in producing allure" (Thrift 2010, 297). Both plays affectively expound that the glamour of objects and its allure turn their characters' bodies into "target practice" (Boles 2018, 59). For instance, Rose in *Eigengrau* is actually scripting her own romcom allure as she tries to win Mark back after he has dropped her, turning herself and Mark into actants of this glamourous game and stating "I know if I believe it hard enough then Mark will love me" (76). "Love" and "sex" as desired objects spring from a vibrant affective arrangement of daydreams, fantasies and alternative worlds denoting a purely imaginary realm in which everything seems possible and attainable (Thrift 2010, 298). Seducing Mark to win him back is, therefore, affectively scripted or arranged by Rose as a glamourous intra-action that turns herself and Mark into object-like intra-actants.

Critics have hinted at the housing crisis as the main subject matter of Bartlett's *Game* (see, most relevantly, Boles 2018 and Birke 2019). Undoubtedly, this is an important sociopolitical frame for the play, but I would like to shift attention to the affinity between what is at work in the play and what Nigel Thrift identified as "the three cultural pillars" of glamour—the object effect, the capacity to create alternative versions of oneself and calculation (2010, 298)—and their transversal intra-action. Firstly, the object effect of Carly and Ashley's new home is the product of daydreams and fantasies; secondly, the object of the "home" is capable of creating alternative versions of the characters; and thirdly, glamour entails calculation, "a willing acceptance of manipulation through 'fake' feeling" (Thrift 2010, 299). For the affective arrangement of glamour, it does not matter at all how "fake" this feeling may be; objects still appear as vibrant intra-actants to the characters. Carly and Ashley's world is interspersed with such lifestyle objects and goods as the high-tech kitchen, its granite worktops, soft-close drawers, induction hub, special pans, hot tub, car, shiny bedroom, big-screen TV, PS4, asparagus, special underwear, iPad, getting a tan, money and eventually going on holiday (7–8, 10–11, 12, 15). All of these nonhuman actants actively create a "world of virtual self-reference" (Thrift 2010, 298) for Carly and Ashley that is as isolated as the "home" situation itself, which is peered into by the punters. At the same time, for both Carly and Ashley, the nonhuman actants allow for material potentials—glamourous special versions of themselves, as it were—that would otherwise seem entirely out of their reach and that, therefore, both of them fall for all too eagerly: "We just have to sign up," says Carly, "we just have to say yes. It's a big thing" (13).

Duration, Disruption and Textures

Given the stereotypical, all in all trivial and, as we shall see, ultimately even resultless character developments in the plotlines of both plays, it seems more than worth interrogating the affective arrangements at work in the intra-action of stage, text, audience and reader that both plays display. The intensities and indeed the fascinatingly gripping effects of both plays are grounded in an aesthetics of affective disruption, in which suspense is created by the relentless challenging of audience/reader expectation. The enactment of a (male) fantasy in *Eigengrau*, for instance, when Rose is on her knees in front of Mark as she lures him into sex, makes the harmless romcom atmosphere of light-hearted humour scatter into pornographic details that are entirely foreign to the genre. Characteristically, it is *not* primarily the cognitive or allegorical *meaning* of the words that Rose uses to lure Mark into sex with her that creates the disruption for the audience and the reader from the romcom frame that has been set up so far, but indeed the *affect* inherent in the sheer, crude materiality of the texture of the words she uses when "a blonde girl comes round" and "offers to *suck* [his] *cock*" (85; italics in the original). This impression continues through both the physicality of the following printed words on the page as well as the graphic visual image that we read or look at, which creates "five minutes of sexual and psychological abjection" (Shore 2010, 286):

> *She takes his dick out. Starts sucking it.*
> *[…]*
> *It seems to go on for an uncomfortably long time.*
> *At last, with a small grunt, Mark comes. Rose sits back. She looks at him, makes a big point of swallowing.* (86)

Intensity is obviously created here as a nonlinear process of duration that rests, very much in Massumi's vein, on "resonation and feedback that momentarily suspend the linear progress of the narrative present from past to future" (Massumi 2002, 26). The crucial word in the stage direction just quoted is, of course, "uncomfortably"—the scene goes on for an *uncomfortably* long time. It is not the meaning of the word that counts, neither the structure of the narrative it relates to, but the vibrancy of the texture, the intensity of the body of the word—its physical impact and its affective potential which, eventually, may be qualified by the reader/spectator thoroughly unpredictably going through the entire arsenal of emotional states that Tomkins conceived of, ranging from (voyeuristic) interest, excitement and surprise to shame, contempt and even disgust (Tomkins 1995, 74; see also Menninghaus [1999] 2002). Texture is "tangible as well as […] visible and/or audible" as it "refers to the surface quality of a text" (Reinfandt 2016, 219). When Rose, after performing the—from her perspective—glamourous act of oral sex on Mark, thanks him "for giving me another chance" (87), the affective threshold to utter embarrassment on the part of readers/spectators may well have been crossed already, but this is immediately outstripped by Mark when he tells her straight after his ejaculation that "I'm seeing someone. Else. *Beat.* Another girl. Sorry. I should have said before" (87), upon which Rose is physically sick:

> *She gets off him. Bends double.*
> […]
> *She is sick. It is mainly come.*
> […]
> *He exits.*
> *Rose stares.*
> *He comes back with a cloth. It's kind of useless. He loiters near the sick but can't touch it.*
> […]
> *She takes the cloth and starts to unwipe.*
> MARK: It makes me (gag) just
> *She cleans.*
> Fuck.

There is a small pause.
She finishes cleaning. (88–89)

Both on stage and on the page, Skinner creates intensity here: intensity-as-texture, a physical as well as a graphic image, a bodily form, the impact of which is distinguished from, but at the same time interlinked with, audience/reader expectation. It is related to structure and qualified emotion, but not logically connected to it. As a matter of fact, there is no more logic in this act and its visual/textual representation than there is logic in, for instance, the coolness factor of fashion. In both cases, affect exists alone in its material intensity. What Skinner makes clear is that affects imply approaches to such stage and/or textual images that go beyond the interpretative levels of semiotics and semantics. Texture as material embodiment of affect highlights the fact that approaches to stage and/or textual images in their *relation* to language are incomplete if they are restricted to a level of meaning and structure that is defined in a purely linguistic or even ideological fashion—a casual jab at gender stereotypes on Skinner's part notwithstanding. It is texture really that corroborates Massumi's postulation that the physical *expression* of an event must not be lost to a search for meaning and structure (2002, 26).

A similar dynamic is at work in Bartlett's *Game*. The affective arrangement of the "game" is a glamourous "safe, professional, five-star reception" for the customers/punters that has to be "distinctly high-end" (Bartlett 2015, 10). The play covers the unusual time frame of seven years. The temporal structure thereby juxtaposes a linear process of development and affective moments of suspense—"temporal sink[s]" or "hole[s] in time" (Massumi 2002, 26), as it were—in which the shootings take place and which are filled with "vibratory motion" (Massumi 2002, 26). As regards the affective arrangement the play sets up for audiences and readers alike, the structure of virtually countless, repetitive shootings over the period of seven years is of less importance than the texture of these repetitions, which features a characteristic escalation pattern to keep the intensity of the game at a high level for both the customers and the spectators/readers. Level one, so to speak, includes shooting the man; level two, for an additional payment, includes shooting the woman; level three includes shooting someone more than once—in Scene Four, Carly is shot four times by a gang of drunken girls celebrating some girl's birthday—with a bulk discount on Wednesdays, which "are so quiet so we get four shots for two" (33). Times to hunt Carly and Ashley, which are originally restricted, become increasingly available until both of them have to expect being shot at all times. In other parts of the country, we hear, other businesses and indeed whole reserves have opened, and "apparently there's a whole village with a gun on a jeep" (54). After seven years, level four includes shooting children, so that Liam, Carly and Ashley's young son, has become a target for customers as well. Finally, near the end of the play, the business has turned bankrupt because the endless escalation necessary to play out the game's full potential has not been able to prevent utter boredom among the customers and, really, the spectators/readers too. The owner of the business, jokingly though, points to a theoretical next level of entertainment: "I think we should make it hurt. [...] Make them actually suffer. Charge more. [...] If this was Holland we could do euthanasia. [...] There's a market" (64–65). As in *Eigengrau*, textures—here, the escalation pattern—provoke in both the spectator and the reader an incalculable range of bodily responses that, again, may trigger likewise invariable emotional states, which a short unsystematic glance at the reviews of *Game* may reflect: Dominic Cavendish observed a "full slap-in-the-face shock" and a "visceral unpleasantness" (2015, 204), while Dominic Maxwell wrote that "with targets as docile as this, this sadistic sport lacks visceral appeal" (2015, 205).

Indeed, the question arises why the characters put up with this situation at all. There are brief glimpses at eventual resistance. At one moment, Ashley seeks to find out from which direction the shots have come that struck Carly down (37); later on, he virtually buys twenty minutes of private sphere from their supervisor David in order to be able to have sex with Carly and to put their wish for a child into practice (41). After Liam is born and old enough to be shot at, Carly professes that "we're not doing this" (50)—and yet, they are, time and again. Liam himself has found his own form of protest when he disturbingly hides under a cardboard box, traumatised perhaps, yet at the same time seeking quiet to twiddle on a handheld games machine. Unable to break free from their intra-action with their situation, they continue on their path, knowing exactly what they would lose if they stopped the game whose benefits they are unable to make up for—the schooling for their child, the house where they live and the living standard they have got used to (62–63). David, the ex-soldier, has moments of resilience, but for the most part he performs well as a complacent instrument of his employer—see, for instance, the brainwashing and the muzzle he gets from the company lawyer Sarah

(53–60). In the final moment of the, really, "too remorseful cop-out ending" (Shuttleworth 2015, 286) of the play, he, first, talks Liam out of his cardboard-box hiding place, tells him to face the "struggle" (75) of life instead and, in a forced symbolic gesture, even hand over his game machine, before he, then, commits suicide because he apparently deems any new start is impossible for himself:

> *He reaches across to his bag.*
> *Takes out a tranquilliser gun.*
> *Puts a dart in the gun.*
> *Sits on the stairs.*
> *Puts the end of the gun in his mouth.*
> *Pulls the trigger.*
> *He convulses for a few seconds.*
> *He dies.* (77)

This moment of madness, as it were, echoes similar consequences taken by Rose in *Eigengrau* after she realises that her strategy of winning Mark back has utterly failed, that is to say, when she feels—rather than realises—that following one's affects can entail opposite effects. In tableau 16, entitled "The Karaoke Bar," Rose is singing a power ballad, bathed in (stereotypically) glamourous pink light reflected by a turning disco ball (Skinner 2010, 94). She is surrounded by offstage voices before she blinds herself with the stiletto heel of her glitzy shoe. I quote the passage at some length to convey the sense of bodily intensity and vibrancy that emanates from its—piercing—texture:

> a van in East London
> West London
> Central
> District
> Jubilee
> Bakerloo
> four minutes
> two minutes
> fifty-two passengers
> no District and Circle
> no service
> no fat blokes
> no ketchup

no gherkins
no Russians
no talking
no
no
I said no
no men
find flat
pick up stuff
sort out teeth
pay bill
call bank
have a wank
fall in love
get a bike
what do you do
get married
what do you do
have kids
where r u
move to the country
what do you do
live happily ever after
two minutes
away
go away
out my way
move away from the platform edge
what do you do
hey darling
hey sweetheart
who are you
hey someone
just someone
please someone
is anyone
any
one
hello?
hello?
is anyone there?

As she nears the climax of the song, Rose pushes the heel of her stiletto into her left eye.
Blood pours down her face.
She does the same to the other eye.
Blackout. (96–97)

The onslaught of voices and the physical list of words raining down on Rose and the spectators/readers alike is the longest of the three occasions where this happens in the play. This list of words/terms uttered by off-stage voices embodies pure "narrative noise" (Massumi 2002, 26) that creates an incoherent, contingent, arbitrary, disruptive, logic-free texture of vibrant matter. Affect-as-texture corresponds to the "shocking and dramaturgically unearned act of self-mutilation" (Spencer 2010, 286) that follows it. For Rose, just as for the list of words preceding the act, there is no cognitive potential available at all, nor apparently a possibility of reflection. All there is is affect or, as the title of the play suggests, "*Eigengrau*," which in psychophysics is also known as "*Eigenlicht*"—dark light, brain grey, light chaos, idioretinal light or, indeed, visual noise (Fechner 1860; Barlow 1972), all denoting the colour that the eye sees in complete darkness and, physiologically speaking, perceived to be lighter than black objects under normal conditions of light. The affects inherent in the passage, therefore, surface as the texture of communicative, narrative, as well as visual noise. In a world, in which, for Rose, seeing is not, nor has ever been, synonymous to the potential of orientation and reflection, the ability to see can be surrendered to total feeling—eyes, as it were, can be gouged for those, like Rose, who believe rather than understand. And only in this sense does it seem sort of consequential that she should later on—hospitalised and in a wheelchair—conceive of her union with simpleton Tim as a "happy ending" to the story. Tim is a believer himself and, in the final tableau of *Eigengrau*, his almost embarrassingly melodramatic spreading of the ashes of his beloved grandmother on Eastbourne pier is grounded in a ridiculously false interpretation: like a true believer he asks for a "sign" (117) before emptying the ash container into the sea. Tim reads—or should I say, "feels"—the cigarette butts that come out of the container as a netherworld message to him from his smoker grandma. Spectators and readers, though, have an advance in knowledge, since we have previously witnessed Cassie irreverently using the container as an ashtray while having it off with Mark in the apartment he shares with Tim. This knowledge ruthlessly exposes Tim's belief for what it really is—a self-delusional lie. Thus confined to their affects, Tim and Rose in *Eigengrau*, just as Carly and Ashley in *Game*—and, in fact, all the rest of the characters in both plays with, perhaps, the half-convincing exception of David—create an almost depressing feeling of total helplessness. By the end of both plays, there is no sense of development for anything or anyone involved. Neither is there a sense of insight or interpretation beyond the intensities of the images and objects that have been intra-acting.

The Appeal Structure of *Eigengrau* and *Game*

An eventual narrativisation of the events, actions, effects and textures is therefore projected entirely on the parts that the spectators and the readers of both plays are invited to inhabit. Skinner and Bartlett orchestrate these parts very carefully, and directors Findlay for *Eigengrau* and Wares for *Game* and their respective teams of set, lighting and sound designers very successfully realised them on stage in the London productions of both plays. Findlay, for instance, used traverse staging at the Bush Theatre, which made half of the audience observe the other half closely to an "exquisitely uncomfortable" (Hitchings 2010, 285) effect, especially in the moments of excruciating sex and self-mutilation discussed above. In an even more elaborate structure, Wares and designer Miriam Buether had the entire space of the Almeida Theatre transformed into four separate seating areas, which worked as "camouflage-draped 'hides'" (Cavendish 2015, 205) for the punters, split off from each other. Walls were inserted featuring windows with lowerable shades through which audience members, who thus shared the space with the customers, could peep into the "home" in which Carly, Ashley and Liam were "performing" and being regularly shot at. Additionally, audience members wore headphones in order to hear not only the conversations between the three targets, but also the voices and actions of the hunters when these were taking place in the other sections or hides. Television monitors added to the synaesthetic theatre experience for the audience (Boles 2018, 58). *Game* obviously is a play whose affective arrangement brings it close to immersive theatre and, indeed, to the structure of video games. The affective arrangements of the sets for both plays produced gripping, viscerally effective shows that triggered intensity and turned the theatre (experience) itself into vibrant matter. Both plays embody affective rollercoaster experiences for spectators and, judging from the reviewers' reactions, both premiere productions provoked different, ever-changing affective responses that undecidedly oscillated between fascination and nausea. Clearly, both sets featured an implied spectator in the role of voyeur, accomplice and/or collaborator and an appeal to the audience to confront their own multiple positionings in such affective and experiential involvement: if witnessing the "uncomfortably long" oral sex scene in *Eigengrau*, for instance, equalled psychological abjection, this would only demonstrate that spectators are prompted to check whether such abjection resonates with their own taboo standards or their own voyeuristic tendencies.

Reading the texts of both plays, as has been shown throughout this essay, not only comprises the confrontation with a textual structure or texture, but also triggers structured acts of reception in which readers are meant to react to the distortions, differences, contingencies and contradictions in the text. Tension and suspense, for instance, are produced by the violation of norms. Deviation from norms, normative behaviour or even normative expectations, as seen in both plays with regard to genre and character psychology, is important for the meaning of the text insofar as it is classifiable in a system of semantics (Iser 1978, 90). My argument, alongside Massumi, is that intensities, that is, the reader's bodily reactions in the reading process, are indeed "outside expectation" and "disconnected from meaning" and "full sequencing" and "narration" (Massumi 2002, 25). The textures of both plays—the thwarted romcom pattern or the long lists of offstage voice utterances in *Eigengrau*; the escalation pattern in the repetitive shooting acts in *Game*—form semantically incomplete fragments, yet highly effective receptional blanks or gaps left for the reader to translate into qualified affects—emotions—and to draw cognitive conclusions from beyond their affective presence (Iser 1974). The semantic gaps created by the expression event of affects in both plays trigger an appeal structure that calls for reading meaning into all instances of indeterminacy in a text, a structure that readers have then to substantiate in the very act of reading. The act of reading implies nothing but the Massumian thinking-feeling. That is, on the one hand, it involves an ongoing process of (re)anchoring the reader's interpretative movements in textual signals that they cognitively face, process, synthesise and react to in their encounter with the text. On the other hand, however, reading text and textures also implies experiencing, living through and, most of all, imagining ever-changing intensities, which, time and time again, may entail suspending the owning and recognition of affect. Reading implies affecting and being affected: when we read literature we are absorbed into what we have been invited to produce through the image. As Wolfgang

Iser puts it, "we cannot help being affected by [our] own production[s]" (1978, 140). Reading text and textures constitutes and implies a vibrant connection to the "affective materiality of words" (Houen 2020a, 18).

Eigengrau and *Game* create visual and mental images of helpless characters unable to reflect on their situation and predicament. Given the fact that, as we have seen already, the characters are unable to accomplish such (self-)reflection, the affective arrangements of both plays project that task onto spectators and readers alike, who are asked to transcend the gaps, blanks and indeterminacies the characters cannot fill and produce meaning out of them. Latour wrote that "one of the affects of capitalism, that is, of thinking in terms of capitalism, is to generate for most of people who don't benefit from its wealth a feeling of helplessness and for a few people who benefit from it an immense enthusiasm together with a dumbness of the senses" (2014, 2). The affective arrangements of both plays, of course, can be read in this vein as critiques of the negative excesses of capitalism. While capitalism appears as a realm of limitless possibilities, at the same time, as both Rose's act of self-mutilation and David's suicide make more than clear, its affective arrangements set up "binding necessities from which there is no escape and a feeling of revolt against them that often results in helplessness" (Latour 2014, 2). Likewise, the object world at work in both plays, for instance, can of course be read in a Marxist fashion as a critique of commodity fetishism, surveillance, loss of control, alienation, underprivileging and exploitation of the masses by a few, as, for instance, synecdochically exemplified in the housing crisis context of *Game*, which may indeed turn the play into "a memento of how a lack of secure and sustainable living conditions is not just an inconvenience, but a deprivation of basic human rights" (Birke 2019, 94). As I have shown above, the sideways look at love in the twenty-first century or the few hints at the issue of (post)feminism in *Eigengrau* collapse into intensity/affect-driven and affect/vibrancy-oriented surrealism and shocking moments of excruciation instead of being elaborated into a serious, comprehensible political ethics or even a moral standpoint. Yes, viewers/readers in their/our complicit status are viscerally addressed and at the same time deliberately desensitised while prompted to reflect on the desensitisation that underpins capitalist systems, but then in their passivity and one-dimensionality, Carly and Ashley, for instance, never become real to the spectator/reader, never invite a touch of empathy for their predicament. As I stated at the beginning of my analysis, the unrivalled protagonists of both plays are their affective arrangements. Some of the reviews of both plays even saw this as a starting point of criticism. Gardner commented in the *Guardian* that *Eigengrau* was "full of dramatic thrills"—in other words, it was centred on intensities and vibrancy of matter on stage and, one may want to add, on the page—but "neglect[ed] to tend its emotional heart" (2010, 286)—that is, all the qualified affect and, ensuing from it, cognitive depth for reflection. *Eigengrau*, in Gardner's mind, ultimately amounts to "ninety minutes whiz by making an immediate visceral impact, but when it's over, it really is over" (2010, 286). In much the same vein, Kate Kellaway wrote in the *Observer* that *Game* was a play that beyond its exploration of thrills was actually lacking in argument, a "show-but-never-tell production"—the play, in her view, needed "more sense, less sensation" (2015, 206).

To conclude, I would like to take up both the allegorical reading of a critique of capitalism and the critique of affect-centredness and demonstrate that an affective reading of *Eigengrau* and *Game* can reveal avenues for a rephrasing of the function and targets of the aesthetics, the appeal structure and the affective arrangements at work in both plays and, beyond that, in stage plays and (dramatic) literature in general. I claim that the affective arrangements of both plays are not primarily concerned with the debunking of capitalist malformations, even though these, of course, are important constituents of their subject matter. As my affective reading of both plays has shown, their emphasis on intensity and vibrancy of matter in the theatre and on the page shows that they share features of the object world that they interrogate. The repulsion from the object world of glamour both plays generate through their affective arrangements and their transpersonal affective dynamics is met by an equal enactment of a fascination with that very object world. While they interrogate the allure of glamour, the intra-actions in both plays actually make for genuinely glamourous shows. Indeed, I would suggest that the box-office success of both plays rests on the affective arrangement, embodiment and marketing of such glamour. It would be hypocritical to assume otherwise. Both plays relish the material vitalism of the affects they embody and create at the same time. The affective arrangements of both plays accentuate the vital immanence of material energy both in a performance-oriented as well as in a textual sense. What their aesthetics of intensity share with philosophical positions put forward by Deleuze/Guattari, Massumi and Bennett is the intention "to paint a positive ontology of vibrant matter, which stretches received concepts of agency, action, and freedom sometimes to the breaking point" (Bennett 2010, x). As I have shown above, the affective arrangements of performative as well as textual matter revealed in both plays—their affectively functioning architectures as well as architextures—offer potential for absorbing and displaying "a drive towards transformative rearrangements of elements, operations, and boundaries" (Slaby et al. 2019, 6). The affective arrangements of both plays draw attention to the vital intra-action between human and nonhuman actants. An affective reading of the kind I have proposed is able to demonstrate that neither play presents the nonhuman actants as dead matter that can easily be instrumentalised. On the contrary, the intensities and vibrancy addressed by and emanating from both plays allow us to realise the full range of nonhuman powers that surround human existence in the twenty-first century. Both plays detect that these vibrant materials "can aid or destroy, enrich or disable, ennoble or degrade us" (Bennett 2010, ix). Both plays, thus, foreground affect—understood here as the bodily expression of intensity and the relational, vibrant force of things. Highlighting the affective efficacy of things is the fundamental condition to identify potentially dangerous matter and, ultimately, to change our patterns of consumption into a more sustainable vein (Bennett 2010, x). This idea is at the centre of the appeal structure and ethical dimension of the affective arrangements at work in both plays: affect-as-intensity may lead us to the "margin of manoeuvrability," to always but "the next experimental step rather than the big utopian picture," the vitality and vibrancy of which, though, are still full of "hope" (Massumi 2015, 3).

Notes

1. For an inventory of actor-network theory, see Latour (1996) and also Jane Bennett (2010, ix).
2. See also Fritz Breithaupt (2017) for the "dark sides" of empathy. The voluntary subjection of the characters in both plays leads the spectator/reader to the limit of any justified empathy.
3. I would very much like to acknowledge that I am indebted here to the numerous discussions with my masterclass participants at the University of Augsburg, especially Eva Ries and Korbinian Stöckl. For the complex cultural and philosophical background of the discourses of love in contemporary British theatre, see Stöckl (2021).

References

Barad, Karen. 2007. *Meeting the Universe Halfway: Quantum Physics and the Entanglement of Matter and Meaning*. Durham, NC and London. Duke UP.

Barlow, Horace. 1972. *Visual Psychophysics*. New York: Springer.

Bartlett, Mike. 2015. *Game*. London: Nick Hern Books.

Bennett, Jane. 2010. *Vibrant Matter: A Political Ecology of Things*. Durham, NC and London: Duke UP.

Birke, Dorothee. 2019. "(Play)Houses of Horror: Addressing the Anxieties of the Housing Crisis." *Journal of Contemporary Drama in English* 7 (1): 89–106.

Boles, William C. 2018. "Theatricalising the National Housing Crisis in Mike Bartlett's *Game* and Philip Ridley's *Radiant Vermin*." *Journal of Contemporary Drama in English* 6 (1): 55–68.

Breithaupt, Fritz. 2017. *Die dunklen Seiten der Empathie*. Berlin: Suhrkamp.

Cavendish, Dominic. 2015. Review of *Game*, by Mike Bartlett. *Daily Telegraph*, March 5. *Theatre Record* 35 (5): 204–05.

Clough, Patricia T. with Jean Halley, eds. 2007. *The Affective Turn: Theorizing the Social*. Durham, NC and London: Duke UP.

Demos, E. Virginia. 1995. *Exploring Affect: Selected Writings of Silvan S. Tomkins*. Cambridge and Paris: Cambridge UP and Éditions de la Maison des Sciences de l'Homme.

Fechner, Gustav Theodor. 1860. *Elemente der Psychophysik*. Leipzig: Breitkopf und Härtel.

Gardner, Lyn. 2010. Review of *Eigengrau*, by Penelope Skinner. *Guardian*, March 19. *Theatre Record* 30 (6): 286.

Greer, Germaine. (1970) 2006. *The Female Eunuch*. London: Fourth Estate.

Gregg, Melissa and Gregory J. Seigworth, eds. 2010. *The Affect Theory Reader*. Durham NC and London: Duke UP.

Hart, Christopher. 2015. Review of *Game*, by Mike Bartlett. *Sunday Times*, March 8. *Theatre Record* 35 (5): 206.

Hitchings, Henry. 2010. Review of *Eigengrau*, by Penelope Skinner. *Evening Standard*, March 16. *Theatre Record* 30 (5): 285.

Houen, Alex. 2020a. "Introduction: Affect and Literature." In Houen 2020b, 1–30.

———, ed. 2020b. *Affect and Literature*. Cambridge: Cambridge UP.

Hurley, Erin. 2010. *theatre & feeling*. Basingstoke and New York: Palgrave Macmillan.

Iser, Wolfgang. 1974. *The Implied Reader: Patterns of Communication in Prose Fiction from Bunyan to Beckett*. Baltimore, MD: Johns Hopkins UP.

———. 1978. *The Act of Reading: A Theory of Aesthetic Response*. Baltimore, MD: Johns Hopkins UP.

Kellaway, Kate. 2015. Review of *Game*, by Mike Bartlett. *Observer*, March 8. *Theatre Record* 35 (5): 206.

Kosofsky Sedgwick, Eve and Adam Frank, ed. 1995. *Shame and its Sisters: A Silvan Tomkins Reader*. Durham, NC and London: Duke UP.

Latour, Bruno. 1996. "On Actor-Network Theory: A Few Clarifications." *Soziale Welt* 47 (4): 369–81.

———. 2014. "On Some of the Affects of Capitalism." Lecture given at the Royal Academy, Copenhagen, February 26. Accessed July 5, 2020.

Marlowe, Sam. 2010. Review of *Eigengrau*, by Penelope Skinner. *Time Out*, March 25. *Theatre Record* 30 (6): 287.

Massumi, Brian. 2002. *Parables of the Virtual: Movement, Affect, Sensation*. Durham, NC and London: Duke UP.

———. 2008. "The Thinking-Feeling of What Happens." *Inflexions: A Journal for Research Creation* 1. Accessed July 5, 2020.

———. 2015. *Politics of Affect*. Cambridge: Polity.

Maxwell, Dominic. 2015. Review of *Game*, by Mike Bartlett. *Times*, March 5. *Theatre Record* 35 (5): 205.

McTiernan, John, dir. 1987. *Predator*. 20th Century Fox.

Menninghaus, Winfried. (1999) 2002. *Ekel: Theorie und Geschichte einer starken Empfindung*. Frankfurt a. M.: Suhrkamp.

Middeke, Martin and Christoph Reinfandt, eds. 2016. *Theory Matters: The Place of Theory in Literary and Cultural Studies Today*. London: Palgrave Macmillan.

Reinfandt, Christoph. 2016. "Reading Textures." In Middeke and Reinfandt 2016, 319–34.

Ross, Gary, dir. 2012. *The Hunger Games*. Lionsgate/Color Force.

Rouse, Joseph. 2002. *How Scientific Practices Matter: Reclaiming Philosophical Naturalism*. Chicago, IL: U of Chicago P.

Seyfert, Robert. 2012. "Beyond Personal Feelings and Collective Emotions: Toward A Theory of Social Affect." *Theory, Culture & Society* 29 (6): 27–46.

Shore, Robert. 2010. Review of *Eigengrau*, by Penelope Skinner. *Metro*, March 18. *Theatre Record* 30 (6): 286.

Shuttleworth, Ian. 2015. Review of *Game*, by Mike Bartlett. *Financial Times*, March 5. *Theatre Record* 30 (6): 286.

Skinner, Penelope. 2010. *Eigengrau*. London: Faber.

Slaby, Jan, Rainer Mühlhoff and Philipp Wüschner. 2019. "Affective Arrangements." *Emotion Review* 11 (1): 3–12.

Spencer, Charles. 2010. Review of *Eigengrau*, by Penelope Skinner. *Daily Telegraph*, March 17. *Theatre Record* 30 (6): 286.

Stöckl, Korbinian. 2021. *Love in Contemporary British Drama: Traditions and Transformations of a Cultural Emotion*. Berlin and Boston: De Gruyter.

Taylor, Paul. 2010. Review of *Eigengrau*, by Penelope Skinner. *Financial Times*, March 17. *Theatre Record* 30 (6): 285.

Thrift, Nigel. 2010. "Understanding the Material Practices of Glamour." In Gregg and Seigworth 2010, 289–308.

Tomkins, Silvan. 1995. "What Are Affects?" In Kosovsky Sedgwick and Frank 1995, 33–74.

Van Alphen, Ernst. 2008. "Affective Operations of Art and Literature." *Anthropology and Aesthetics* 53/54: 20–30.

CHAPTER 11

Entanglements: Transaction and Intra-action with the Devil in *How to Hold Your Breath*

Julia Boll

The published script of Scottish playwright Zinnie Harris's play *How to Hold Your Breath* (2015) opens with the main character, Dana, standing alone on stage, speaking to the audience.[1] In this speech, she paints a haunting picture of defeat, vulnerability and resignation, the abject personified that we fear to become, and that she will become herself over the course of the play:

> I am stand at the back. Don't look out. Gets shouted at for looking down. I am eyes closed, head bent in every gathering. I am knees bowed, chest to the floor. I am a flower by the wall, grass in the shade. I am back turned, shoulders hunched, face hollowed. I am a scream. A howl. I am a snake on the plane, a hyena, an antelope. I am ant under a stone, beetle scurrying away. I am beaten at birth, blackened. I am sand. I am soil. I am earth. I am less than earth. I am poor. I'm so poor my skin is my clothes. I am uncovered. Ashamed. The land can't feed me. I am the end. The dead. The carcass by the roadside. I am the abyss into which people dread to fall. (Harris 2015, 13)

J. Boll (✉)
Universität Hamburg, Hamburg, Germany
e-mail: julia.boll@uni-hamburg.de

M. Aragay et al. (eds.), *Affects in 21st-Century British Theatre*,
https://doi.org/10.1007/978-3-030-58486-3_11

This opening monologue did not appear in the play's first production at London's Royal Court Theatre.[2] Inserted at the beginning of the script, though, we can consider it a prologue poignantly framing a play that dramatises contemporary Western society's insecurity and its fear of social decline.

How to Hold Your Breath is the story of a young woman who proposes her research project to a European funding body and is offered the opportunity to apply for an international research position in Alexandria. While she is on her way to the interview in North Africa, Europe experiences a major financial crisis and descends into chaos, prompting thousands of Europeans to try and reach a more stable environment as the surrounding countries close their borders. The critical discussion of Harris's play has mostly analysed its particular depiction and framing of the "inverted" migrant narrative (see, for example, Aston 2017 and Cornford 2018). This chapter focuses on the play's depiction of neoliberal self-development marketing and its portrayal of interpersonal relationships as transactions, leading to a broader discussion of the politics of emotion and happiness as posited by Sara Ahmed, who critically examines the discourse of happiness as an individual's responsibility and as a marketable commodity in the context of understanding one's life as a business project (2010, 10). Further, it discusses how this understanding of emotions as commodities correlates with physicist and feminist theorist Karen Barad's work on quantum entanglement and intra-action (2007, 2010) in relation to the performance of ethics. The chapter will chart the two entangled narratives of affect woven through the play: one chronicling the main character's efforts to adjust and achieve the flexibility to insert herself into a structure that values subject-centred narratives and downplays the fact that individuals are tied into different and interrelated systems; the other, drawing on Barad, inviting us to consider the encounters and entanglements between humans, nonhumans and indeed systems as mutually affecting and coconstitutive.

Advocating strongly against a division between body and mind, Barad's approach can be read as a possible bridge between different strands in current critical thought on affect theory. I will argue that the main characters in Harris's play can be regarded as entangled systems whose ability to act and rework their worlds emerges from their intra-action, demonstrating that the encounter between subject and system not only changes the subject, but also the system. I will then draw a line back to Ahmed's thesis on happiness and her suggestion to rewrite the political will to be affected by unhappiness as political freedom.[3]

Happiness and Life as a Project

Early in the play, Dana pitches her research project to a funding interview panel somewhere in Europe.[4] She proposes imbuing customer-business relationships with the same emotional value as personal relationships by sorting all human interactions into the same analytical framework and regarding the customer-business contact as a variant of "other basic human interactions, such as [...] friendship" (36). Pointing out that customer exchange and business correspondence have already seeped into all the channels originally set up for personal communication, she claims that

> there is no distinction in these channels between other communications that the customer might receive. You might in the same second get a text from your partner, and then from your bank. To maximise the feeling of mutuality, should the text from your bank feel *more* on your team than from your partner? It is *your* bank, there to listen to you. It may take a role and a flavour, a character if you like. I think with the right modelling Customer Dynamics could go beyond the transactional nature of the interaction to look at emotions, intent and desires. (37–38; italics in the original)

By proposing to equate personal and business relationships, Dana's project effectually proposes turning all relationships into commodities. And while the exact structure and research question, even the academic field, of her proposed project remain vague throughout the play, its larger objective and conceptual framework seem to be aligned with the neoliberal tendency to personalise the market, a trend on which Stuart Hall observes: "*it* [the market] 'thinks' this, 'does' that, 'feels' the other, 'gets panicky,' 'loses confidence,' 'believes' [...]. Every social relation can be bought and sold, has its 'price' and its 'costs.' Everything can become a commodity" (2011, 722; italics in the original). This extends to the contemporary individual's relationship to society in the context of citizenship as defined by fitting into the market, by being employed. In her social study about the effects of Britain's neoliberal policies on its excluded, Imogen Tyler discusses widespread social insecurity as an "essential component of neoliberal governmentality, as it introduces competition (marketization) into every sphere of social life" (2013, 191) and so redesigns citizenship "around the axis of work/worklessness, whereby poverty and disadvantage have become associated with 'poor self-management'" (2013, 198). Citizenship thus has been redefined as leading a successful life and being productive, which implies being well, not drawing on welfare or healthcare, and demonstrating this well-being by displaying the feeling of happiness.

In her 2010 study *The Promise of Happiness*, Ahmed relates the concept of happiness to the performance of well-being as a civic duty—we have a duty to become happier for others—and criticises the positive psychology movement for instrumentalising happiness for a marketisation of the self:

> Not only does happiness become an individual responsibility, a redescription of life as a project, but it also becomes an instrument, as a means to an end, as well as an end. We make ourselves happy, as an acquisition of capital that allows us to be or to do this or that, or even to get this or that. [...] Happiness becomes, then, a way of maximizing your potential of getting what you want, as well as being what you want to get. Unsurprisingly, positive psychology often uses economic language to describe happiness as a good. [...] Happiness gets you more in the bank; happiness depends on other forms of capital (background, personality, networks) as well as acquiring or accumulating capital for the individual subject. (2010, 10)

Demonstrating happiness is not only profitable but essential, because being—or appearing to be—happy and well means being able to work, and often even being able to find work in the first place. Hall similarly points out that "[t]he care-of-the-self-fashioning industries [...] feed massively off these trends" of turning everything, including the self, into a marketable product (2011, 722). More recently, this reflection has been revisited and expanded in essays by Laurie Penny, who discusses the way self-care has become corrupted into a neoliberal commodity (2016), and Miya Tokumitsu, who traces how the "marketization of every aspect of our lives" (2018) is entangled with an increasing demand on the individual to self-optimise and engage in self-care, thus shifting the responsibility for well-being away from society and the community and onto the individual, who is asked to demonstrate flexibility and the ability to withstand stress and insecurities, forging herself into the perfect neoliberal subject.

Carl Cederström and André Spicer equally argue that wellness has become an ideology linked to a person's individual market value and that "the failure to conform becomes a stigma" and will not only negatively impact one's personal market value, but lead to being cast as "a direct threat to contemporary society" (2015, intro). They maintain the same logic holds true for happiness, the assumption being that "happy workers are more productive" (2015, intro).

In *How to Hold Your Breath*, Dana's initial pitch of her project is successful: she is put forward for an international award, for which she will be interviewed in Alexandria in Egypt. She decides to turn this trip into a leisurely minibreak with her sister Jasmine. During their train journey south, a financial crisis dips Europe into chaos, and they find themselves stranded somewhere in Europe, in the fictive town of Hartenharten, unable to access their funds.[5] There, Dana encounters the Librarian, whom she first met at her local library, but who regularly appears to her throughout her odyssey, as a figure seeking to give advice in the form of ever more outlandish self-help books. At night in the shabby overheated hotel, the Librarian offers her titles such as *How to Get Sleep in a Room that is Now Too Hot*, *How to Stay Asleep and Still Even if it Feels Like You Are in an Oven* or *How to Lie Awake and Not Breathe in the Air* (104–05).

The Librarian's continuous suggestions of self-improvement satirise the self-help ideology, suggesting Dana is the problem to be fixed, not the room, as if Dana only needed to adjust herself. The scene lampoons what the propagation of wellness as an ideology means on a larger scale: shifting the responsibility for wellbeing and happiness onto the individual depoliticises the human struggle for the good life within the community, as if factors wholly out of the individual's control could be influenced by just trying harder. In their investigation of neoliberal subjectivity in relation to the concept of self-development, Salman Türken et al. trace the discourse that constructs the subject as human capital. They map the ways in which she has become "an entrepreneur of herself" who "is expected to act to increase her value" by perpetually reworking and improving the self "to fit the demands of the advanced liberal society" (2016, 34). In this endeavour, they add, the individual is "largely responsible for her own successes and failures, the individual's well-being and development becomes the sole responsibility of the neoliberal entrepreneurial subject. Discursively detached from the structural constraints of society and isolated from contextual and historical conditions, the neoliberal subject then has no one else to blame but herself if she fails to achieve goals or make ends meet"

(2016, 34).[6] This resonates with Catherine Malabou, who succinctly writes on the plasticity of the human brain and its ability to adapt to the ever more challenging and brutalising demands of late capitalism, which requires people to "be connected to a network, to be capable of modulating one's efficacy. We know very well that every loss of suppleness means rejection, pure and simple" (2008, 10)—suggesting that contemporary capitalism has perfected taking advantage of the brain's ability to forge and adjust neuronal connections to enable the subject's political and social functioning.

As the sisters in Harris's play find themselves adrift, it is illuminating to consider Ahmed's brief genealogy of the term *unhappy* and its connection with the phrase "wretched in mind": as she reminds us, "wretch" also used to refer to "a stranger, exile, or banished person" (2010, 17). In her tracing of the genealogy, we also find parallels to the language of abjection and defeat used in Dana's opening monologue, allowing for a further link to be established with Tyler's proposal of a social "theory of abjection," where "abjection" is understood as a mechanism of governance through aversion (2013, 17).

Some of the reasons for the fairly widespread public unwillingness to engage with, and accept responsibility for, the refugees trying to reach Europe spring from the current dominant discourse that dictates everyone be responsible for their own fate; that people, if they just tried hard enough, should be able to live decent lives in the countries whence they flee and should not have an incentive to come to Europe as "economic migrants." The assumption is that migration is a question of attitude and not a consequence of systemic, globalised neoliberal policy. It should be noted that *How to Hold Your Breath* is not actually a play depicting or discussing what has come to be called "the European migrant crisis," which began in the early 2010s and reached a tragic climax in the summer of 2015. The play posits the question, what if it were us?, but does not touch on the colonial and neocolonial interdependencies that lie at the root of the ongoing mass migration.[7] I contend, though, that the play makes a very strong and clear argument about global neoliberalism and the way it isolates and strips the individual of all social and political support, while casting her as solely responsible for her fate and threatening her with exclusion.

In the midst of their odyssey, stranded without funds and with her sister Jasmine struggling to recover from a miscarriage, Dana tries to raise money by selling herself for sex. Disturbingly, the scene morphs into one in which she has to explain herself to the interview panel for her research grant. The ensuing discussion, during which Dana tries to persuade the funding body to help her arrive at her interview in Alexandria in time, or at least to issue her with some sort of proof that she has been invited for an interview, demonstrates how absolute mobility and flexibility has become the unchallenged prerequisite for even being considered for a position:

INTERVIEWER 2: if we are to hold this research grant for you—
DANA: I'll be there
[…]
as soon as I can. Can you help me get to the border?
INTERVIEWER 2: we leave travel arrangements up to the individuals. We understand that this is a difficult time for those coming from the European Union, but—
DANA: they have more or less closed the border into Turkey, and if we go by boat—
[…]
could you give me a piece of paper saying that you have invited me?
INTERVIEWER 1: we aren't really sure
INTERVIEWER 3: the administrative burden
DANA: if you could give me a piece of paper saying that I have a position to go to
INTERVIEWER 2: but you don't have a position. That is just the matter that we are discussing.
INTERVIEWER 3: you might have a position. (135–36)

Aligning the job-search situation with Dana's desperate attempts to raise money by selling her body, the play foregrounds how she has to turn herself into a commodity in order to survive on the market. Anthropologist Anna Tsing discusses how human concentration of wealth has been achieved through an alienated relationship with the environment that turns "both humans and nonhumans into resources for investment" (2015, 5). She argues that this development has inspired investors to imbue both people and things with alienation, that is, the ability to stand alone as if the entanglements of living did not matter, because "[t]hrough alienation, people and things become mobile assets; they can be removed from their life-worlds in distance-defying transport to be exchanged with other assets from other life-worlds, elsewhere" (2015, 5). Tsing stretches Karl Marx's use of "alienation" to describe how both nonhumans and humans are cut off from their life-worlds "to become objects of exchange" (2015, 121).[8]

Dana and Jasmine finally manage to find a boat that will take them across the sea to Alexandria. This harrowing moment in the play alludes to the countless life-threatening journeys across the Mediterranean in small, often unsafe, mostly overcrowded dinghies that have become habitual news items in the second decade of the twenty-first century. The sisters' passage is equally dangerous; the sea is stormy, and the Librarian appears to Dana with more books, insisting she take one called *How to Hold Your Breath for a Very Long Time* and urging her to start doing precisely that, hold her breath. As the ship capsizes and Dana is drowning, she finds herself once more in front of the funding body's interview panel:

INTERVIEWER 1:	you seem not to be breathing.
DANA:	I am breathing. I'm holding my breath
INTERVIEWER 1:	you seem to be going under [...] if this means you can't give your presentation, this will cause us no end of headache
DANA:	I'll give my presentation
INTERVIEWER 2:	you seem to be still, Ms Edwards [...] you needed to hold your breath earlier. (151–52)

Dana pitches her project while embodying the self-sustained "subject *par excellence*" (Hall 2011, 723), who will agree to everything, adapt to anything, ask for nothing—not even air.

Entanglements and Intra-action

The neoliberal subject as depicted in *How to Hold Your Breath* struggles against this constant demand to demonstrate and prove her own value, to improve and streamline herself, to be independent and mobile to a fault, to adjust in the way Malabou describes when she speaks of a "culture that celebrates only the triumph of flexibility" (2008, 79). But the play also shows that not even endless flexibility and self-improvement will guarantee a place within the structure—nor, indeed, will they keep it from collapsing. William E. Connolly argues that instability and fragility are inherent to capitalism as an economic and sociopolitical system and that to underplay "the role of noise and loose remainders *within* the markets [...], the ways capitalism alters nonhuman force fields and the independent power of nonhuman forces *acting upon* capitalism" is a grave mistake (2013, 26; italics in the original). He advocates connecting critical thought rooted in a philosophy of becoming with ideas about "the ecology of late capitalism" to properly consider how capitalism as a system overlaps and even meshes with other force fields, which are often "nondiscursive systems with impressive powers of their own" (2013, 30). In a passage that chimes with Tsing's suggestion that precarity is in fact the condition of our time (2015, 20), he writes that "we inhabit a world in which the fragility of things—from the perspective of the endurance and quality of life available to the human estate in its entanglements with other force fields—becomes apparent, while the categories and sensibility with which we habitually come to grips to [*sic*] the world make it difficult to fold that sense deeply into theory and practice" (2013, 31).

In view of Connolly's argument that thinking alongside and within traditional—which often means binary—frameworks fails to address the way complex systems are imbricated, it is worth returning to Barad's seminal work on quantum physics and entanglement to reconsider human and nonhuman relationships and the way in which these are constructed and reconstructed through continuous, iterative intra-actions. Barad argues that human agency does not pre-exist separately or independently, but emerges from relationships in intra-actions—a concept markedly different from interaction, as the latter indicates action between pre-existing entities that maintain a certain level of independence, whereas the intra-action of two bodies denotes action that is coconstitutive, coming "from within." Addressing the prevailing subject-centred narrative, which foregrounds the individual as a preexisting, autonomous entity and downplays the way individuals are tied into several different, but related—entangled—systems and force fields, Barad criticises the apparent need for both social and physical theories "to write matter and meaning into separate categories" (2007, 25). This reverberates with the individualising, subject-centred narrative of the individual alienated from her environment as analysed and criticised by Ahmed, Malabou and Tsing, and can also be extended to a critique of a theory of affect that firmly separates body and mind. Instead, Barad advocates what she calls a "'diffractive' methodology" in order to read insights from different areas of studies "through one another" (2007, 25). She draws on different fields from the sciences and social and critical theory to forge a philosophical framework in which she argues for the need to eschew binary thinking so as to rethink fundamental concepts such as "notions of matter, discourse, causality, agency, power, identity, embodiment, objectivity, space, and time" (2007, 26). "To be entangled," she writes, "is not simply to be intertwined with another, as in the joining of separate entities, but to lack an independent, self-contained existence. Existence is not an individual affair. Individuals do not preexist their interactions; rather, individuals emerge through and as part of their entangled intra-relating" (2007, ix).

Structurally entangled with and therefore coconstitutive to the narrative centred on European migrants trying to leave the European Union, a second narrative emerges in Harris's play, evolving from the first scene and developing into the emotional conflict of the play. It is the affective intra-action between these two intertwined narratives which shapes and defines the play. Before Dana and her sister begin their journey, before Dana gives her presentation to the funding board, even, we see her waking up next to Jarron, a man she met the night before, who now seems quite eager to distance himself from her. At first, he claims to be a UN official on his way to Alexandria. In keeping with the premise of Dana's proposed research project, which suggests shifting business relationships to a personal plane and thus instilling a sense of intimacy, he prefers to keep personal relationships transactional to avoid any entanglement based on duty, debt or feelings.[9] If Jarron and Dana were to treat their personal encounter as a business relationship, it would follow that this temporary personal relationship would conclude after the transaction and all emotional value attached to it, if any, would automatically dissolve. And so, convinced Dana is a sex worker, Jarron offers her money as he leaves in the morning, as a means to complete the business transaction. But Dana reacts angrily to his attempts to pay her: her emotional involvement or noninvolvement is not for sale, nor is her body. In direct contradiction of her own research project, she refuses to enter a commercial transaction and thereby view what she understands to be a personal connection as a customer-business contact.

Jarron, though, is not just any old guy trying to buy sex with no strings attached: it turns out he is a demon, fundamentally opposed to owing anybody anything. As the Librarian points out, he is "the original transactional creature" (45). From their first encounter, Dana takes away an actual Devil's mark that festers and grows. While the symbolism is perhaps a bit unsubtle here, it can also be read as the physical manifestation of what Tsing describes as being "contaminated" by our encounters: "they change who we are as we make way for others. As contamination changes world-making projects, mutual worlds—and new directions—may emerge" (2015, 27). In *How to Hold Your Breath*, it becomes clear that the contamination works both ways, as Jarron carries Dana's "mark" inside him and it causes him to evolve. They have another encounter after Dana's first project pitch. Unused to having an emotional connection, Jarron again tries to pay her in order for her to release him, as he is sure the exchange of money will cancel his feelings for her:

JARRON: [...] this sensation I have
this uncomfortable sensation,
why I can't control my thoughts as I should—
[...]
I'll pay you to undo it, how about that? 45 euros, it's not a payment for the other night, it's a payment for your unlocking services
[...]
DANA: you want me to stop you from loving me?
JARRON: who talked about love?
DANA: that's the sensation you described
JARRON: it's not love
DANA: what is it?
JARRON: a curse of some kind. You've made me obsessed by you (49–51)

Jarron's unwillingness to "owe anyone anything" (45) is rooted in his inability to understand relational, indeed affective, encounters as anything else than trade-based transactions, for which an exchange of equal values has to take place. For a self-styled cosmic entity of some description, the demon has a remarkably limited understanding of what quantum entanglement entails. With regard to his and Dana's coconstitutive relationship, it involves that, if we regard Dana as system A and Jarron as system B combined in a single mathematical term, their entangled state "cannot properly be understood as a composite system, for example, a mixture, composed of two independent components, that is separately determinate systems A and B. Rather, the entangled state of A and B [...] *must be understood as a single entity*" (Barad 2007, 271; italics in the original). We can therefore claim, borrowing from the wave function (ψ) in quantum physics,[10] that when visualised on an axis representing the two systems' emotional energy, Dana's *eigenvalue*—the characteristic set of parameters, the "essence" of Dana-as-system-A, which in quantum physics is interpreted as measuring a particle's energy—is "up" and Jarron's is "down," but this term is entangled and thus coconstituted with the *eigenvalues* visualised on an axis representing the transactional energy (or intensity, if you will) measured for systems A and B—and here, Jarron's *eigenvalue* is "up" and Dana's is "down." Importantly, neither of the two systems A and B—Dana and Jarron—have independent, preexisting identities that have merely interacted with each other to come to this state of entanglement. Instead, they have intra-acted and their respective identities are in a constant state of becoming in relation to their respective Other: their ability to act emerges from within the relationship, not outside of it. Barad defines agency not as something that something or someone has, but rather as an enactment. Therefore, it

> cannot be designated as an attribute of subjects or objects (as they do not preexist as such). It is not an attribute whatsoever. *Agency is 'doing' or 'being' in its intra-activity. It is the enactment of iterative changes to particular practices [...] through the dynamics of intra-activity.* [...] Particular possibilities entail an ethical obligation to intra-act responsibly in the world's becoming, to contest and rework what matters and what is excluded from mattering. (2007, 178; italics in the original)

That both Dana and Jarron find themselves "marked" by the encounter can also be interpreted by reading it through Barad's theory of intra-action, as the result of measuring a particle's energy is "permanent marks on bodies" (2007, 178). Barad posits these measurements are not restricted to the laboratory, but rather result from any intra-action: "What we usually call a 'measurement' is a correlation or entanglement between component parts of a phenomenon, between the 'measured object' and the 'measuring device'" (2007, 337). Intra-action can thus be regarded as contamination and ongoing affective contagion, from which, as Tsing suggests, spring possibilities to change directions and build mutual worlds. Returning to Dana's description of her research project, which takes as its premise "the transactional nature of the interaction" (38), it becomes clear now why this understanding of the relationship proves to be unfeasible. Declaring the two constituents of the transaction as independent ignores their entanglement, which manifests as emotions, intent and desires, and precludes how their intra-action shifts the particular positions—the *eigenvalues*, if you will—of the constituents.

Over the course of the play, Jarron repeatedly attempts to trick and coerce Dana into taking his money. For a while, the play tries to fool us into believing, along with Dana, that the chaos following the financial crash and the sisters' ensuing descent into extreme precarity are directly linked, in the way of a linear cause-and-effect dynamic, to Dana's refusal to allow the demon to treat her as a commodity by paying her off. Actually, though, we can observe the entanglement of a socioeconomic system and an interpersonal one: the crumbling of the European Union and Dana's push-pull relationship with Jarron are not two independent and separately determinate phenomena, with the trajectory of the one subordinately caused by the development of the other. Rather, they are entangled and must be understood as a single entity. Jarron's insistence on the existence of the debt also draws attention to the fundamental mechanism of debt underlying the sociopolitical world we inhabit.

Crucially, Barad proposes to radically rethink the traditional notion of causality by considering agential intra-action as the dynamic determining the relationships, boundaries and properties of what constitutes different systems (2007, 333–34). She argues for a notion of causal relationship that "exceeds any linear conception of dynamics in which effect follows cause end-on-end, and in which the global is a straightforward emanation outward of the local" (2007, 170). Dana's and Jasmine's situation is determined by their privileged western European lives' entanglement with the refractions and reverberations of global capitalism—a fact of which they seem to be, at first, gloriously unaware:

> DANA: why are you so calm?
>
> JASMINE: because we live in Europe, because nothing really bad happens. We both have jobs, the worst of this is, is a bit of an inconvenience and perhaps not such a good mini-break but really in the grand scheme of life, not so bad. (92)

Within the theatrical canon of the past three decades, there is an echo here of David Greig's pivotal 1994 play *Europe*, which is set in an unnamed small border town somewhere in the middle of Europe and presents the effects of modernity and globalisation on local communities while also relating these developments to transnationalism and the question of refugees and displacement. It also examines the mythical ideal of Europe, where war and conflict are regarded as an anomaly. Sava, one of Greig's displaced characters, says to his daughter, "we're not in some savage country on the other side of the world. Look around you, look at the architecture. Listen to the sounds from the street. You can smell the forest. We're a long way from home but we're still in Europe. We'll be looked after. Our situation will be understood" (Greig 2002, 29).

In Harris's play, Dana demonstrates an equally unshaken faith in (European) civilisation as an equalising, self-contained system and a robust belief that someone will come and help them, an attitude that unleashes Jarron's cynicism: "*The demon laughs at that. Long and hard*" (103). *How to Hold Your Breath* does not explicitly address the entanglements of the Western European privileged cosmopolitan lifestyle—which relies strongly on securities, easy movement between countries and a stable and accessible infrastructure—with a globalised financial market, the exploitation of third-world countries and the exclusion of the nonprivileged through ever-tightening border closures. Yet these entanglements are implicitly touched upon, precisely by means of the inverted migrant narrative that draws attention to the entanglement *ex negativo*.

Responsibility and the Freedom to be Unhappy

Barad establishes a logical connection between the concept of quantum entanglement and, by extension, the notion that nothing is entirely separate from anything else, and the responsibility individuals have for each other before and beyond choosing, suggesting that, as a consequence of the emergence of agency from intra-actions, responsibility is distributed amongst the coconstitutive entities (2007, 2010). She argues against reading responsibility as an obligation *chosen* by the subject. Rather, she suggests it should be understood as an embodied relation preceding "the intentionality of consciousness. Responsibility is not a calculation to be performed. [...] It is an iterative (re)opening up to, an enabling of responsiveness" (2010, 265). Maintaining that entanglements are "relations of obligations," she concludes that ethics have to be regarded as integral to the act of becoming rather than a set of human values superimposed onto the ontology of the world, stating that "the very nature of matter entails an exposure to the Other" (2010, 265). Returning to Malabou's contention that late capitalism demands people's connection to a network, it is constructive to note that Barad's conception of entanglement not only endorses this assessment, but also suggests recognising this very entanglement allows for prospective change: we are not only connected to networks, we are entangled with them and coconstitute them, and thus, we influence and affect them as well. On her part, Ahmed comments on "how threatening it can be to imagine alternatives to a system that survives by grounding itself in inevitability" (2010, 165) and suggests that

> [t]he political will to be affected by unhappiness could be rewritten as a political freedom. We would radicalize freedom as the freedom to be unhappy. The freedom to be unhappy is not about being wretched or sad, although it might involve freedom to express such feelings. The freedom to be unhappy would be the freedom to be affected by what is unhappy, and to live a life that might affect others unhappily. (2010, 195)

After Dana has almost drowned during the attempted crossing of the Mediterranean and is on the verge of dying, she is laid out in a sort of limbo while the demon Jarron and the Librarian argue over her body and about the respective role they played in her demise. Returning to Tsing's statement on the transformative effect of contamination, Jarron's frustration at Dana's death and his helpless inability to decide what to do with her indicate he has been profoundly affected by his encounter with her, and that he continues evolving. Neither Jarron nor the Librarian is taking proper responsibility for her suffering, but Jarron wishes to remove it from her timeline entirely to give her another chance at life:

JARRON: […] She made it to this side. We could wake her up. Give her some clothes. She could do her presentation, get the job, decent salary, buy a flat
She is one of the lucky ones
She could have everything
[…]

LIBRARIAN: but her eyes are open now, as you said, she can't shut them again. Even you can't shut them. What she has seen—she thought that men and women were basically good, human nature in essence benign. Then she saw it wash all away, one crisis and the jungle came at her, she heard the hyenas howling, saw hell etched on other people's faces.
[…]

JARRON: [...] we make her forget. We put her in a trance, we wash it off. She is as good as dead, we wash her in the river between the two worlds if we have to. (155–57)

Jarron decides to send Dana back to the moment she gave her first presentation to the funding body's interview panel, implying that she will pitch them exactly the same project on customer-business relationships. If Dana succeeds in her interview, she might be offered a position straight away or might decide to fly to the interview in Alexandria, thus circumventing getting physically caught up in the European crisis. She would then indeed be "one of the lucky ones" who "could have everything," while there will inevitably continue to be many who will have nothing, meaning the whole abusive, brutalising system will be perpetuated. By erasing Dana's memories and sending her back in front of her funding panel to give her presentation, Jarron does not only confirm the neoliberal doctrine that There Is No Alternative (TINA), he also robs her of the fundamental knowledge of having experienced global capitalism in its ruins and having endured "the sorrow of the stranger" (Ahmed 2010, 17). For all its criticism of the consumer-oriented society, the play thus remains safely nonradical.[11] Jarron sends Dana back into the role of a happy, functioning, therefore successful subject instead of allowing for the information she gained to be transformed into—and to transform her into—a potentially empowering instrument for change. To allow Dana to slip back into oblivion means taking away her choice to be unhappy and her potential for political change; she will once more have what Ahmed calls "the freedom to look away from what compromises one's happiness" (2010, 196). Allowing Dana to keep her memories of suffering and unhappiness would render her a constant reminder of the suffering Jarron prefers she left behind—for her sake, but also for his. As Ahmed points out, the wish to dispense with suffering "means that those who persist in their unhappiness become causes of the unhappiness of many. Their suffering becomes transformed into our collective disappointment that we cannot simply put such histories behind us" (2010, 216).

Elaine Aston sees a parallel between *How to Hold Your Breath* and Sarah Kane's 1995 play *Blasted* on account of their mutual departure from "a private sexual encounter that descends into global atrocities" and their formal rejection of mimetic realism (2017, 304). Yet the causality in *Blasted* is presented as much more linear—Kane herself confirmed that the connection between "a common rape in a Leeds hotel room" and what was happening in Bosnia had been obvious to her: "One is the seed and the other is the tree" (quoted in Buse 2001, 186)—whereas the relationship between the two systems in *How to Hold Your Breath* is one of entanglement. In Harris's play, mimetic realism is formally rejected insofar as the latter mostly relies on sequential structures, not on the concept of space-time. This is foregrounded by Harris's choice to loop the play back to the beginning. Indeed, *How to Hold Your Breath* revisits Harris's frequently used technique of narrative loop, which underpinned the war trilogy formed by *Midwinter* (2004), *Solstice* (2005) and *Fall* (2008) and played a significant role in *The Wheel* (2011) (Boll 2013). None of Harris's plays make an open, prominent argument about the nonlinearity of time, the fact that, in accordance with Albert Einstein's special theory of relativity, "time is but a fourth spatial dimension, and the usual couple 'space and time' becomes the single term 'space-time'" (Barad 2007, 437). But in both *The Wheel* and *How to Hold Your Breath*, the main character, facing death, is returned to an earlier point in her timeline and faces other possible outcomes, which resonates with both the nonlinearity of time and physicist Hugh Everett's many-worlds interpretation (1957).[12]

Following Barad's notion of responsibility, we can draw from the scene above, and indeed from the whole play, the conclusion that "there are no individual agents of change" because responsibility requires "an ongoing responsiveness to the entanglements of self and other" (2007, 394):

> If, as Levinas suggests, "proximity, difference which is non-indifference, is responsibility," then entanglements bring us face to face with the fact that what seems far off in space and time may be as close or closer than the pulse of here and now that appears to beat from a center that lies beneath the skin. The past is never finished once and for all and out of sight may be out of reach but not necessarily out of touch. (2007, 394)

Notably, in *How to Hold Your Breath* Jarron does not send Dana to a point in time before they meet, so their encounter and thus their intra-action will always already have happened and have left its mark on them. It remains open whether Jarron's decision to send her "back" is motivated by a wish to "contest and rework what matters" (Barad 2007, 178), and whether he believes resetting her timeline will efface the marks they have acquired as a result of their entanglement. Having witnessed her unhappiness and yet choosing not to erase the encounter, however, he has chosen the freedom to be affected by her unhappiness and to let himself be changed by it, too. This chosen openness to change and a different future, as Ahmed suggests, may present itself as potentially revolutionary:

> In imagining what is possible, in imagining what does not yet exist, we say yes to the future. In this yes, the future is not given content: it is not that the future is imagined as the overcoming of misery; nor is the future imagined as being happy. The future is what is kept open as the possibility of things not staying as they are, or being as they stay. Revolutionaries must dream; if their imaginations dwell *on* the injustice of how things stay, they do not simply dwell *in* what stays. (2010, 197; italics in the original)

On a structural level, *How to Hold Your Breath* points at multiple causal entanglements that not only affect the characters' choices and their trajectories, but also make up the core structure of the society and indeed the universe in which they move and operate. In its exploration of the construction of the individual as human capital, the play traces how a person adapts to ever more brutalising circumstances while she is being isolated and made to lose access to any and all infrastructural and affective/emotional support, until she is fully alienated from her life world. The desolate vision of a lone, disconnected figure conjured in the monologue opening the play, defined as she is by having failed at the civic duty to present as happy and well, to be the perfect neoliberal subject and thus a valuable citizen of the global society, stands in stark contrast to the intertwined second narrative in the play, which shows how fragile the capitalist system really is and how, suddenly, we may find ourselves living in its ruins. In the process, the play reveals the entanglement of different world-making systems and questions linear, one-directional notions of causality. The affective/emotional coconstitutive intra-relation between individuals is explored as an alternative conception to the individualising narrative of personal relationships as market-based transactions.

I suggest that Barad's focus on intra-action as becoming and transformation invites us to read her application of quantum entanglement as a possible way to reconcile diverse strands of affect theory. Barad argues that responsibility is preontological precisely because individuals and phenomena can only emerge from intra-actions, from entanglement. She therefore does not subscribe to a dualism between body and mind, nor, by extension, between affect and emotion. In logical conclusion, affect can also not be regarded as autonomous and "uncontaminated." Reading *How to Hold Your Breath* alongside Barad, but coming from Ahmed, allows for an alignment of quantum entanglement and the individualising self-care culture of late capitalism, the latter being revealed as continuously alienating the individual from acknowledging her affective/emotional relationships and intra-actions with other human and nonhuman forces. Linking the two approaches reveals the individualising narrative analysed and criticised by Ahmed, Connolly and Malabou and exemplified in one of the two main narrative strands of *How to Hold Your Breath* to be ultimately futile and counterproductive. Barad's approach foregrounds the entanglement of all systems and human and nonhuman actors and their ability to act as emerging precisely from their encounters and entanglements, as opposed to viewing a system's constituents as individual units devoid of any mutual involvement. Happiness can thus only be reclaimed as part of the individual if and when its emergence from intra-action is acknowledged and both relationships and affects/emotions cease to be treated as autonomous, marketable commodities.

Notes

1. I would like to thank all three editors for their invaluable comments and suggestions, as well as my colleague Nina Engelhardt for essential feedback and advice.
2. *How to Hold Your Breath* premiered on February 4, 2015, at the Royal Court's Jerwood Theatre Downstairs, under the direction of Vicky Featherstone. It ran for six weeks.
3. Several of these ideas were formed in dialogue with the students of my "Theatre/Theory" honours seminar at the University of Konstanz (2017–2018). I would specifically like to acknowledge Svetlana Kulikov's unpublished work on neoliberalism and gender in *How to Hold Your Breath* and Shakespeare's *As You Like It*, in which she argues that migration is used as a neoliberal tool shaping perfect, self-sufficient neoliberal selves (2018).
4. Several passages in the script indicate this could be Berlin in Germany.
5. The name is Germanic enough to suggest a traveling route through the Czech Republic, Austria and Hungary, if starting from Berlin. While the exact setting of the play is not directly relevant either to the play itself or to the argument of this chapter, it is nevertheless interesting to note that one of the few British plays addressing the interdependencies between current refugee movements and the recent global economic crisis is quite deliberately *not* set in Britain.
6. Here Türken et al. draw on Lynne Layton (2010).

7. In a passage analysing the Royal Court production's casting choices, Tom Cornford questions the production's problematic "abjection of racialized migrant-figures" and how the play's valid critique of "the imbrication of consumerism and structural violence" nevertheless stripped the ensemble-cast refugee figures of their subjectivity (2018, 105).
8. I thank my colleague Timothy C. Baker for suggesting I "read more Anna Tsing." His deployment of Tsing's thought on friction and precarity (Baker 2019) has certainly influenced my thinking about encounters, contamination and the prospect of change.
9. The pattern of shifting responsibility onto the victim is anticipated early in the play, when Jarron tells Dana, whom he mistakes for a sex worker when they first meet, "you ought to wear more when you go out / you ought to be more careful about the message you send" (20). The parallel to the victim blaming behaviour inherent to rape culture is obvious here.
10. In quantum physics, particles do not have exactly defined positions and velocities. They are described by the so-called wave function, which contains everything there is to know about a particle: its position and its velocity.
11. Commenting on Dana's revival and the erasure of the painful memories of her journey, Aston also criticises what she terms "the greater flaw" of the play: "[Dana] comes to stand for all of us whose economic privilege occludes the suffering that could be, but is not avoided" (2017, 305).
12. Everett first presented his Theory of the Universal Wave Function, later named "many-worlds" by Bryce DeWitt, in his thesis at Princeton University in 1956. It assumes the existence of a universal wave function by which all possible events and histories are real but happen in an infinite number of distinct universes all embedded within a greater multiverse.

References

Ahmed, Sara. 2010. *The Promise of Happiness*. Durham, NC and London: Duke UP.

Aston, Elaine. 2017. "Moving Women Centre Stage: Structures of Feminist-Tragic Feeling." *Journal of Contemporary Drama in English* 5 (2): 292–310.

Baker, Timothy C. 2019. *Writing Animals: Language, Suffering and Animality in Twenty-First Century Fiction*. London: Palgrave Macmillan.

Barad, Karen. 2007. *Meeting the Universe Halfway: Quantum Physics and the Entanglement of Matter and Meaning*. Durham, NC and London: Duke UP.

———. 2010. "Quantum Entanglements and Hauntological Relations of Inheritance: Dis/continuities, SpaceTime Enfoldings, and Justice-to-Come." *Derrida Today* 3 (2): 240–68.

Boll, Julia. 2013. "Last Girl Standing: On Zinnie Harris's War Plays." *International Journal of Scottish Theatre and Screen* 6 (1): 37–53.

Buse, Peter. 2001. *Drama and Theory: Critical Approaches to Modern Drama.* Manchester: Manchester UP.

Cederström, Carl and André Spicer. 2015. *The Wellness Syndrome.* Cambridge: Polity. Kindle edition.

Connolly, William E. 2013. *The Fragility of Things: Self-Organizing Processes, Neoliberal Fantasies, and Democratic Activism.* Durham, NC and London: Duke UP.

Cornford, Tom. 2018. "Experiencing Nationlessness: Staging the Migrant Condition in Some Recent British Theatre." *Journal of Contemporary Drama in English* 6 (1): 101–12.

Everett, Hugh. 1957. "'Relative State' Formulation of Quantum Mechanics." *Review of Modern Physics* 29 (3): 454–62.

Greig, David. 2002. *Plays: 1.* London: Bloomsbury.

Hall, Stuart. 2011. "The Neo-Liberal Revolution." *Cultural Studies* 25 (6): 705–28.

Harris, Zinnie. 2004. *Midwinter.* London: Faber.

———. 2005. *Solstice.* London: Faber.

———. 2008. *Fall.* London: Faber.

———. 2011. *The Wheel.* London: Faber.

———. 2015. *How to Hold Your Breath.* London: Nick Hern Books.

Kane, Sarah. (1995) 2002. *Blasted.* London: Methuen.

Layton, Lynne. 2010. "Irrational Exuberance: Neoliberal Subjectivity and the Perversion of Truth." *Subjectivity* 3: 303–22.

Malabou, Catherine. 2008. *What Should We Do with Our Brain?* Translated by Sebastian Rand. New York: Fordham UP.

Penny, Laurie. 2016. "Life-Hacks of the Poor and Aimless: On Negotiating the False Idols of Neoliberal Self-Care." War of Nerves series. *The Baffler*, July 8. Accessed February 22, 2019.

Tokumitsu, Miya. 2018. "Tell Me It's Going to be OK: Self-Care and Social Retreat under Neoliberalism." *The Baffler* 41. Accessed February 22, 2019.

Tsing, Anna Lowenhaupt. 2015. *The Mushroom at the End of the World: On the Possibility of Life in Capitalist Ruins.* Princeton, NJ: Princeton UP.

Türken, Salman et al. 2016. "Making Sense of Neoliberal Subjectivity: A Discourse Analysis of Media Language on Self-Development." *Globalizations* 13 (1): 32–46.

Tyler, Imogen. 2013. *Revolting Subjects: Social Abjection and Resistance in Neoliberal Britain.* London: Zed Books.

CHAPTER 12

Theatre at the End of the World

Mark Robson

The Future of the End of the World

Two voices in the dark. The first says: "The future of the world is not my future."

How is this to be heard? To state that the future of the world is not mine is to recognise an inevitability, or rather, to begin to prise apart the layers of what is all too often given as an inevitability: the world is not mine to dominate, even in imagination, and the future is not something that I can "know." Or, instead, the sentence may be taken as saying: I know that what is called the world was here before me, and that this world will outlive me, since both the world and I are finite, but it is impossible not to see that those finitudes do not coincide. Or else, flatly, it says: after I am dead, the world will no longer be my concern. Or again but differently, a claim that acts as a disclaimer: I am not one of the rulers of the world, my actions in the present are not meaningfully shaping the future that seems to be coming, perhaps I have even spent my life trying to resist that future, so I cannot be held responsible for whatever comes to pass. These questions of responsibility claimed and disclaimed will echo through this discussion.

M. Robson (✉)
University of Dundee, Dundee, UK
e-mail: m.robson@dundee.ac.uk

M. Aragay et al. (eds.), *Affects in 21st-Century British Theatre*,
https://doi.org/10.1007/978-3-030-58486-3_12

Perhaps it is not primarily a matter of how future is defined, but instead a consideration of the constitution of the world, making this a simpler statement of philosophical idealism, which can be distinguished from psychology or solipsism: there is nothing that I might meaningfully call a "world" without my consciousness of it, and therefore, for me, the world cannot meaningfully be said to have a future without me.

Another voice—let us imagine in response, although it was not conceived as one—says: "To be human we need to experience the end of the world."

To say that it is not only possible but necessary to experience the end of the world works wholly otherwise than the first statement, whichever of its modalities we pick. The world divides. To be able to experience the end of the world, it must be possible to project a space or time "beyond" the end, to survive it, at least in imagination—even if that survival may not feel like survival. Such experience is necessarily poetic, made not found, that is, crafted rather than given. But for this second speaker everything hinges on this experience, including being human, since it is what makes it possible to conceive of the fact that there is more than one world and that the world that was "known" was not what it appeared to be.

These two statements, both by playwrights but not torn from plays—one from Heiner Müller (1984, 140); the other, Hélène Cixous (1993, 10)—do not encapsulate their work, dramatic or intellectual. I am not reading them as expressive of a personality, but rather as markers of a complexity around the relation of the future to the end of the world.

One way of trying to think these two sentences together is to recognise the specifically fable-like characteristic of the end of the world. Just as Jacques Derrida underlines the "fabulously textual" nature of the idea of nuclear catastrophe, since it is something that, having not yet occurred, for the time being can only be talked about (2007, 393), so he is equally insistent that this should prompt reconsideration of the power of rhetoric, particularly its harnessing of reason and affect to produce opinion and belief in ways that act performatively. Suspending distinctions between truth and fiction, belief in the fable of the end of the world leads to techno-military-politico-diplomatic investments that reveal the worldly power of affect, even where that cannot be translated into knowledge.

Catastrophe

Certain British playwrights have made the affective dimension of theatre an explicit question within their work in recent years, and here I will cite only some particularly striking examples that have appeared on Scottish stages. In addition to my two main examples in this chapter—Stef Smith's *Swallow* (Traverse Theatre, Edinburgh; first performed on August 9, 2015) and Kieran Hurley's *Heads Up* (first presented at Summerhall, Edinburgh, in August 2016; no precise date in the script)—plays such as David Greig's *The Events* (2013), which explores the limits of empathy in the wake of an atrocity, or Zinnie Harris's *This Restless House* (2016), an adaptation of the *Oresteia* that is recast in terms of contemporary debates around mental health, and *Meet Me at Dawn* (2017), a lyrical piece on grief, have probed the affective resources of the Western theatrical tradition.

The turn to affect that such plays embody has been accompanied by another strophic figure, what might be thought of as a poetics of catastrophe.[1] Perhaps this should not be surprising. The earliest sense of the word *catastrophe* given by the *Oxford English Dictionary* is the name given to the final turn or twist that precedes the dénouement of a drama. Not in itself the conclusion, it is that from which conclusion flows. It is only later that this dramatic term transfers to events in the world, and in this drift from the dramatic it also shifts to the end, that is, to *become* the end or conclusion rather than prompting it. A species of dramaturgy is employed to give shape to events in the world that without the framing power of form may appear simply random or meaningless. Catastrophe becomes the structure for that which lacks structure or in which no structure is apparent. Does this entail a dramatisation or theatricalisation of what might otherwise be called the real? Not as such. Catastrophe is a *form* of explanation. But this form has its own affective dimension: catastrophe is experienced as unhappiness or misery, and the threat of it arouses fear or anxiety. That threat lies in part in catastrophe's power of interruption, its tendency to be associated with systemic change, or with the falling away of "things as they are." This is the end of the world as the recognition that the world that presented itself as natural was not the only possible world. Catastrophe is an explanatory ordering that is substituted for the order of things. It is not reassuring, even if it opens on to a vision of another world that at least makes apparent that an alternative to the present order is possible. Another name for this threat, then, might be hope. It should not be forgotten that what for one group of people is a catastrophe may be interpreted by another as an opportunity (Klein 2007).

For theatre to turn to catastrophe is to enact a return, to go back to a dramatic form from which the everyday sense of catastrophe emerges. In itself, the strophe of catastrophe contains both a turn and a (poetic) structure, marking the break without which there could be no structure. The break is what makes continuity perceptible. There is a rhythmic dimension. If this is the case, is turning to the end of the world what makes the continuity of drama possible? Drawing together affect and catastrophe, I will begin to unfold some of these ideas with the help of Smith's *Swallow* and Hurley's *Heads Up*. First, though, I would like to place the specific forms of affect conjured by catastrophe in a wider—but still very limited—context of affect and performance.

And the Sky Can Still Fall on Our Heads

In a revealing moment in one of the most influential theatre texts of the twentieth century, Antonin Artaud, writing in 1933, explains that he is proposing what he names a "theatre of cruelty" because "[w]e are not free. And the sky can still fall on our heads. And theatre has been created [est fait] to teach us that, first of all" (1993, 60, 2004, 552 for the inserted French text). Far from any vision of emancipation, Artaud stresses an unfreedom that is given shape by a metaphor of catastrophe, one which he uses frequently in *The Theatre and Its Double* to describe the contemporary world. In turn, this metaphor is given force by being tied to a primary pedagogic function: that the sky may fall is what theatre has been "created"—by whom?—to teach us "first of all." This is what we might call catastrophe as first pedagogy.

For theatre to have a pedagogic function presupposes that there is a relation between what appears in performance and the realm inhabited by the spectators. This seems self-evident, but it is worth thinking about the nature of this relation in a text such as Artaud's. The sky can still fall on our heads: this is a vision of a *shared* fate that is insistently reinforced by "we," "our," "us." As Samuel Weber points out, there is something curiously Aristotelian in Artaud's insistence on the didactic function of theatre, and this is not diminished even when coupled with the idea that actions that appear on the stage cannot simply be repeated elsewhere (Weber 2004, 279). Artaud's avowed anti-Aristotelianism—unlike Brecht's, for instance—is rooted in a rejection of a psychological rather than a political tradition—although there is a point at which psychology and politics cross and structure each other. The pedagogical dimension of drama is linked to a conception of mimesis that, as Weber puts it, "proceeds more through feeling, *pathos*, than through conceptual understanding" (2004, 281). It is necessary to be cautious about identifying the nature of what might appear to be a universalising invocation of the "we," however. Artaud's true target in rejecting psychologism is not individualism per se but rather humanism. What he is attempting to displace or unsettle is a stability to the cosmos that seeks its guarantee in the essentialised privileging of "man." That stable cosmos, says Weber, is the focus of Artaud's comment about the sky falling on our heads. As Weber puts it: "the *actuality* of the Theater of Cruelty lies not in its practical feasibility but in its *coupling of violence with virtuality*—which is to say, in its relation to the future as *risk*" (2004, 284; italics in the original).

As this chapter progresses, I will circle around these notions of futurity and risk, of the relation between theatre and world, of violence and the invocation of a "we," "our" or "us." The notion of affect emerging here is intimately linked to a sense of world. In the theatre, affect appears "in the room," in that curious unlocatable location that opens up between performance and audience in a given space. Affect rests on structures of identification and dis-identification between the audience and the onstage world that cannot be limited to a narrowly "aesthetic" response, but which are rooted in older notions of *aesthesis*; in other words, it makes apparent the combination of sensory response and reason in aesthetic judgment (Robson 2005). The cultivation of affect in the theatre has been a crucial element in the articulation of theatre's function from the earliest discussions in the Western tradition, often precisely in order to be able to claim that theatre *has* effects on its audiences. One of the consequences of this is that theatre's political resonances have conventionally rarely strayed far from what might for shorthand be thought of as a Horatian aesthetic, with its roots in Aristotle: the purpose of theatre is to teach and to delight. To take a somewhat brutal shortcut, we might say that in the Western tradition, theatre's history is a history of oscillation between reinforcement of and resistance to that sense of pedagogico-political purpose.

Of course, and at the same time, what is wrong with theatre, what makes it truly objectionable, is that it is bound up on so many levels with affect. As I have discussed elsewhere, it is the affective dimension of theatrical performance that is tied to political instability in Plato's *Republic*, and this suspicion of theatre's capacity for affect has cast a long shadow across the Western dramatic tradition and its critical reception (Robson 2018). Precisely to the extent that theatre involves actors speaking about things that they do not themselves "know," that is, that they have not experienced or in which they have no expertise, dramatic performance places itself at a remove from truth. The problem is the familiar objection to representation. The frame for Plato's objection to theatrical representation needs to be recalled, however. The discussion in the *Republic* has as its primary concern the need to think about political effectiveness. In this context, art and the aesthetic have no value in themselves. Political forms such as democracy that rely on the response of a crowd to a discourse that can be persuasive without being true are always in danger of a catastrophic fall into tyranny. There is an echo here of what Derrida says of the fable and its suspension of the distinction between truth and fiction, although Derrida does not move from this into a negative reading of fable. An inevitable crossover between these thoughts means that for Plato politics is not something to be added to theatre; rather, it subtends theatrical form.

In the antitheatrical, antipoetic logic of the *Republic*, theatrical performance and political rhetoric come together such that affect has ineluctable political implications. For Plato, tragedy in particular arouses excessive emotions in both the actors who perform it and the audience who mimetically amplify this pathos, to their own detriment and that of the *polis*. This political, even moral, reading persists in the usages of the word *affect* that stress its separation from reason, that avert to the emotional forces that lead to a distorted sense of the world. Framed in this way, the notion of the *theatrum mundi* might be read as an accusation.

Political Affect

In a conversation with Pierre-Philippe Jandin that takes place under the heading of "Political Affect," Jean-Luc Nancy makes the following observation: "if one thinks about all the relations together—beginning with 'relation' itself—then one must also consider that any relation is a relation of affect: it's acceptance or refusal, assimilation or rejection, retraction, fear, identification, preference ..." (2017, 76; ellipsis in the original). Keeping in mind the terms concatenated in this list, I want to remark a curious inversion of expectation. Affect implies relation, one might think—that is, it would seem to be what the phenomenologists would call *intentional* in that it invites us to think in terms of a subject-object relation. But relation, says Nancy, *is* affect. A fold appears: affect is relational but relation is affect. The English translation introduces an uneasy repetition as if to emphasise this fold: "any relation is *a relation of* affect," says the English, splitting or doubling "relation" in its attempts to grasp the relation between one language and another. The language of the translation strains to hold apart what Nancy's French text collapses: "tout rapport *est* affect" (2013, 76; italics added). To say "any relation is a relation of" puts the brakes on the "as such"—"en tant que tel" (2013, 76), which is not quite "itself"—of any, every, perhaps the whole of relation—"tout rapport" (2013, 76).[2] In a more material way, Nancy goes on to suggest how different governmental forms entail different affective relations. Political affect in this account is not a subdivision of affect but rather a structural element of the political that cannot but come into play as the political seeks to frame affect.[3]

What underpins this understanding of affect is Nancy's—as always—equivocal reading of Martin Heidegger (Critchley 1999). Recognising both the impact of *Being and Time* (*Sein und Zeit*, 1927) and the need for it to be rethought in order to avoid some of the by now well-known political and ethical ramifications of Heidegger's thinking of political community, Nancy nonetheless retains Heidegger's fundamental thinking about being-in-the-world (*In-der-Welt-sein*) and being-with (*Mitsein*)—a project *Etre singulier pluriel* (Nancy 1996) could be said to begin. That is, Nancy continues to think subjectivity as intersubjectivity. Relation is not something that befalls being but is what constitutes being. Heidegger states in *Being and Time*, for example, that, "[t]he world of Dasein is a *with-world* [*Mitwelt*]. Being-in is *being-with* [*Mitsein*] others. The innerworldly being-in-itself of others is *Dasein-with* [*Mitdasein*]" (2010, 116; italics in the original). Heidegger places with-ness at the centre of his thinking in this part of *Being and Time*, and stresses that others are encountered "environmentally," that is, as (coming) out of the world. While Heidegger writes of care and solicitude (*Sorge* and *Fürsorge*), "empathy" ("*Einfühlung*," always in this section of Heidegger's text held in inverted commas) is not seen as an ontological bridge to the other, but is rather rejected as a form of projection in which the other is simply treated as a duplicate (*Dublette*) of the self on the basis of a dubious imposition of similitude for which there is no evidentiary basis. Heidegger says: "'Empathy' does not first constitute being-with, but is first possible on its basis, and is motivated by the prevailing deficient modes of being-with in their inevitablility" (2010, 121).[4] If empathy is rejected as a basis in itself for relating to the other, it remains unclear precisely how that relation is to be defined, although Heidegger insists that the other is to be known existentially by what she *does* (2010, 122–26).

As Nancy suggests in his interview with Jandin, the recognition of the other is a major lapsus in much political thinking in the Western tradition, not least in Heidegger. Nancy's sense is that Heidegger did vital work "because he dismissed all the other ways of recognizing the other, which were based on reasoning or empathy, by maintaining that what's given from the start is myth" (2017, 83).[5] But Heidegger does not then adequately interrogate the thinking of myth itself.[6] If Nancy is drawing on the idea that relation is constitutive of being, but then proposing that relation is affect, then perhaps we need to think of affect as constitutive of being.

It is worth recognising some provisional distinctions within the category of affect. Drawing differently on Heidegger, Sara Ahmed opens up a distinction between fear and anxiety, for example, by thinking about the differing relations to objects in each case. Ahmed proposes that fear "projects us from the present into a future" in the anticipation of a pain to come (2014, 65). Fear can entail fixation. Precisely because it is not attached to a specific object, however, anxiety can attach itself to multiple objects: "One thinks of more and more things to be anxious about; the detachment from a given object allows anxiety to accumulate through gathering more and more objects, until it overwhelms other possible affective relations to the world [...]. Anxiety becomes *an approach to objects* rather than, as with fear, *being produced by an object's approach*" (Ahmed 2014, 66, italics in the original; see also Bauman 2006). Anxiety is not one affect among others in this scenario, but one that potentially absorbs any other, just as it dissolves the relation to a particular object into relation to objects *tout court*. The end of the world more obviously produces fear than anxiety, so my emphasis will lie there, but the tendency to treat present objects as signs of the approach of the end makes the line between anxiety and fear somewhat permeable.

I want to briefly trace the trail that leads Ahmed to this point and go back to Heidegger. In *Being and Time*, Heidegger treats fear from the perspective of a frame of mind or "attunement"—*Befindlichkeit*—which he subdivides into (a) that which provokes fear—*Wovor*—(b) fearing and (c) that about which we fear—*Worum*—which is more easily understood in English as fearing *for* another person or thing. The fearsome—*das Furchtbare*—he proposes "is always something encountered within the world [ein innerweltlich Begegnendes]" (Heidegger 2010, 136; for the German text, Heidegger 2006, 140). Fear is always fear in relation to the world, then. This is not a matter of discovering an object to be feared, nor of being scared and finding something to explain that fear, but rather, "[a]s a dormant possibility of attuned being-in-the-world, fearing, 'fear-fulness' has already disclosed the world with regard to the fact that something like a fearful thing can draw near to us from this fearfulness" (Heidegger 2010, 137).[7] The disclosure of the world as containing the potential to be experienced fearfully tells us about the world as much as our inner selves. As Rei Terada puts it, in another context, "[f]ear not only expresses the inner state of the frightened person, but forms a hypothesis about something in the outside world as well" (2001, 57).

Heidegger notes that his discussion of fear is based on a section of Aristotle's *Rhetoric* that also discusses fear as a frame of mind. Aristotle begins by suggesting that "[f]ear may be defined as a pain or disturbance due to imagining some destructive or painful evil in the future" (1995, 2202), and goes on to suggest—as Heidegger repeats—that this fear is only triggered when this evil seems close at hand. In this section of the *Rhetoric*, Aristotle also clarifies the relationship between pity and fear, stating: "Speaking generally, anything causes us to feel fear that when it happens to, or threatens, others causes us to feel pity" (1995, 2203). Pity is generated by Heidegger's *Worum*, fear *for* rather than fear *of* another.[8] It is no doubt obvious where a reading that extends this into the understanding of the effects of tragedy in the *Poetics* might begin.[9]

If fear is linked to proximity, does this help us to think through fear of the end of the world? Some moments in world history, or in the personal histories of those individuals and groups confronted by catastrophe, may make the end seem closer than others. But this question of closeness may lead to a misstep in thinking of the end. As Nancy puts it in *After Fukushima*, "[t]he end is always far away; the present is the place of closeness—with the world, others, oneself," but in fact the present "has its end in itself in both senses of the word end: its goal and its cessation" (2015, 37).[10] In a more recent cowritten text, this is expressed as, "[t]he end has always already begun" (Ferrari and Nancy 2018, 17).[11]

From Pity to Com-Passion

Nancy's *Being Singular Plural* opens with an extraordinary preface, dated to the summer of 1995 and written in the shadow of the "martyr-name" Sarajevo (2000, xiii). Nancy lists the places and groups that he sees in the "theater of bloody conflicts among identities" (2000, xii). In this world "lacking in world, and lacking in the meaning of world" (2000, xiii),[12] Nancy suggests that what is needed is compassion, but this must immediately be specified: "What I am talking about here is compassion, but not compassion as a pity that feels sorry for itself and feeds on itself. Com-passion is the contagion, the contact of being with one another in this turmoil. Compassion is not altruism, nor is it identification; it is the disturbance of violent relatedness" (2000, xiii).

"La contiguité brutale" (Nancy 1996, 12)—violent relatedness, yes, but also the shock of stark contiguity, allowing a sense of spatial proximity, of a shaking (as of foundations in an earthquake), sudden and exposing. Com-passion, like Nancy's use elsewhere of *comparution*—literally "co-appearance," but with a specific legal sense of appearing as if summoned to court, captured in the Scottish-English term *compearance* (Nancy 1992)—underlines a logic of the "with" that carries its own affect, located in the fact of relation rather than in an object. There is no assurance that this is a purely positive acknowledgement of relatedness. If relation is affect, then negative affect reveals negative relation.

The End of Empathy

Hurley's *Heads Up* weaves together a city's narratives at the end of the world, in which a sense of violent relatedness is undisguised. It is a one-man show, which I saw performed by Hurley as part of a tour at the Traverse Theatre, Edinburgh, in 2017. The piece is best described as storytelling rather than naturalist drama. A table, chair, microphone, desk lamps, candle and audio samplers stand in place of a set. The imaginative work of the audience is primarily focused on conjuring the scenes that "Kieran"—the name given to the speaker in the script—describes as he sits at the table.[13]

It is clear from the outset that this is a story of the end of the world—the second line of the script says so explicitly—and a juxtaposition is immediately established in the first scene, introducing a character called Mercy who deals in Futures. Mercy has a Biblical quotation about wonders and signs (Acts 2.19) on her desk that reveals as it conceals, since it stops in midverse, before the signs are named: blood, fire and smoke. The initial effect of the piece is unsettling since Kieran addresses the first scene to a "you," inviting the audience to align themselves with the one addressed. The future is where it all happens, says Kieran, but that future is "just a deal we make between ourselves now and an imagined future moment" (Hurley 2016, 9). Mercy is one of Naomi Klein's disaster capitalists, trading in catastrophe and crisis (Klein 2007). The "you" shifts, unfolding a collection of characters who share moments in time and the space of the city. a girl playing a computer game called Ash, who likes destroying her creations in the game with disasters; a coke-driven musician, Léon, who wants to save the bees; Abdullah, who works for a coffee chain that wants to be able to define his behaviour in exchange for minimum wage and whose everyday life is a state of emergency.

This sharing is far from equal, and what makes that inequality apparent is in part the varying degrees of control that these characters have over their affective lives. In the place of Abdullah, Kieran tells us: "You remember reading something about paracetamol, how it doesn't just block up pain, it blocks up how you see pain. In others. Not just physical pain, like emotional suffering. You can't actually recognise it or tell what it is in the same way, under the drugs. You think: like we need to feel pain, then. To be able to understand each other, to know each other, to live together" (21–22). Hurley's text is close to Cixous here, echoing her suggestion that to be fully human we have to experience pain, perhaps even the end of the world, if we are to recognise the world as shared (1993, 10). But there is a limit and, as in Heidegger, it is bound to empathy. A moment later in the scene, Abdullah thinks: "too much empathy is a fucking killer. In fact empathy can gigantically go and fuck itself" (22).

Heads Up knits together narratives of crisis, states of emergency, the deadening demands of work, rolling news, everyday humiliation and bullying, until the "you" addressed dissolves into the nonhuman, the inanimate, becoming part of the city and its detritus. As Liz Tomlin suggests, it is the narrative rather than the staging that has the strongest "affective charge" for an audience as the end of the world—and the performance—approaches (2019, 111). The future is rooted in the present with which "you" become(s) serially identified. Then the "you" turns on itself, describing Kieran. His purpose in storytelling is explained by one simple phrase: "it's easier to imagine the end of this world than it is to imagine what a new one might look like" (47). The sky can fall on our heads. In fact, Hurley's text is asking the audience to recall an infamous phrase—attributed variously to Fredric Jameson or Slavoj Žižek and shaping significantly Mark Fisher's *Capitalist Realism* (2009)—that has somehow lost its moorings in the thought of any individual to become a contemporary catch-all diagnosis: it is easier to imagine the end of the world than the end of capitalism (see also Rebellato 2017).

Hurley's piece embeds a form of reflexivity: Ash plays games that involve building a world that she then destroys and Hurley admits that the world of the performance is one created in order to be annihilated. Created to be destroyed, the fictional world fictions its end. Symbolically, this takes a ritual form in performance: the candle is lit just before the first line is spoken and blown out at the end. The point is not, I think, to offer a vision of an alternative world, but rather to recognise that alternatives to this world are possible even as all the signs point to its apparently inevitable destruction—Mercy's premonitions, the disappearance of the bees and so on. Hurley is not proposing a utopian future but a potential for resistance already in the present that needs to be realised through the present's negation.

Someone Just Like Me

Imagination takes on a very different resonance in Smith's *Swallow*. The printed text carries the following epigraph, taken from an interview with Frida Kahlo published in *Vogue* magazine in 1937. Kahlo says:

> I used to think I was the strangest person in the world but then I thought there are so many people in the world, there must be someone just like me who feels bizarre and flawed in the same ways I do. I would imagine her, and imagine that she must be out there thinking of me too. Well, I hope that if you are out there and read this now and know that, yes, it's true I'm here, and I'm just as strange as you. (Smith 2015, 3)

Everything hinges on imagination and identification. Thinking is prompted by feeling. The logic of Kahlo's comment is a kind of virtuous circle: the shift is from believing that I am the strangest one to knowing that, however strange I am, there is someone else—that there may be many others, in fact—quite as strange as me. There is some comfort in being one of the strange rather than the strangest one, and to knowing that to believe oneself to be bizarre and flawed is shared. But how does Kahlo arrive at this consolation? It is a deduction based on probability—"so many people"—which is then used as the springboard for a kind of thought experiment in which not only is the other person imagined, but that imagined person is also gifted a speculative imagination—I imagine her imagining me. What does not enter into this deduction is a critical relation to the initial feeling: what if Kahlo is in fact neither bizarre nor flawed? There is a slippage between feeling strange and being strange, an affirmation of strangeness that also stakes a claim to it. Empathy, sympathy and ultimately telepathy are at stake. In the empathy at work here, there is a sensed distance from the world that is assuaged by something in the world. Rather than prompting a rejection of the world, then, the answer to estrangement is imaginative immersion in a world in which strangeness is shared (out).

In *Swallow*, three strangers, Sam, Anna and Rebecca, each attempting to leave their former lives and to create a new one, gradually find ways out of destructive and self-destructive behaviours. The set design for the Traverse production, by Fred Meller, began by emphasising their isolation. As the play unfolds, they begin to interact, with each other and with the world. Around two-thirds of the way through, Anna, who has not left her flat for more than a year, is prompted by Rebecca to explain what has happened to her. She gives a speech that is striking for its compelling unbelievability, that is, for its ability to convey an affective truth that could never be translated into a "rational" one:

> You know the Twin Towers?
> I was there. 9/11.
> You know those London bombings? I was
> there too.
>
> Lockerbie. I saw the plane fall from the sky.
> Chernobyl. I watched the trees melt. The truth is I
> was forced to dig the graves for Auschwitz.
>
> I also have cancer and HIV and bird flu. I've
> burned books and bodies. I've recruited child
> soldiers. I've stoned women to death. I injected
> heroin into pregnant mothers and I've evicted
> people on their birthdays. I've also placed pillows
> over the faces of newborns, set homeless people
> on fire, starved families and withheld drinking
> water, buried people alive and left them to rot and
> I've plunged puppies into boiling water.
>
> I've hung people from hooks and watched them
> bleed to death. I heard them cry. I heard them
> shout. I heard them plead for their lives and still I
> helped build the first nuclear bomb. I set it off.

> I mean I gave Pocahontas smallpox.
> I gave Myra Hindley that haircut and I told her she
> looked nice.
> I rejected Hitler from art school.
> And, I drowned the last dodo.
>
> That's what happened to me. (29–30)

Terrorism, nuclear accidents, the Holocaust, sickness and disease, exploitation, violence, murder, torture, serial killers, dictators, extinction. The speech treads the line between the impossible and the all too possible. Rebecca's understated response is perfectly judged: "I'm not sure that's actually what happened" (30). Everything is in the word "actually."

What brings Anna pain is her identification with the perpetrators of crimes rather than the victims. Watching the performance, I am reminded of Primo Levi's luminous reading of the final scene of Kafka's *The Trial* ([1925] 2009), in which the guilt of K. is explained by his ability to identify with those who are about to execute him. What K. feels, says Levi, is the shame of being a man, that is, the shame of being capable of what these humans are about to inflict on him (1991, 109).[14] Negative affect revealing negative, violent relatedness. In two later plays, *Human Animals* (2016) and *Girl in the Machine* (2017), Smith confronts catastrophe directly. In *Swallow*, it seems that the catastrophe has already happened and the play unfolds the aftermath. These are past crimes, and Anna's withdrawal from the world into the solitude of her flat is both painful and necessary if she is to find resources for an alternative to an obsessively imagined repetition of these crimes.

The first part of Anna's speech echoes Sarah Kane's *4.48 Psychosis* in its listing of crimes (Kane 2001, 227), but the quasi-comic turn to Hindley, Hitler and the dodo at the end of the speech produces a very different effect on stage. What gives the speech in *Swallow* its power is both the discomfiting mixture of cliché and imaginative horror with ridiculous overextension, and also the almost immediate deflation by Rebecca. Her "actually" evaporates Anna's sense that the world is necessarily as it seems to her in this moment. The exchange hovers between pathos and bathos, but also troubles the line between reason and emotion. The power of the affective response is conveyed by the impossibility of taming it by thinking it away, but it is not simply endorsed. In the Traverse production directed by Orla O'Loughlin—in which Anna was played by Emily Wachter,

Rebecca by Anita Vitesse and Sam by Sharon Duncan-Brewster—the speech was delivered in a way that allowed the audience to believe that it sincerely communicated Anna's state of mind while it was simultaneously impossible to believe what she literally said. In speeches such as this, performative force escapes the constative truth or falsity of what is said, to put it in J. L. Austin's terms, and it is this performative dimension that carries the affective charge and in which the claim to affective truth lies. But this does not cancel truth.

Swallow finds its way towards a positive ending. Opening with destruction, the way is cleared for something else to emerge from the wreckage of that former lifeworld. In a final speech, Sam says, "Back in the world now. Reconnect" (49). Having experienced the end of the world, it is possible to live (in) another.

Coda

Contemporary theatre faces an aporia. Any critical relation to the present is affective as well as critical, even as criticism conventionally claims to transcend affect, since—following Nancy—relation *is* affect. This plays out in a tendency for theatre to present the present as either inescapably tied to the (negative) actions of the past or else as containing the kernel of a (negative) future. To fabulate the end of the world is to negate the present in the name of the future, but by that negation to open up the possibility of a future the traces of which the present already contains, even if only in negative form. To feel the end of the world is to experience that future as hope.

Notes

1. What I am considering here is a more literal sense of a theatre of catastrophe than that envisaged by Howard Barker (Barker 1997).
2. The full passage in the French source reads: "si on pense à l'ensemble des rapports—c'est à dire d'abord au 'rapport' en tant que tel—alors il faut aussi considérer que tout rapport est affect: il est acceptation ou refus, assimilation ou rejet, dédire, crainte, identification, préférence …" (Nancy 2013, 76).
3. This might map on to Frédéric Lordon's Spinoza-inspired arguments around the, for him, false distinction between political rationality and supposedly nonrational political passion. For a summary of views worked out over several books, see Lordon (2016).

4. In the German source, "'Einfühlung' konstituiert nicht erst das Mitsein, sondern ist auf dessen Grunde erst möglich und durch die vorherrschenden defizienten Modi des Mitseins in ihrer Unumgänglichkeit motiviert" (2006, 125).
5. In Nancy's French text, "dismissed" is *écarté*—so swerved or put a space or distance from—and "other" is *autri* (2013, 81).
6. Nancy has attempted this work, and his primary conclusion is that the thinking of myth in Western thought is so to speak mythical. In other words, our dominant understanding of myth is a myth, and one which has been used to underpin some disastrous political projects, including that of Heidegger (Nancy 1991).
7. In the German source, "Das Fürchten als schlummernde Möglichkeit des befindlichen In-der-Welt-seins, die 'Furchtsamkeit,' hat die Welt schon darauf hin erschlossen, daß aus ihr so etwas wie Furchtbares nahen kann" (Heidegger 2006, 141).
8. Marc Crépon usefully distinguishes between terror and fear, suggesting that fear functions at the level of the individual, in anticipation of suffering alone. A sense of solitude is part of suffering. Terror, on the other hand, is always experienced collectively. Both can be cultivated for political ends, conjoined to form a culture of fear (2008, 13).
9. Pity inevitably recalls Aristotle's handling of catharsis in the *Poetics*, but it is important to remember Theodor W. Adorno's statement that "[c]atharsis is a purging action directed against the affects and an ally of repression" (1997, 238). "[A]lly of repression" translates the German source's "einverstanden mit Unterdrückung" (Adorno 2003, 354).
10. In the French source, "closeness" is *proximité* and "end," *fin* (Nancy 2012, 63).
11. My translation from the French original. There is not the space to pursue this here, but this offers an opening to the work of Catherine Malabou, who has convincingly demonstrated the complication of historically specific notions of futurity, not least within the work of Hegel (Malabou 2005).
12. The French original reads, "un monde en mal du monde et de sens du monde" (Nancy 1996, 12)—*sens* here as "meaning," but also as "sense" and "direction."
13. Hereafter "Hurley" refers to the author-performer; "Kieran," to the speaker in the piece. Hurley's piece appeared in the same venue as Ontroerend Goed's *World Without Us* (2016; published in Ontroerend Goed 2019, 146–200) during the Edinburgh Festival Fringe, which would also be pertinent here, were they not a Belgian company. See Robson (2019) for a discussion of this piece in another context.
14. Giorgio Agamben presents another possibility, claiming that Kafka's text makes most sense if we understand that the rumours about K. with which the novel opens can only have been started by K. himself against himself (2009, 34). On shame in affective performance, see Denise Varney (2017).

References

Adorno, Theodor W. 1997. *Aesthetic Theory.* Translated and edited by Robert Hullot-Kentor. Minneapolis: U of Minnesota P.

———. 2003. *Ästhetische Theorie.* Frankfurt: Suhrkamp.

Agamben, Giorgio. 2009. *Nudità.* Milan: Nottetempo.

Ahmed, Sara. 2014. *The Cultural Politics of Emotion.* 2nd ed. Edinburgh: Edinburgh UP.

Aristotle. 1995. *The Complete Works of Aristotle.* Vol 2. Edited by Jonathan Barnes. Princeton, NJ: Princeton UP.

Artaud, Antonin. 1993. *The Theatre and Its Double.* Translated by Victor Corti. London: Calder.

———. 2004. *Œuvres.* Edited by Évelyne Grossman. Paris: Gallimard.

Barker, Howard. 1997. *Arguments for a Theatre.* 3rd ed. Manchester: Manchester UP.

Bauman, Zygmunt. 2006. *Liquid Fear.* Cambridge: Polity.

Cixous, Hélène. 1993. *Three Steps on the Ladder of Writing.* Translated by Sarah Cornell and Susan Sellers. New York: Columbia UP.

Crépon, Marc. 2008. *La Culture de la peur.* Tome 1, *Démocratie, identité, sécurité.* Paris: Galilée.

Critchley, Simon. 1999. *Ethics-Politics-Subjectivity: Essays on Derrida, Levinas and Contemporary French Thought.* London: Verso.

Derrida, Jacques. 2007. *Psyche: Inventions of the Other.* Vol 1. Edited by Peggy Kamuf and Elizabeth Rottenberg. Stanford, CA: Stanford UP.

Ferrari, Federico and Jean-Luc Nancy. 2018. *La Fin des fins: Scène en trois actes.* Paris: Kimé.

Fisher, Mark. 2009. *Capitalist Realism: Is There No Alternative?* Alresford: Zero Books.

Greig, David. 2013. *The Events.* London: Faber.

Harris, Zinnie. 2016. *This Restless House.* London: Faber.

———. 2017. *Meet Me at Dawn.* London: Faber.

Heidegger, Martin. 2006. *Sein und Zeit.* 19th ed. Tübingen: Max Niemeyer Verlag.

———. 2010. *Being and Time.* Translated by Joan Stambaugh, revised by Dennis J. Schmidt. Albany: SUNY P.

Hurley, Kieran. 2016. *Heads Up.* London: Oberon.

Kafka, Franz. (1925) 2009. *The Trial.* Translated by Mike Mitchell and edited by Ritchie Robertson. Oxford: Oxford UP.

Kane, Sarah. 2001. *Complete Plays.* London: Methuen.

Klein, Naomi. 2007. *The Shock Doctrine: The Rise of Disaster Capitalism.* Harmondsworth: Penguin.

Levi, Primo. 1991. *The Mirror Maker.* Translated by Raymond Rosenthal. London: Minerva.

Lordon, Frédéric. 2016. *Les Affects de la politique*. Paris: Éditions de Seuil.
Malabou, Catherine. 2005. *The Future of Hegel: Plasticity, Temporality and Dialectic*. Translated by Lisabeth During. London and New York: Routledge.
Müller, Heiner. 1984. *Hamletmachine and Other Texts for the Stage*. Translated and edited by Carl Weber. New York: PAJ.
Nancy, Jean-Luc. 1991. *The Inoperative Community*. Translated by Peter Connor et al. Minneapolis: U of Minnesota P.
———. 1992. "La Comparution/The Compearance." Translated by Tracy B. Strong. *Political Theory* 20 (3): 371–98.
———. 1996. *Etre singulier pluriel*. Paris: Galilée.
———. 2000. *Being Singular Plural*. Translated by Robert D. Richardson and Anne E. O'Byrne. Stanford, CA: Stanford UP.
———. 2012. *L'Équivalence des catastrophes (Après Fukushima)*. Paris: Galilée.
———. 2013. *La Possibilité d'un monde: Dialogue avec Pierre-Philippe Jandin*. Paris: Les petits Platons.
———. 2015. *After Fukushima: The Equivalence of Catastrophes*. Translated by Charlotte Mandell. New York: Fordham UP.
———. 2017. *The Possibility of a World: Conversations with Pierre-Philippe Jandin*. Translated by Travis Holloway and Flor Méchain. New York: Fordham UP.
Ontroerend Goed. 2019. *Pieces of Work: 5 Theatre Performances*. London: Oberon.
Rebellato, Dan. 2017. "Of an Apocalyptic Tone Recently Adopted in Theatre: British Drama, Violence and Writing." *Sillages critiques* 22. Accessed March 30, 2017.
Robson, Mark. 2005. "Jacques Rancière's Aesthetic Communities." *Paragraph* 28 (1): 77–95.
———. 2018. "Performing Democracy." *Anglia: Journal of English Philology* 136 (1): 154–70.
———. 2019. *theatre & death*. London: Red Globe Press.
Smith, Stef. 2015. *Swallow*. London: Nick Hern Books.
———. 2016. *Human Animals*. London: Nick Hern Books.
———. 2017. *Girl in the Machine*. London: Nick Hern Books.
Terada, Rei. 2001. *Feeling in Theory: Emotion after the "Death of the Subject."* Cambridge, MA: Harvard UP.
Tomlin, Liz. 2019. *Political Dramaturgies and Theatre Spectatorship: Provocations for Change*. London: Bloomsbury.
Varney, Denise. 2017. "Feeling, Sensation, and Being Moved: Case Studies in Affective Performance." *Modern Drama* 60 (3): 322–41.
Weber, Samuel. 2004. *Theatricality as Medium*. New York: Fordham UP.

CHAPTER 13

Affects and the Development of Political Subjectivity: From Resilience to Agency in Kae Tempest's *Wasted*

Clara Escoda

Introduction

Kae Tempest's *Wasted* (2011; published 2013) has been described as "a witty and clever play from a major voice in new urban writing" about youngsters "looking for meaning in a modern urban life" (Davies 2015).[1] Divided into five scenes that take place in the course of a day, it explores the life and feelings of middle-class Londoners Charlotte, Danny and Ted, who meet on the anniversary of the death of their friend Tony around a tree that stands for his memory, the same place where they gathered in the past when they were a tightly-knit group. The three protagonists work in monotonous jobs that barely pay "the bills" (Tempest 2013, 12). Their youth and energy, and the fact that they have an education, makes them feel entitled to imagine a better future, yet at the same time they fear that, if they make changes to their life, they may lose what little they have, and

C. Escoda (✉)
University of Barcelona, Barcelona, Catalonia
e-mail: clescodag@ub.edu

M. Aragay et al. (eds.), *Affects in 21st-Century British Theatre*,
https://doi.org/10.1007/978-3-030-58486-3_13

this makes them reluctant to reinvent themselves and the world. Thus, they hover between the possibility of starting their lives from scratch, perhaps in another country, or remaining in London, close to their friends and families, even if clinging to their precarious jobs and their routines would be the easiest nonchoice. Empowered by the symbolism of the tree, they all imagine trying to "change it up" (16) by following their affective inclinations, and Charlotte even takes some steps towards reshaping her life, albeit she pulls back at the end.

This chapter will argue that the three young protagonists of Tempest's play are shown attempting to resist the pull of the neoliberal discourses of "resilience" (Chandler and Reid 2016a, 1) and "self-development" (Türken et al. 2016, 34) in order to begin to transform their lives.[2] Resilience requires a subject defined by diminished autonomy and agency who submits to the requirement to adapt to "an endemic condition of global insecurity" (Chandler and Reid 2016a, 1–2), while self-development implies the subject's continual reworking of the self as a way to "manage" life and adjust to a flexible, unstable market. At no point, however, does Charlotte, Danny or Ted feel empowered enough to aspire to actively change the world around them, that is, to become political subjects. I follow David Chandler and Julian Reid's conception of political subjectivity (2016a, 4), which entails a vision of the world as changeable and a sense of the self as capable of acting on and transforming it according to their ethical inclinations. I will argue that the possibility of developing a political subjectivity is presented to spectators in the play's closing moments, where they are interpellated by the chorus—made up of figures One, Two and Three, to be played, as the opening stage directions point out (4), by the same actors as the three characters, since it clearly embodies their feelings and desires—and a highly affective mise en scène.[3]

What Charlotte, Danny and Ted find missing, as they state at various points, is a society formed by relational, mutually dependent, affective beings that exceeds a concern with mere survival. Instead, *Wasted* constructs "a picture of an atomised society" (Bowie-Sell 2011) populated by self-contained, individualistic subjects. In his essay "The Intruder" ([2000] 2008), Jean-Luc Nancy gives an account of his experience undergoing a heart transplant, which led him to elaborate a view of subjectivity as characterised by exposure. For Nancy, letting the donor's heart—which he calls "the intruder"—into his body blurred the distinction between what is "one's own" and what is "alien" and led him to conclude that "identity is defined by immunity, the one is identified with the other. To lower the one is to lower the other" (2008, 167). Nancy thus rejects the unified, highly immune notion of identity at the core of neoliberal discourse in favour of a dis-integrated subjectivity constituted by multiple alterities.[4]

Wasted portrays how an emphasis on individualism and immunity leads the three protagonists to experience "negative affects" (Ngai 2005, 3) of dejection, anxiety and loneliness. This chapter traces the clash in the play between such negative feelings and the positive affects that enable mutual care and allow the young protagonists to acquire a degree of agency that increases their power to act on their lives and in the world. I draw additionally on Lauren Berlant's *Cruel Optimism* (2011) and Adriana Cavarero's "Inclining the Subject: Ethics, Alterity and Natality" (2011) in order to show how, as a consequence of the pressure exerted by the aforementioned neoliberal discourses of resilience and self-development, for the play's protagonists negative affects of anxiety and dejection ultimately prevail over positive ones that "incline" the subject towards a mutually caring relationship with others.

I believe that Berlant's affective analysis of the contemporary, post-2008 financial crisis moment can illuminate aspects of recent theatre and performance practice. Berlant's understanding of the present as a "mediated affect" (2011, 4), that is, as dependent on the regulation of affect conducted by neoliberalism, can help account for Tempest's characters' affective responses, which end up conforming their reality at the end of the play. According to Berlant, since the 2008 financial crisis, the present is mostly felt as a moment of extended impasse or "crisis ordinariness" (2011, 10)—crisis, that is, has become embedded in the ordinary. This is certainly how Charlotte, Danny and Ted sense their present situation, although they are not able to fully articulate it. In this light, I contend that the three young people in *Wasted* fear losing their attachments to jobs, partners and routines even if they are experienced as and shown to be "cruel" (Berlant 2011, 24)—that is, even if these attachments deprive them of the very conditions of happiness they are striving for. Such fear is linked to an anxiety about increased precarity, as well as to the sense that, as Berlant puts it, the continuity of a subject's attachments "provides something of [its] sense of what it means to keep on living on and to look forward to being in the world" (2011, 24).

My use of "incline" is drawn from Cavarero's "Inclining the Subject: Ethics, Alterity, and Natality." From Kant to Hobbes and Descartes to

Canetti, Cavarero claims, the modern understanding of the self is "enthralled by the dream of its own autonomy and integrity" (2011, 16). Inherently rational, calculating and self-referential, the modern subject is characterised by "vertical[ity]" (2011, 195), as it "neither exposes itself nor leans out" (2011, 199–200). In contrast, Cavarero mobilises Hannah Arendt's notion of "inclination," where birth is seen as "the naked fact of our original, physical appearance" (Arendt 1998 [1958], 179), that is, as signalling a fundamental, shared human condition that makes human beings equally vulnerable and thoroughly relational. On this basis, Cavarero emphasises the urgent necessity to redefine the subject as being "inclined" (2011, 195) towards the Other. Inclination is a disposition towards positive, caring affective relationality, which seems central to the way Tempest evokes an alternative mode of understanding the nucleus of human subjectivity vis-à-vis the "immune" (Nancy 2008, 167) neoliberal individual.

The Stickiness of Affects, Immunity and Political Subjectivity

Charlotte, Danny and Ted try to cope with a context of generalised precarity and crisis ordinariness. In the context of the play, they all represent neoliberalism's resilient subjects: even though they feel strongly dissatisfied and would like to break with their cruel attachments, they adjust to their life of insecurity, "pressuppos[ing] the unknowability of the world [...] as a condition for partaking of [it]" (Chandler and Reid 2016a, 4) and ultimately dismissing any possibility of "acting agentially or politically in relation to their environments" (Chandler and Reid 2016a, 5). Ted, for instance, claims that he feels "miserable" (11), because "although he's on the career ladder," he is convinced that in reality "he's going nowhere" (12). Still, he accepts that his monotonous stock-taking and data entry job is "paying the bills" (12). Danny works in an unspecified job and takes refuge in his music band and in drugs to escape from his feelings of dejection and insecurity. Finally, Charlotte, Danny's girlfriend, works at a school with lower-class children and believes she cannot make a difference nor help them in any meaningful way. She is also reluctantly tied to Danny, who is not able to fully commit to her.

As Chandler and Reid contend, neoliberalism's emphasis on resilience "has transformed and undermined the role and possibilities of politics," since politics "requires a subject capable of conceiving the transformation of its world and the power relations it finds itself subject to" (2018, 4). Political interventions demand an empowered subject who is capable of seeing the world as changeable, not one whose imagination is managed and circumscribed by a world to which they must constantly accommodate and in relation to which they stand enslaved. In *Wasted*, as Charlotte, Danny and Ted remember their past together, they begin to break out of the prison house of neoliberal resilience through sharing positive affects, that is, affects that incline subjects towards mutually caring relationships with others. As James Thompson asserts, (positive) affects are connected "to a capacity for action and to a sense of aliveness, where it is that vitality that prompts a person's desire to connect and engage (perhaps with others or ideas)" (2009, 119). This enables them to emerge out of their hopelessness and begin to build up the strength to try to change their conditions, thus (potentially) developing a political subjectivity.

In this regard, Sara Ahmed's notion of the "stickiness" of affects may illuminate how Tempest's protagonists are temporarily able to subvert the mediated affects of neoliberalism and imagine themselves as agential and capable of changing their life. In *The Cultural Politics of Emotions*, Ahmed rephrases the basic question of "what emotions are" into "what emotions do," thus opposing both psychological notions of emotions, which assume that emotions originate within the individual, and the assumption that they come from without and move inward. Instead, she views emotions as relational, since they "circulate between bodies, [...] they stick as well as move" (Ahmed [2004a] 2014, 4), creating the very effect of the surfaces or boundaries of bodies and worlds. Affects, in other words, are "sticky," Ahmed argues, and what makes such "stickiness" possible is the fact that they circulate between objects instead of residing in individual people.

Wasted also shows that affects are not a private, individual matter, but that they "stick" to, and circulate, between the protagonists. Initially, the characters are all scattered, as shown by the fact that each speaks individually to Tony's tree, and they all believe that the "negative affects" (Ngai 2005, 3) they experience are theirs alone. Progressively, however, by talking to one another, they are able to transform their feelings of anger and dejection into positive ones that prompt them to connect and engage with others. On the day of the anniversary of Tony's death, for instance, Charlotte, Danny and Ted individually go to where Tony's tree is planted, looking for comfort and intimacy, and they confess their feelings of anxiety secretly and individually to Tony. This shows that anxiety is the dominant, "negative affect" (Ngai 2005, 3) in the group. Slowly, however, as the rest of the members of the group also galvanise around the tree, they all begin to remember their past together, when they "cared about each other [...] it was exciting [...] [and] [i]t felt real" (21), and are progressively empowered to imagine the possibility of improving their lives.

In the same manner, at the start of scene two, Charlotte demonstrates her inclination when, prompted by a desire to live life "from her guts" (22), she buys a ticket to "go teach somewhere completely new," where she "could be helping people" (36). Charlotte is finally able to muster the strength to go abroad after talking to Tony about it—who, for the group, represents memories of past affective intensity—and discussing it with Ted, who also prompts her to pursue her aims. From this point of view, *Wasted* confirms, as Ahmed puts it, that "all actions are reactions, in the sense that what we do is shaped by the contact we have with others" ([2004a] 2014, 4). Indeed, it is by sharing positive affects that enable mutual care and responsibility that Charlotte, Danny and Ted feel empowered enough to *imagine* the possibility of leading a life that may be truer to their relational affective inclinations. Of the three, however, Charlotte is the only one who develops the capacity to *act* in order to affectively transform her life.

Beyond Resilience: The Power to Affect and Be Affected

Wasted evokes alternatives to neoliberal immunity. As they participate in the flow and passage of affect around Tony's tree, Charlotte, Danny and Ted are able to subvert, albeit only temporarily, the mediated affects of neoliberalism. The site of Tony's tree progressively begins to stand for the positive affects of joy and pleasure the characters shared in the past, and becomes a symbol of possibility that will outlive the changes and incidents in the characters' individual lives. Progressively, Charlotte, Danny and Ted feel as one again and gain the strength to share their desire for a life that may be truer to their relational affective leanings. Charlotte, in particular, dares to break away from her job as a teacher. In her case, however, her decision seems to be motivated by an attempt to escape, rather than to embrace, the problems at the school as well as affects of care and responsibility for others. Her monologue in scene two is an account of her decision to break away from her cruel attachments, taken while she was in the classroom with the kids:

> And so, I'm staring out at the kids […] and suddenly I'm remembering the other day […] heading into town, and there's a group of ten or fifteen boys on some kind of field trip with their teacher, and they're wearing nice uniforms, they must have been from a private school or something. I mean, I listened to them talking to each other […] in perfect English, and helping each other with equations and fuckin' algebra and asking each other questions about how to say this or that particular thing in French, and it didn't seem fair. I thought of the kids here, in my class […] and I feel like bursting into tears and telling them all to run out on the streets and smash windows or something, do something I want to tell them they're perfect and they're strong and tell them to go out and live every minute of their lives from their guts, to go after what they want, to own this fuckin' terrible city and get all they can out of their life. […] And so here I am, in front of the class, and the classroom's hot and I feel like I'm drowning and I walk out of the classroom. […] It's raining gently. It's good. I'm walking to the bus stop. I'm leaving I'm making a decision. I'm changing things. (22)

Charlotte's epiphany, her desire to enact a change in her life, is prompted by a sense of the future that awaits the children in her class, which is even more uncertain and may be more "wasted" than her own, and by her intuition that she will probably not be able to help her students in any meaningful way. Specifically, it is triggered by the important class distinction she notices between her kids and the more privileged ones she observes during her field trip, and by her awareness of the class obstacles that will stand in the way of her kids' development. Indeed, just before her monologue, she intimates that even the teachers at her school, who "hate everything about [their job]," "secretly […] hope" their kids will "come to nothing" (20). However, by leaving the kids Charlotte will be able to do even less for them. Her decision to leave the school and "go teach somewhere completely new" (36), therefore, is a selfish, irresponsible choice, perhaps motivated by the fear to fail in her attempt to help the children. Rather, it is her staying and rising up to the challenge that would be the more difficult option and an example of inclination towards others.

Charlotte's vision of the children "run[ning] out on the streets and smash[ing] windows or something" and "to go[ing] out and liv[ing] every minute of their lives from their guts" uncannily anticipates the London riots, which broke out on August 6, 2011, a mere three weeks after the premiere of *Wasted*, and were led mainly by teenagers and young people.[5] The riots were caused by the racial and class tensions, economic decline and unemployment that austerity policies had brought about, and expressed a sense of waste and frustration similar to the one Charlotte describes. In Iván Morales's 2017 production at Barcelona's Sala Beckett, Charlotte's monologue was staged as a moment of personal breakdown where she became progressively unnerved, until she finally left the stage and went on screaming her words from the backstage area, as if she was no longer a character but maybe a member of the staff or even the audience, while spectators were left to stare at an empty stage. This disruption of the naturalistic fourth wall affectively conveyed the notion that neoliberal societies have reached a breaking point, even as they drive dissent "offstage."

Charlotte, Danny and Ted's desire to share positive affects is apparent from scene one, where Danny suggests that they should do something to celebrate the anniversary of Tony's death, thereby turning the negative affects often associated with mourning into creative, empowering ones linked to remembrance. In scene three, they thus attend a party in Peckham in an attempt to recover the feeling of togetherness they used to share in the past. This is when they realise that empathy and solidarity are affective states that can lead towards collective feeling and action. At the start of the scene, the stage directions indicate that the characters are "*completely munted. But not in a caricature kind of way. In a way that suggests they've been getting munted for many years*" (28). As the chorus puts it, they are in the habit of taking "drugs to feel" (51), which points to their rather desperate search for the affective intensity and inclination that are denied in commodified, neoliberal London. They stand under strobe lights that make them "*look a bit monstrous [...] a bit alien*" (28). Further,

> *Danny and Ted are sitting together with their backs against the speakers, on the floor, grinning, with their arms round each other's necks looking a bit like they're ten years old. There should be a massive difference in their physicality compared to earlier when they were sat on the bench together. They should be open and tactile. [...] Ted throws his arms around both of their necks, they're all together, in a little love huddle, raving, and munted, looking up to the lights, swallowing, grinning, touching each other.* (28–29)

In my view, the "love huddle" formed by the three protagonists dramatises an understanding of the subject as characterised by what Nancy calls "ecstasy" (Nancy [1986] 1991, 6). The ecstatic subject transgresses its self-contained individuality in order to expose itself or stand outside itself. Insofar as ecstasy implies non-absoluteness, relationality and incompletion, the scene clearly defies the neoliberal definition of subjectivity, characterised by immunity and verticality, and gestures towards a new affective horizon defined by inclination towards others. Arguably, however, the scene also suggests that the characters need to be "*completely munted*" in order to experience positive affects of coresponsibility and mutual care, and thus signals to the difficulties involved in attaining the necessary ecstatic state of being within the neoliberal affective regime. The ecstatic, profoundly relational fusion between Charlotte, Danny and Ted is anticipated by the chorus at the end of scene two, when they claim that "[w]e just want to lose our names and our edges. / We just want to lose our minds / And lose the lines that draw the borders" (28). In this regard, Morales's production turned this specific moment at the party into stage poetry. The stage, which was mostly bare, was flooded with intense red light while the music sounded at full volume and the performers' movements were choreographed in such a way as to suggest their unceasing attempt to merge into one single body. This stage image of affective intensity powerfully interpellated spectators, both visually and aurally, by drawing attention to the characters' search for new, profoundly relational affective horizons.

The scene also suggests that affects are central to the development of a fully political subject who may be able to move beyond mere resilience and adaptation to neoliberal parameters. Right after the party, Ted admits that, although he did not feel like "[c]om[ing] out and party[ing]" (30), he felt fully present and alive at the party and laments that over the years he has "lost contact with a lot of people" (30). At this moment, Ted is momentarily able to break free from his former immune self and question the mediated affects of neoliberalism. Revealingly, he is able to see Danny—whose job remains unspecified and who seems to spend most time with his band, taking drugs—differently and even admire his potential as someone who does not have "those kind of worries, do you? The fuckin' rush hour on the Tube, and the telly and the pub quiz. You just naff around being interesting, and I think, what a prick" (30).

"Negative Affects": Swaying Between Change and the Known

According to Berlant, in the wake of the 2008 financial crisis, the pull of "conventional good-life fantasies […] of enduring reciprocity in couples, families, political systems, institutions, markets, and at work" (2011, 2) has grown stronger, even when there is ample evidence of their fragility. In *Wasted*, to such cruel attachments is added the characters' fear of increased precarity should they decide to step fully away from the dictates of the neoliberal discourse of resilience and self-development.

In scene two, for instance, at the site of Tony's tree, Ted confesses that he feels "miserable" (11), but resists affects of dejection by imagining the possibility of changing his life. As he puts it, "We're still young, for fuck's sake. We could sell the car. Leave the flat. Fuck off for a year. We could live in Spain, I could get a job in a bar. She could be a waitress. We could swim naked in the sea. We could get drunk in the afternoons and sleep it off on the beach, we could…" (12). In scene three, however, he admits to Danny that he hardly goes out or leaves his routine now, in contrast with his past exhilarating experiences with the group. This retreat towards immunity makes him anxious—"[i]t's been really getting me down recently, you know. […] [W]ork, and the routine, and Sally and me, the flat, and who's doing the washing up, and who's making the dinner or, you know. It's. I dunno. I ain't really been seeing a lot of anyone else" (31)—yet he accepts it as an inevitable fact of life—"It's life though, innit. Getting older" (31)—which suggests he has given up on his dreams of a more fulfilling life, truer to his affective inclinations.

Revealingly, at the end of the play, Danny applies the vocabulary of self-development, which demands a "continual self-improvement to fit the demands of the advanced liberal society, often in terms of a flexible and unstable market" (Türken et al. 2016, 34), to his own life and objectives. In scene five, he tells Charlotte that he is "gonna fuckin' do it" (54) with the band, and that he will train "six hours a day" and practise a "martial art too. For the discipline," as well as start "yoga or something" (54). Self-development implies "'lifelong learning'" (Türken et al. 2016, 34) as a route to successful life and a subject that is "autonomous yet governable via continual self-monitoring and self-disciplining" (Türken et al. 2016, 34). In this sense, Danny increasingly construes himself as "an entrepreneur" (Türken et al. 2016, 34), a free, autonomous, individualised, self-regulating actor "understood as a source of capital; as human capital" (Türken et al. 2016, 34).

Charlotte's case, however, is different, since in spite of her daring decision to "travel. Live abroad. Teach" (36), she finally chooses the more difficult option of staying, an indication not of resilience, but rather of her inclination towards others. Revealingly, Charlotte finally tells Danny, her reluctant, non-committing boyfriend, that "I'm gonna go back to school and teach. Properly. Coz I love them kids. And they deserve so much more. They really do. Last thing they need is another person walking out on them. I'm gonna put all my energy into it, Dan, I'm gonna be a teacher. A really fuckin' good one" (53), realising that "walking out" on her underprivileged kids would be an irresponsible option. Charlotte, therefore, twice finds the strength to act in order to affectively transform her life, finally deciding to stay true to her desire for coresponsibility.

At the end of the play, especially Ted and Danny pull themselves back to 'known ground', which they see as safer than pursuing intangible, unknown possibilities. Indeed, Ted keeps his job and his girlfriend, and Danny is still "*sniffing lines with his mates*," both looking "[*l*]*onely*" (57). On her part, it is not clear whether Charlotte finally leaves Danny, since, in scene five, they are still seen talking to one another in search for comfort. In Berlant's terms, to a greater or lesser extent in each case, the characters remain tied to their attachments in a relation of cruel optimism, compromising the present for a future that will supposedly make their feelings of loneliness, anxiety and fear worth it (2011, 24). The good-life fantasy they remain attached to is based on reciprocity in romantic relationships, satisfaction in the work place and consumerism. Thus, Ted and presumably Charlotte decide to keep their strained relationship with their partners, Danny opts for self-improvement as the way to find his job meaningful, and at the very end of the play, Ted is seen shopping in IKEA, the ultimate consumer's paradise.

Ted and Danny's surrender to neoliberal discourses of self-development and resilience shows that, as Chandler and Reid put, in a neoliberal context "the area of the individual's transformative activity is essentially reduced to a disciplining of the inner self" (2016a, 5). Instead, Charlotte's decision to stay with her underprivileged school children, and Charlotte, Danny and Ted's deep ambivalence towards their cruel attachments indicate that social and personal tensions are far from resolved through neoliberalism's disciplinary rhetoric of self-development and resilience. Significantly, the play ends with Charlotte and Danny confiding to one another that they feel "fuckin' wasted" (55), as "*Danny puts his arms around* [*Charlotte*]" (55). Morales's production underlined the deep political ambivalence that lies at the heart of the play by replacing the embrace by a passionate, almost violent kiss. The kiss conveyed both Charlotte and Danny's anxiety vis-à-vis the negative affects of dejection and fear dominating their lives and their enduring, albeit suppressed, capacity for positive, creative affects enabling connection and sharing. Further, I would suggest that the kiss's sheer affective force extended an invitation to spectators to realise their own potential to transcend immunity and build affective connections that incline them towards coresponsibility and mutual care.

Self-Empowerment, the Chorus and Spectatorship

In the play's closing moments, especially Danny and Ted's attempts to break free of their cruel attachments are seen to fail as they accommodate to the individualistic demands of neoliberal immune subjectivity. In this context of neoliberalism's affective mediation, the chorus, however, invites spectators to realise that the potential to engage in a mutually caring, affective relationship with others lodges within them as much as it does within the characters. By alerting spectators as to the importance of transforming the negative affects of anger and disgust the protagonists are overcome by into positive affects that incline the subject towards caring engagement with others, the chorus's interpellation, in combination with a highly affective mise en scène, presents spectators with the possibility of cultivating a political subjectivity in Chandler and Reid's sense of the term.

Throughout the play, the chorus both externalises the characters' feelings of waste and meaninglessness and addresses spectators directly and affectively through poetry. As the opening stage directions indicate, the protagonists, "*as well as being the characters, are also the Chorus. [...] They should speak directly to the audience [...] smiling at the audience, or looking at them dead in the eye. They should speak in their own accents, and be aware of the meter beneath their words, in the way that you are aware of a beat when you dance to a song. [...] [T]hey are everyone that's ever felt how the characters feel*" (4). At the start of the play, the chorus describes the waning of affects fostering connection and their replacement by externally imposed desires:

ONE: Hearts beating
THREE: Slower than they used to, stressing over bills to pay,
TWO: A million distractions just to fill the day,
THREE: Faces greyer than before. It's not our world no more
ONE: It's someone else's.
[...]
TWO: And the rest of us stride on and through
THREE: The mess,
TWO: The rust,
THREE: The flesh,
TWO: The lust,
THREE: The lies.
[...]
TWO: The way we hide from the truth that is inside. (8–11)

Through poetry and direct audience address, the chorus expresses the importance of not giving up the struggle for a fuller affective life, truer to one's deep relational inclinations, in an increasingly fragmented, materialistic London. It also invites spectators to become attuned to both the positive affects that enable mutual care and coresponsibility, and may ultimately enable social justice, and the negative feelings—such as dejection, anxiety or fear—that constitute the human subject in neoliberal societies. In scene two, after Charlotte decides to tell Danny about her decision to leave, the chorus both celebrates people's potential for change and alerts spectators as to the fragility of such potential:

> Change coming! [...] / I swear, we can change something. / We change nothing. / Change is puffing off its chest. / Change is jumping to its death. / [...] [O]ur smiles are contorted/And we forget our epiphany / The minute that we thought it. (26–28)

The play ends with the chorus exhorting spectators to be true to their affective inclinations—"We came here to share the feeling / [...] Whatever moves you—you must chase it— / [...] Your life is for/Much more / Than getting / Wasted" (56–57)—while very precise stage directions describe how Danny and Ted, and even Charlotte, go on with the inertia of their daily lives. Simultaneously, images are projected on stage that evoke the January 2011 revolution in Egypt against president Hosni Mubarak's regime and that, like Charlotte's monologue earlier, also seem to uncannily foreshadow the August 2011 London riots:

> *We see projections of supermarket aisles, pubs, people in a party, then riots, revolts, soldiers, burning cars, etc, interspersed with the three characters, buying cigarettes, lying on the floor of their flat, watching telly, time-lapse footage of London, pizza boxes, traffic jams, market stalls, queue in the bank, then Ted, in IKEA, pushing a trolley loaded up with loads of massive flat pack boxes, struggling, Egypt after the revolution, Tony's tree, kids in a classroom, visuals flicker off […]. Music still playing, the characters are back on stage in their first positions, it's Monday again, nothing changes, Ted's still at work, Charlote is still in the classroom, Danny is still up sniffing lines with his mates. They look tired. Lonely. End.* (57)

In this manner, *Wasted* links Charlotte, Danny and Ted's situation to that of other young people, including young people in other parts of the world, who, as opposed to the protagonists, have rebelled in response to widespread precarity or oppressive regimes. In the wake of the 2008 financial crisis and at a time when the empowering affective energy set in motion by the Arab Spring was still very much in the air, the play thus provides a glimpse of the potential for change that, as the chorus suggests at the start of the play, dwells in individuals.[6] Admittedly, however, the images of "*riots*," "*soldiers*" and "*burning cars*" are pictures of unfocused, chaotic uprisings—as was the case with the London 2011 riots—rather than focused, meaningful revolt. The flickering images of "Egypt after the revolution" are themselves also deeply ambiguous. While the revolution led to Egypt's first free presidential election in May 2011, with the Muslim Brotherhood's Mohammed Morsi declared the winner in June, and that he pushed ahead with a referendum on the draft constitution, Morsi later rescinded most of his decree, and opposition groups continue to accuse him of betraying the goals of the revolution (Amnesty International 2014). Ultimately, the play acknowledges the extreme fragility of the protagonists' potential for change by ending with an image of stagnation, as "*the characters are back on stage in their first positions, it's Monday again, nothing changes, Ted's still at work, Charlotte is still in the classroom, Danny is still up sniffing lines with his mates. They look tired. Lonely*" (57).

Each staging needs to navigate the playtext's ambivalence. Morales's production at Barcelona's Sala Beckett found a way of both acknowledging the fragility, while at the same time inciting spectators to search for ways of countering it. Upon entering the auditorium, spectators were given a copy of what looked like Tony's memorial card. Each spectator, individually, was therefore invited to become part of the group, to feel for the loss and maybe seek affective support from the other group members, including the actors and other spectators. On the card's cover there appeared the play's title, *Wasted*, together with Tony's name—Catalanised to "Toni"—the initials of his surnames and his birth and death dates: "Toni P. G. 1992–2007." On the inside of the cover were the production details, and on the next page was a text that prompted spectators to imagine a different world: "Thank you for coming. Life is shit. Life is awesome. Do we still bear the beatings they inflict on our legs? Even as we stand tall, here? Shall we have to trust again? And place ourselves at the forefront? Is this our home? Who does the world belong to, now? Who is embracing strongly now? Who the fuck will save us? Why do I desire to dream? Dreaming so strongly hurts terribly bad."[7] The text contrasted the positive affective potential of human life, as suggested by the claims that "life is awesome," that human subjects "stand tall" and have the capacity to "dream strongly," with the violent regulation of the affective capacities of individuals by power, evoked by "the beatings they inflict on our legs." This foregrounded opposition thus framed Morales's entire production, prompting spectators to contemplate the possibility of (re)defining themselves as affective beings driven by agency and imagination into developing a political subjectivity based on mutual trust and coresponsibility, in the face of political regimes or ideologies that try to seize on and control their potential to do so.

Conclusion

This chapter has argued that *Wasted* explores how positive affects may lead to the development of an empowered, agential subject and, eventually, to the possibility of collective empowerment. The positive affects Charlotte, Danny and Ted experience when sharing their intimacy and remembering their past experiences next to Tony's tree, or when attending the party together in scene three, are seen to give them a degree of agency, and in Charlotte's case, to increase her power to act and consciously decide on her life, which the play sees as key to the cultivation of a political subjectivity. Whereas Charlotte stays closer to her affective inclinations, Danny and Ted are finally unable to break away from their cruel attachments and succumb to neoliberal discourses of resilience and self-development.

Through highly affective, poetic images of the porous, incomplete, relational subject reinforced by the chorus's direct interpellation of spectators, however, *Wasted* points towards an alternative understanding of subjectivity constituted by ecstatic exposure and affective inclination towards others, thus suggesting that when affects of mutual care circulate between bodies and objects, they enable an increased sense of autonomy and a capacity to engage with others that bear a strong revolutionary potential. Positive affects are therefore viewed in Tempest's play as the adhesive inclination or "*clinamen*" (Nancy [1986] 1991, 3; italics in the original) between individual subjects that enables them to exist as relational, mutually dependent beings, and ultimately develop a political subjectivity in Chandler and Reid's sense of the term—namely, a way of being in the world that is thoroughly invested with the possibility of change.

In this sense, and despite its title, *Wasted* may be read as an affirmative play that offers glimpses of the subject's potential to break away from the affects of immunity fostered by neoliberal globalisation. Through the formal and aesthetic means examined in this chapter, the play makes a political intervention in the prevailing climate of neoliberal crisis ordinariness, one that gestures towards the importance of positive relational affects for the development of a potentially transformative collective identity. Ultimately, the play summons spectators to ponder their own potential contribution to creating a new affective topology of the possible.

Notes

1. Commissioned by Paines Plough, the play premiered at Latitude Festival on 15 July 2011, directed by James Grieve.
2. Like Stuart Hall, I use the term "neoliberal" to refer to an economic model grounded "in the idea of the 'free, possessive individual'" where "[s]tate-led 'social engineering' must never prevail over corporate and private interests" (2011, 706), while also taking into account that it is a reductive term, that sacrifices "attention to internal complexities and geo-historical specificity" (2011, 706). For a summary of the main theoretical approaches to neoliberalism and an attempt to come to terms with the blanket applicability of the term, see also Clarke (2008). Like Berlant, I also believe that the present, neoliberal conjuncture is perceived affectively, and that neoliberalism's "mediated affective responses exemplify a shared *historical* sense" (2011, 3; italics in the original).
3. Even though this chapter carries out an essentially textual analysis of the play, occasional references are made to Iván Morales's 2017 production at Barcelona's Sala Beckett (17 February-12 March 2017). Morales's *Wasted* was the first production of a play by Tempest to take place in Catalonia (as well as in Spain).

4. The concept of immunity has also been discussed by Jacques Derrida (2005) and Donna Haraway (1991), among others.
5. The 2011 England riots, more widely known as the London Riots, started when thousands of people rioted in cities and towns across England, resulting in the deaths of five people. As Paul Lewis puts it, "[w]hat began as a gathering of around 200 protesters demanding answers over the death of Mark Duggan, who was shot dead by police on Thursday, culminated twelve hours later in a full-scale riot that saw looting spread across north-London suburbs" (2011).
6. The Arab Spring, which started in Tunisia with Mohamed Bouazizi's decision to set fire to himself in order to protest against police officers shutting down his business, was "a wave of pro-democracy protests and uprisings that took place in the Middle East and North Africa beginning in 2010 and 2011, challenging some of the region's entrenched authoritarian regimes" (*Encyclopaedia Britannica* 2020). In all cases, the protests were violently repressed, and "demonstrators expressing political and economic grievances faced violent crackdowns by their countries' security forces" (*Encyclopaedia Britannica* 2020). With protests against authoritarianism and exploitation continuing to take place globally—e.g., in Chile as recently as October 2019–February 2020—*Wasted* may indeed be described as uncannily prescient. In both these cases, too, empathy is seen as the key to constructing a mutually caring society—Chilean protesters asking for more empathy on the part of the financial elites resonates with the chorus in scene one of Tempest's play claiming that "[w]e're less empathetic and more / Selfish, / Less independent and more / Helpless" (9).
7. My translation from the Catalan source, which reads: "Gràcies per venir. La vida és una merda. La vida és collonuda. Encara aguantem hòsties a les cames? Ben drets, aquí? Haurem de tornar a confiar? Posar-nos al davant? Això és casa nostra? De qui és el món ara? Qui s'abraça tan fort ara? Qui cony ens salvarà? Per què vull somiar? Somiar tan fort fa mal."

References

Ahmed, Sara. (2004a) 2014. *The Cultural Politics of Emotion*. Edinburgh: Edinburgh UP.

Amnesty International. 2014. "Egypt after the 2011 Revolution." *Amnesty International UK*, August 4. Accessed May 1, 2020.

Arendt, Hannah. (1958) 1998. *The Human Condition*. Chicago, IL: U of Chicago P.

Berlant, Lauren. 2011. *Cruel Optimism*. Durham, NC and London: Duke UP.

Bowie-Sell, Daisy. 2011. Review of *Many Moons*, by Alice Birch. *Telegraph*, June 1. Accessed August 23, 2019.

Campbell, Timothy and Adam Sitze, eds. 2013. *Biopolitics: A Reader.* Durham, NC and London: Duke UP.

Cavarero, Adriana. 2011. "Inclining the Subject: Ethics, Alterity and Natality." In Elliot and Attridge 2011, 194–204.

Chandler, David and Julian Reid. 2016a. "Introduction: The Neoliberal Subject." In Chandler and Reid 2016b, 1–8.

Chandler, David and Julian Reid, eds. 2016b. *The Neoliberal Subject: Resilience, Adaptation and Vulnerability.* London and New York: Rowman and Littlefield.

Clarke, John. 2008. "Living with/in and without Neo-Liberalism." *Focaal: Journal of Global and Historical Anthropology* 51: 135–47.

Davies, Lewis. 2015. Review of *Wasted*, by Kae Tempest. *Wales Arts Review*, November 22. Accessed November 17, 2019.

Derrida, Jacques. 2005. *Rogues: Two Essays on Reason.* Translated by Pascale-Anne Brault and Michael Naas. Stanford, CA: Stanford UP.

Elliot, Jane and Derek Attridge, eds. 2011. *Theory After 'Theory.'* London and New York: Routledge.

Encyclopaedia Britannica. 2020. "Arab Spring." Accessed May 1, 2020.

Hall, Stuart. 2011. "The Neoliberal Revolution." *Cultural Studies* 25 (6): 705–28.

Haraway, Donna. 1991. "The Biopolitics of Postmodern Bodies: Constitutions of Self in Immune System Discourse." In Campbell and Sitze 2013, 274–309.

Lewis, Paul. 2011. "Tottenham Riots: A Peaceful Protest, then suddenly all Hell Broke Loose." *Guardian*, August 7. Accessed November 17, 2019.

Nancy, Jean-Luc. (1986) 1991. *The Inoperative Community.* Translated and edited by Peter Connor. Minneapolis: U of Minnesota P.

———. 2008. *Corpus.* Translated by Richard A. Rand. New York: Fordham UP.

———. (2000) 2008. "The Intruder." In Nancy 2008, 161–70.

Ngai, Sianne. 2005. *Ugly Feelings.* Cambridge, MA: Harvard UP.

Thompson, James. 2009. *Performance Affects: Applied Theatre and the End of Affect.* Basingstoke and New York: Palgrave Macmillan.

Tempest, Kae. 2013. *Wasted.* London: Bloomsbury.

Türken, Salman et al. 2016. "Making Sense of Neoliberal Subjectivity: A Discourse Analysis of Media Language on Self-development." *Globalizations* 13 (1): 32–46.

Index[1]

[1] Note: Page numbers followed by ‘n’ refer to notes.

M. Aragay et al. (eds.), *Affects in 21st-Century British Theatre*, https://doi.org/10.1007/978-3-030-58486-3

Printed by Printforce, the Netherlands